Early Praise for *Programming Phoenix*

Programming Phoenix is an excellent introduction to Phoenix. You are taken from the basics to a full-blown application that covers the MVC layers, real-time client-server communication, and fault-tolerant reliance on 3rd party services. All tested, and presented in a gradual and coherent way. You'll be amazed at what you'll be able to build following this book.

➤ **Xavier Noria**
Rails Core Team

I write Elixir for a living, and *Programming Phoenix* was exactly what I needed. It filled in the sticky details, like how to tie authentication into web applications and channels. It also showed me how to layer services with OTP. The experience of Chris and José makes all of the difference in the world.

➤ **Eric Meadows-Jönsson**
Elixir Core Team

A valuable introduction to the Phoenix framework. Many small details and tips from the creators of the language and the framework, and a leader in using Phoenix in production.

➤ **Kosmas Chatzimichalis**
Software Engineer, Mach7x

Programming Phoenix is mandatory reading for anyone looking to write web applications in Elixir. Every few pages I found myself putting the book down so I could immediately apply something I'd learned in my existing Phoenix applications. More than merely teaching the mechanics of using the Phoenix framework, the authors have done a fantastic job imparting the underlying philosophy behind it.

➤ **Adam Kittelson**
Principal Software Engineer, Brightcove

Programming Phoenix

Productive |> Reliable |> Fast

Chris McCord
Bruce Tate
and José Valim

The Pragmatic Bookshelf

Dallas, Texas • Raleigh, North Carolina

Many of the designations used by manufacturers and sellers to distinguish their products are claimed as trademarks. Where those designations appear in this book, and The Pragmatic Programmers, LLC was aware of a trademark claim, the designations have been printed in initial capital letters or in all capitals. The Pragmatic Starter Kit, The Pragmatic Programmer, Pragmatic Programming, Pragmatic Bookshelf, PragProg and the linking *g* device are trademarks of The Pragmatic Programmers, LLC.

Every precaution was taken in the preparation of this book. However, the publisher assumes no responsibility for errors or omissions, or for damages that may result from the use of information (including program listings) contained herein.

Our Pragmatic courses, workshops, and other products can help you and your team create better software and have more fun. For more information, as well as the latest Pragmatic titles, please visit us at *https://pragprog.com*.

The team that produced this book includes:

Jacquelyn Carter (editor)
Potomac Indexing, LLC (index)
Eileen Cohen (copyedit)
Gilson Graphics (layout)
Janet Furlow (producer)

For customer support, please contact *support@pragprog.com*.

For international rights, please contact *rights@pragprog.com*.

Printed in the United States of America.
ISBN-13: 978-1-68050-145-2
Printed on acid-free paper.
Book version: P1.0—April 2016

Contents

Part I — Building with Functional MVC

Part II — Writing Interactive and Maintainable Applications

Acknowledgments

Most of this book is written in a collective voice, but acknowledgments are deep and personal things. For this chapter alone, we'll speak some as a team but also in each of our individual voices. You'll notice that Chris has more to say than the rest of us, and as the creator of Phoenix, it's right and proper that he does so.

As a team, we'd like to thank this production crew. It's been the finest any of us have ever worked with. Potomac Indexing, LLC handled our indexing, Eileen Cohen did our copyedit, and Janet Furlow managed the endless production details.

These contributions were invaluable, but we'd also like to single a couple out for deeper praise. Jackie Carter, our longtime friend and editor, has as much to say about the quality of this book as any of the authors on this team. Your voice is constant, and your gentle encouragement pushed us at the right times and in the right ways. Also, Dave Thomas did the layout and cover for this book, but he's also served as a tireless advocate for Elixir and Phoenix and has shared many plates of Indian food with this team. Your friendship and guidance are always appreciated. We might not have had the opportunity to write this book without your tireless contributions. The next plate of Indian is on us. And we mean it.

Our reviewers worked hard to provide excellent feedback, even though the code serving as the foundation for this book was constantly shifting. Bryan Weber, Eric Meadows-Jönsson, Colby Blaisdel, Adam Guyot, Adam Kittelson, Jason Stiebs, Ian Warshak, Xavier Noria, George Guimaraes, Carlos Antonio da Silva, Bernardo Chaves, Ian Dees, Vince Foley, Brian Hogan, and Lauro Caetano all did various levels of reviews for us. Xavier Noria stands out for providing extraordinary service while going through broken examples and also providing excellent feedback for the concepts in this book. Thanks also to the beta readers who did great work for us.

José Valim

Elixir has been a labor of love and a project that has exceeded my wildest expectations. Elixir wouldn't exist without the support of my partners at Plataformatec. They were the first to believe Elixir could make a dent in the world, and their investments in the community have helped Elixir grow with strength and grace.

Getting this far wouldn't be possible without the unconditional support of my wife, Małgosia. Most of Elixir was written on a small desk placed in the corner of our bedroom. Of all the corners in the world, I can't imagine a better one. Finally, I want to thank my parents and friends for teaching me the lessons that still guide me on this journey.

Bruce Tate

I would like to thank my family as always, especially Maggie. You inspire me; you make bad days better and good days impossibly great. I couldn't do any of this without you. Also, thanks to Paul Janowitz at icanmakeitbetter.com. While going through an acquisition, you allowed me research time to spend on projects like this one. We both believe that the world is a better place when we can give back to the projects that contribute to our success. Thanks for putting your money where your mouth is. Ian, your journey continues to inspire me. It's been great having you in this community, and I can't wait for the great things you'll do here. Also, to the Elixir Mafia, *molte grazie*. You know who you are.

Chris McCord

First, I would like to thank José Valim for creating Elixir, for his contributions to Phoenix, and for building a community that has been such a pleasure to be a part of. It goes without saying that Phoenix wouldn't be possible without his work on Elixir, but it goes deeper than that. He has my deepest gratitude for setting in motion my dream career, sharing his wisdom on running large open source projects, and being a helpful friend in between hectic releases. He has shared with the world a true gift, and I can't wait to see where his creativity leads.

Thanks also go to Bruce Tate for contributing his superb writing skills, helping to form the abstractions behind Phoenix, and encouraging me to seek out José's help with the project. His craftsmanship in this book really shows, and it's been a pleasure having him on the team.

I extend my warmest thanks to Brian Cardarella and DockYard, for making early bets on Phoenix, supporting the project's development to get to where we are today, and giving me the chance to work with some of the finest folks in the industry.

Behind many of the open source projects or books you reference day to day is an understanding spouse who bears late nights and all too much laptop time. My deepest love and appreciation goes out to my lovely wife, Jaclyn, for all her support and encouragement throughout the years along the path to Phoenix and writing this book. A life with you is a truly happy one.

And finally, to the community for this great project, I extend both heartfelt appreciation and bright hope that we might continue to build something special, together.

## CHAPTER 1

Introducing Phoenix

In the first few paragraphs to open this book, you probably expect us to tell you that Phoenix is radically different—newer and better than anything that's come before. We know that Phoenix is a bold name for a bold framework, but look. By now, you've likely seen enough web frameworks to know most of our ideas aren't new. It's the combination of so many of the best ideas from so many other places that has so many people excited.

You'll find metaprogramming capabilities that remind you of Lisp and domain-specific languages (DSLs) that remind you at times of Ruby. Our method of composing services with a series of functional transformations is reminiscent of Clojure's Ring. We achieved such throughput and reliability by climbing onto the shoulders of Erlang and even native Cowboy. Similarly, some of the groundbreaking features like channels and reactive-friendly APIs combine the best features of some of the best JavaScript frameworks you'll find else-where. The precise cocktail of features seems to fit, where each feature multiplies the impact of the next.

We spent time on the right base abstractions for simplicity, and later we noticed that things weren't just fast, but among the fastest in the industry. When we pushed on performance and concurrency, we got functions that composed better and were simpler to manage. When our focus was on the right abstractions, we got better community participation. We now find our-selves in a firestorm of improvement. *Phoenix just feels right.*

After using and writing about frameworks spanning a half a dozen languages across a couple of decades, we think the precise bundle of goodness that we'll share is powerful enough for the most serious problems you throw at it, beautiful enough to be maintainable for years to come, and—most impor-tant—fun to code. Give us a couple of pages and you'll find that the framework represents a great philosophy, one that leverages the reliability and grace of

Elixir. You'll have a front-row seat to understand how we made the decisions that define Phoenix and how best to use them to your advantage.

Simply put, Phoenix is about fast, concurrent, beautiful, interactive, and reliable applications. Let's break each of these claims down.

Fast

Let's cut to the chase. Elixir is both fast and concurrent, as you'd expect from a language running on the Erlang virtual machine. If you're looking for raw speed, Phoenix is hard to beat. In July 2015, we (Chris McCord) compared Phoenix with Ruby on Rails. The firebird was nearly an order of magnitude faster than the locomotive, and it used just over one fourth of the processing power and just under one sixth of the total memory. Those numbers are staggering, but not many Rails users are after naked power.

Let's compare Phoenix with some other popular frameworks. Check out the measurements of some major web frameworks at the Phoenix/mroth showdown.[1] Those results are impressive, rivaling the best in the industry. Among these servers are some of the fastest available. As these numbers rolled in, the core team got increasingly excited. Little did we know that the story was only beginning.

We kept noticing that as you add cores, *the story gets even better*. Another run of this benchmark on the most powerful machines at Rackspace[2] tells an even more compelling story. Check the link for details, but you can see the bare bones here:

Framework	Throughput (req/s)	Latency (ms)	Consistency (σ ms)
Plug	198328.21	0.63	2.22
Phoenix 0.13.1	179685.94	0.61	1.04
Gin	176156.41	0.65	0.57
Play	171236.03	1.89	14.17
Phoenix 0.9.0	169030.24	0.59	0.30
Express Cluster	92064.94	1.24	1.07
Martini	32077.24	3.35	2.52
Sinatra	30561.95	3.50	2.53
Rails	11903.48	8.50	4.07

---

1. https://github.com/mroth/phoenix-showdown/blob/master/README.md
2. https://gist.github.com/omnibs/e5e72b31e6bd25caf39a

Throughput is the total number of transactions, latency is the total waiting time between transactions, and consistency is a statistical measurement of the consistency of the response. Phoenix is the fastest framework in the benchmark and among the most consistent. The slowest request won't be *that* much slower than the fastest. The reason is that Elixir's lightweight concurrency removes the need for stop-the-world garbage collectors. You can see results for Plug, the Elixir library that serves as a foundation for Phoenix, as well as results for two different versions of Phoenix. You can see that over time, Phoenix performance is getting *better*, and the performance is in the same ballpark with the lower-level Plug.

You'll see several reasons for this blindingly fast performance:

- Erlang has a great model for concurrency. Facebook bought WhatsApp for $21 billion. That application achieved two million concurrently running connections on a single node.

- The router compiles down to the cat-quick pattern matching. You won't have to spend days on performance tuning before you even leave the routing layer.

- Templates are precompiled. Phoenix doesn't need to copy strings for each rendered template. At the hardware level, you'll see caching come into play for these strings where it never did before.

- Functional languages do better on the web. Throughout this book, you'll learn why.

Performance with Phoenix isn't an afterthought. Nor will you have to trade beautiful, maintainable code to get it.

Concurrent

If you're using an object-oriented web framework, chances are that you're watching the evolution of multicore architectures anxiously. You probably already know that the existing imperative models won't scale to handle the types of concurrency we'll need to run on hardware with thousands of cores. The problem is that languages like Java and C# place the burden of managing concurrency squarely on the shoulders of the programmer. Languages like PHP and Ruby make threading difficult to the point where many developers try to support only one web connection per operating-system process, or some structure that is marginally better. In fact, many people that come to Phoenix find us precisely because concurrency is so easy.

Consider PhoenixDelayedJob or ElixirResque—complex packages that exist only to spin off reliable processes as a separate web task. You don't need one. Don't get us wrong. In Ruby, such packages are well conceived and a critical part of any well-crafted solution. In Elixir, those frameworks turn into primitives. The Elixir programming model makes reasoning about concurrent systems almost as easy as reasoning about single-threaded ones. When you have two database fetches, you won't have to artificially batch them together with a stored procedure or a complex query. You can let them work *at the same time:*

```
company_task  = Task.async(fn -> find_company(cid) end)
user_task     = Task.async(fn -> find_user(uid) end)
cart_task     = Task.async(fn -> find_cart(cart_id) end)

company = Task.await(company_task)
user = Task.await(user_task)
cart = Task.await(cart_task)

...
```

You don't have to wait for the combined time for three database requests. Your code will take as long as the single longest database request. You'll be able to use more of your database's available power, and other types of work—like web requests or long exports—will complete much more quickly.

In aggregate, your code will spend *less time waiting* and *more time working.*

Here's the kicker. This code is more reliable. Elixir is based on the libraries that form the backbone of the most reliable systems in the world. You can start concurrent tasks and services that are fully supervised. When one crashes, Elixir can restart it in the last known good state, along with any tainted related service.

Reliability and performance don't need to be mutually exclusive.

Beautiful Code

Elixir is perhaps the first functional language to support Lisp-style macros with a more natural syntax. This feature, like a *template for code*, is not always the right tool for everyday users, but macros are invaluable for extending the Elixir language to add the common features all web servers need to support.

For example, web servers need to map routes onto functions that do the job:

```
pipeline :browser do
  plug :accepts, ["html"]
  plug :fetch_session
  plug :protect_from_forgery
end
```

```
pipeline :api do
  plug :accepts, ["json"]
end

scope "/", MyApp do
  pipe_through :browser
  get "/users",     UserController, :index
  ...
end

scope "/api/", MyApp do
  pipe_through :api
  ...
end
```

You'll see this code a little later. You don't have to understand exactly what it does. For now, know that the first group of functions will run for all browser-based applications, and the second group of functions will run for all JSON-based applications. The third and fourth blocks define which URLs will go to which controller.

You've likely seen code like this before. Here's the point. You don't have to sacrifice beautiful code to use a functional language. Your code organization can be even better. In Phoenix, you won't have to read through dozens of skip_before_filter commands to know how your code works. You'll just build a pipeline for each group of routes that work the same way.

You can find an embarrassing number of frameworks that break this kind of code down into something that is horribly inefficient. Consultancies have made millions on performance tuning by doing nothing more than tuning route tables. This Phoenix example reduces your router to pattern matching that's further optimized by the virtual machine, becoming extremely fast. We've built a layer that ties together Elixir's pattern matching with the macro syntax to provide an excellent routing layer, and one that fits the Phoenix framework well.

You'll find many more examples like this one, such as Ecto's elegant query syntax or how we express controllers as a pipeline of functions that compose well and run quickly. In each case, you're left with code that's easier to read, write, and understand.

We're not here to tell you that macros are the solution to all problems, or that you should use a DSL when a function call should do. We'll use macros when they can dramatically simplify your daily tasks, making them easier to understand and produce. When we do build a DSL, you can bet that we've done our best to make it fast and intelligent.

Simple Abstractions

One continuous problem with web frameworks is that they tend to bloat over time, sometimes fatally. If the underlying abstractions for extending the framework are wrong, each new feature will increase complexity until the framework collapses under its own weight. Sometimes, the problem is that the web framework *doesn't include enough*, and the abstractions for extending the framework aren't right.

This problem is particularly acute with object-oriented languages. Inheritance is simply not a rich enough abstraction to represent the entire ecosystem of a web platform. Inheritance works best when a single feature extends a framework across a single dimension. Unfortunately, many ambitious features span several different dimensions.

Think about authentication, a feature that will impact every layer in your system. Database models must be aware, because authentication schemes require a set of fields to be present, and passwords must be hashed before being saved. Controllers are not immune, because signed-in users must be treated differently from those who are not. View layers, too, must be aware, because the contents of a user interface can change based on whether a user is signed in. Each of those areas must then be customized by the programmer.

Effortlessly Extensible

The Phoenix framework gives you the right set of abstractions for extension. Your applications will break down into individual functions. Rather than rely on other mechanisms like inheritance that hide intentions, you'll roll up your functions into explicit lists called *pipelines*, where each function feeds into the next. It's like building a shopping list for your requests.

In this book, you'll write your own authentication code, based on secure open standards. You'll see how easy it is to tune behavior to your needs and extend it when you need to.

The Phoenix abstractions, in their current incarnation, are new, but each has withstood the test of time. When it's time to extend Phoenix—whether you're plugging in your own session store or doing something as comprehensive as attaching third-party applications like a Twitter wrapper—you'll have the right abstractions available to ensure that the ideas can scale as well as they did when you wrote the first line of code.

Interactive

Chris started the Phoenix project after working to build real-time events into his Ruby on Rails applications. As he started to implement the solution, he had a threading API called Event Machine and noticed that his threads would occasionally die. He then found himself implementing code to detect dead threads.

Over time, the whole architecture began to frustrate him. He was convinced that he could make it *work*, but he didn't think he could ever make it *beautiful* or *reliable*.

If you're building interactive applications on a traditional web stack, you're probably working harder than you need to. There's a reason for that. In the years before web programming was popular, client-server applications were simple. A client process or two communicated to its own process on the server. Programmers had a difficult time making applications scale. Each application connection required its own resources: an operating-system process, a network connection, a database connection, and its own memory. Hardware didn't have enough resources to do that work efficiently, and languages couldn't support many processes, so scalability was limited.

Scaling by Forgetting

Traditional web servers solve the scalability problem by treating each tiny piece of a user interaction as an identical request. The application doesn't save state at all. It simply looks up the user and simultaneously looks up the context of the conversation in a user session. Presto. All scalability problems go away because there's only one type of connection.

But there's a cost. The developer must keep track of the state for each request, and that burden can be particularly arduous for newer, more interactive applications with intimate, long-running rich interactions. As a developer, until now, you've been forced to make a choice between applications that intentionally forget important details to scale and applications that try to remember too much and break under load.

Processes and Channels

With Elixir, you can have both performance and productivity, because it supports a feature called *lightweight processes*. In this book, when you read the word *process*, you should think about Elixir lightweight processes rather than operating-system processes. You can create hundreds of thousands of processes without breaking a sweat. Lightweight processes also mean lightweight connections, and that matters because *connections can be conversations*. Whether you're building a chat on a game channel or a map to the grocery store, you won't have to juggle the details by hand anymore. This application style is called *channels*, and Phoenix makes it easy. Here's what a typical channels feature might look like:

```
def handle_in("new_annotation", params, socket) do
  broadcast! socket, "new_annotation", %{
    user: %{username: "anon"},
    body: params["body"],
    at: params["at"]
  }

  {:reply, :ok, socket}
end
```

You don't have to understand the details. Just understand that when your application doesn't need to juggle the past details of a conversation, your code can get much simpler and faster.

Even now, you'll see many different types of frameworks begin to support channel-style features, from Java to JavaScript and even Ruby. Here's the problem. None of them comes with the simple guarantees that Phoenix has: isolation and concurrency. Isolation guarantees that if a bug affects one channel, all other channels continue running. Breaking one feature won't bleed into other site functionality. Concurrency means one channel can never block another one, whether code is waiting on the database or crunching data. This key advantage means that the UI never becomes unresponsive because the user started a heavy action. Without those guarantees, the development bogs down into a quagmire of low-level concurrency details.

Building applications without these guarantees is usually possible but never pleasant. The results will almost universally be infected with reliability and scalability problems, and your users will never be as satisfied as you'd like to make them.

Reliable

As Chris followed José into the Elixir community, he learned to appreciate the frameworks that Erlang programmers have used to make the most reliable applications in the world. Before Elixir, the language of linked and monitored processes wasn't part of his vocabulary. After spending some time with Elixir, he found the missing pieces he'd been seeking.

You see, you might have beautiful, concurrent, responsive code, but it doesn't matter unless your code is reliable. Erlang applications have always been more reliable than others in the industry. The secret is the process linking structure and the process communication, which allow effective supervision. Erlang's supervisors can have supervisors too, so that your whole application will have a tree of supervisors.

Here's the kicker. By default, Phoenix has set up most of the supervision structure for you. For example, if you want to talk to the database, you need to keep a pool of database connections, and Phoenix provides one out of the box. As you'll see later on, we can monitor and introspect this pool. It's straightforward to study bottlenecks and even emulate failures by crashing a database connections on purpose, only to see supervisors establishing new connections in their place. As a programmer, these abstractions will give you the freedom of a carpenter building on a fresh clean slab, *but your foundation solves many of your hardest problems before you even start*. As an administrator, you'll thank us every day of the week because of the support calls that don't come in.

Now that we've shown you some of the advantages of Phoenix, let's decide whether this book is right for you.

Is This Book for You?

If you've followed Phoenix for any period of time, you already know that this book is the definitive resource for Phoenix programming. If you're using Phoenix or are seriously considering doing professional Elixir development, you're going to want this book. It's packed with insights from the team that created it. Find just one tip in these pages, and the book will pay for itself many times over. This section seeks to answer a different question, though. Beyond folks who've already decided to make an investment in Phoenix, who should buy this book?

Programmers Embracing the Functional Paradigm

Every twenty years or so, new programming paradigms emerge. The industry is currently in the midst of a shift from object-oriented programming to functional programming. If you've noticed this trend, you know that a half dozen or so functional languages are competing for mindshare. The best way to understand a programming language is to go beyond basic online tutorials to see how to approach nontrivial programs.

With *Programming Phoenix*, we don't shy away from difficult problems such as customizing authentication, designing for scale, or interactive web pages. As you explore the language, you'll learn how the pieces fit together to solve difficult problems and how functional programming helps us do it elegantly. When you're done, you might not choose Phoenix, but you'll at least understand the critical pieces that make it popular and if those pieces are likely to work for you.

Rails Developers Seeking Solutions

If you follow the Rails community closely, you know that it has experienced some attrition. Bear in mind that this team believes that Ruby on Rails was great for our industry. Rails still solves some problems well, and for those problems it can be a productive solution. The problem for Rails developers is that the scope of problems it's best able to solve is rapidly narrowing.

In fact, the early growth of Elixir is partially fueled by Rails developers like you. The similar syntax provided an attractive base for learning the language, but the radically improved programming paradigms, introspectable runtime, and concurrency models all provide the solid foundation that those who push Rails the hardest find lacking.

Phoenix measures response times in microseconds, and it has been shown to handle millions of concurrent WebSocket connections on a single machine without sacrificing the productivity we've come to appreciate.

If you're pushing Rails to be more scalable or more interactive, you're not alone. You're going to find Phoenix powerful and interesting.

Dynamic Programmers Looking for a Mature Environment

Like the authors of this book, you may be a fan of dynamic languages like Ruby, Python, and JavaScript. You may have used them in production or even contributed to those ecosystems. Many developers like us are looking for similar flexibility but with a more robust runtime experience. We may love the programming experience in those languages, but we often find ourselves worn out by the many compromises we have to make for performance, concurrency, and maintainability. Phoenix resonates with us because many of the creators of this ecosystem built it to solve these problems.

Elixir is a modern dynamic language built on the three-decades-old, battle-tested Erlang runtime. Elixir macros bring a lot of the flexibility that Ruby, Python, and JavaScript developers came to love, but those dynamic features are quarantined to compile time. With Elixir, during runtime, you have a consistent system with great type support that's generally unseen in other dynamic languages.

Mix these features with the concurrency power, and you'll see why Phoenix provides such excellent performance for everything on the web, and beyond.

Java Developers Seeking More

When Java emerged twenty years ago, it had everything a frustrated C++ community was missing. It was object-oriented, secure, ready for the Internet, and simple, especially when compared to the C++ alternatives at the time. As the Java community flourished and consolidated, the tools and support came. Just about everyone supported Java, and that ubiquity led to a language dominance that we'd never seen before.

As Java has aged, it's lost some of that luster. As the committees that shaped Java compromised, Java lost some of the edge and leadership that the small leadership team provided in early versions. Backward compatibility means that the language evolves slowly as new solutions emerge. All of that early ubiquity has led to a fragmented and bloated ecosystem that moves too slowly and takes years to master, but delivers a fraction of the punch of emerging languages. The Java concurrency story places too much of a burden on the developer, leaving libraries that may or may not be safe for production systems.

New languages are emerging on the JVM, and some of those are rich in terms of features and programming models. This team respects those languages tremendously, but we didn't find the same connection there that we found elsewhere. We also had a hard time separating the good from the bad in the Java ecosystem.

If you're a Java developer looking for where to go next, or a JVM-language developer looking for a better concurrency story, Phoenix would mean leaving the JVM behind. Maybe that's a good thing. You'll find a unified, integrated story in Phoenix with sound abstractions on top. You'll see a syntax that provides Clojure-style metaprogramming on syntax that we think is richer and cleaner than Scala's. You'll find an existing ecosystem from the Erlang community that has a wide range of preexisting libraries, but ones built from the ground up to support not only concurrency, but also distributed software.

Erlang Developers Doing Integrated Web Development

Curiously, we're not seeing a heavy proliferation of Erlang developers in the Elixir community so far. We expect that to change. The toolchain for Phoenix is spectacular, and many of the tools that exist for Erlang can work in this ecosystem as well. If you're an Erlang developer, you may want to take advantage of Mix's excellent scripting for the development, build, and testing workflow. You may like the package management in Hex, or the neat composition of concerns in the Plug library. You may want to use macros to extend the language for your business, or test with greater leverage. You'll have new programming features like protocols or structs.

If you do decide to embrace Elixir, that doesn't mean you need to leave Erlang behind. You'll still be able to use the Erlang libraries you enjoy today, including the Erlang process model and full OTP integration. You'll be able to access your OTP GenServers directly from the Elixir environment, and directly call libraries without the need for extra complex syntax. If these terms aren't familiar to you, don't worry. We'll explore each of them over the course of the book.

Heat Seekers

If you need raw power supported by a rich language, we have a solution and the numbers to back it up. You'll have to work for it, but you'll get much better speed and reliability when you're done. We've run a single chat room on one box supporting two million users. That means that each new message had to go out two million times. We've run benchmarks among the best in the industry, and our numbers seem to be improving as more cores are added. If you need speed, we have the tonic for what ails you.

Others

Certainly, this book isn't for everyone. We do think that if you're in one of these groups, you'll find something you like here. We're equally confident that folks that we haven't described will pick up this book and find something valuable. If you're one of those types, let us know your story.

Online Resources

The apps and examples shown in this book can be found at the Pragmatic Programmers website for this book.[3] You'll also find the community forum and the errata-submission form, where you can report problems with the text or make suggestions for future versions.

In the next chapter, you'll dive right in. From the beginning, you'll build a quick application, and we'll walk you through each layer of Phoenix. The water is fine. Come on in!

---

3. http://pragprog.com/book/phoenix/programming-phoenix

Part I

Building with Functional MVC

In Part I, we'll talk about traditional request/response web applications. We'll walk through the basic layers of Phoenix in great detail. You'll learn how to structure your application into small functions, with each one transforming the results of the previous ones. This pipeline of small functions will lead to the controller, from where we call models and views, but splitting the responsibilities slightly differently from what you've seen elsewhere. You'll explore a new, functional take on the existing model-view-controller pattern. You'll also learn to integrate databases through the Ecto persistence layer and even build your own authentication API. Then, you'll learn to test what you've built so far. In short, you'll learn to build traditional applications that are faster, more reliable, and easier to understand.

## CHAPTER 2

The Lay of the Land

Welcome to Phoenix. In this chapter, we're not going to try to sell you too hard. We think that once you begin the work of learning this framework, the benefits will quickly become evident.

You can think of any web server as a function. Each time you type a URL, think of it as a function call to some remote server. That function takes your request and generates some response. *A web server is a natural problem for a functional language to solve.*

When all is said and done, each Phoenix application is made of functions. In this chapter, we're going to break down a typical web request, and we'll talk about what happens from the moment the user types the URL to the moment Phoenix returns some result.

Simple Functions

Phoenix is built on Elixir, which is a beautiful language, so we're going to use Elixir to talk about the way the layers of Phoenix fit together. In Elixir, we might have a couple of functions like these:

```
def inc(x), do: x + 1
def dec(x), do: x - 1
```

We can chain together several different function calls like this:

```
2 |> inc |> inc |> dec
```

The |>, or *pipe operator*, takes the value on the left and passes it as the first argument to the function on the right. We call these compositions *pipes* or *pipelines*, and we call each individual function a *segment* or *pipe segment.*

There's a side benefit, though. Pipelines are also functions. That means you can make pipelines of pipelines. This idea will help you understand how the various layers fit together. Let's take a look at what a Phoenix program might look like, using pipes:

```
connection |> phoenix
```

Most of the time, you'd write phoenix(connection), but bear with us for a moment. We're going to expand that phoenix function in a bit. We don't care how the request gets to Phoenix. At some point, we know that a browser establishes a connection with an end user, and then there's this big hairy function called phoenix. We pipe the connection into phoenix, it does its magic, and we're done.

In Phoenix, that connection is the whole universe of things we need to know about a user's request. It is a *struct*, which is a map with a known set of fields. The connection comes in with information about the *request*: whether it's HTTP or HTTPS, what the URL is, what the parameters look like. Then, each layer of Phoenix makes a little change to that connection. When Phoenix is done, that connection will have the response in it.

Where Are All of the Diagrams?

In this book, we're going to try something a little different. We're going to use an experimental alternative to architectural diagrams.

For example, let's say we're showing you how to bake a cake. We could have a little diagram with boxes representing process steps that have beautiful bevels or drop shadows or other embellishments. Such a diagram would give you a quick mental picture of what's happening. Then, you could mentally translate that diagram into code.

We can do better, though. Instead, we could choose to express the same idea with an Elixir pipe, like this:

```
ingredients
|> mix
|> bake
```

That code isn't as beautiful as a blinking diagram with fountain fills, but it's tremendously exciting. That ugly text shows you exactly what the layers are, and also how the functions work together. It also helps you build a mental picture of what's happening, because in Phoenix it *is what's happening.* When you understand *that* diagram, you understand Phoenix. You'll actually see code like that throughout the Phoenix framework, so we think it's an excellent way to show how the parts fit together.

Now you know what the API of *every layer of Phoenix looks like*. Functions call other functions, and the first argument for each of those other functions is the connection.

The Layers of Phoenix

Let's take our simplified version of Phoenix and break it down a bit. Let's say that the request is a classic HTTP-style request. (The book will cover the more interactive channels API a little later, but the basic premise will be the same.) As we drill down to the next layer of detail, here's what you see:

```
connection
|> endpoint
|> router
|> pipelines
|> controller
```

Each request comes in through an endpoint, the first point of contact. It's literally the end, or the beginning, of the Phoenix world. A request comes into an endpoint. From there, requests go into our router layer, which directs a request into the appropriate controller, after passing it through a series of pipelines. As you might expect, a pipeline groups functions together to handle common tasks. You might have a pipeline for browser requests, and another for JSON requests.

Inside Controllers

Web frameworks have been around for a long time. The main pattern we use has been around even longer. The Smalltalk language introduced a pattern called *model-view-controller* (MVC). Models access data, views present data, and controllers coordinate between the two. In a sense, the purpose of a web server is to get requests to functions that perform the right task. In most web frameworks, including Phoenix, that task is called an *action*, and we group like functions together in controllers.

To give you a little more perspective, the controller is also a pipeline of functions, one that looks like this:

```
connection
|> controller
|> common_services
|> action
```

This view of the world may look much like what you'd expect from a typical web framework. The connection flows into the controller and calls common services. In Phoenix, those common services are implemented with Plug. You'll get more details as we go. For now, think of Plug as a strategy for building web applications and a library with a few simple tools to enable that strategy.

In this book our actions will do many different things, from accessing other websites to authenticating a user. Most often, our actions will access a database and render a view. Here's what an action to show a user might look like:

```
connection
|> find_user
|> view
|> template
```

If you're using a database in Phoenix, you'll probably use Ecto, the persistence layer. In Phoenix, whenever it's possible, we try to limit side effects—functions that touch and possibly change the outside world—to the controller. We'll try to keep the functions in our models and views pure, so that calling the same function with the same arguments will always yield the same results.

If you're a diehard MVC person, you might have to reimagine the job of the model layer. In Phoenix, you'll want to separate the code that calls another web server, or fetches code from a database, from the code that processes that data. We process data in the model; we read or write that data through the controller. Ecto allows us to organize our code in this way. It separates the code with side effects, which changes the world around us, from the code that's only transforming data.

There you have it. You don't have to memorize all of these layers now, but you've seen the major pieces, and you know how they fit together. After a few pages of theory, you're probably eager to roll up your sleeves and get started.

Installing Your Development Environment

Like many great programming projects, Phoenix builds on some of the best open source projects available. You'll install all of those dependencies now, using the best resources you can find for your own environment.

Elixir Needs Erlang

Erlang provides the base programming virtual machine. It supports our base programming model for concurrency, failover, and distribution. It also provides an exhaustive programming library that's the foundation of the Elixir language.

Go download Erlang,[1] choosing the best installation for your environment. You'll want version 17 or greater.

Phoenix Needs Elixir

The Elixir programming language powers Phoenix. You can find installation instructions on the Elixir[2] site. You'll want version 1.1.0 or greater. Before you work through this book, it would be helpful to know Elixir. Good online resources[3] exist, but we recommend the excellent book *Programming Elixir [Tho14]*, by Dave Thomas, which will get you all of the way through concurrency concepts and OTP. For now, think of OTP as the layer for managing concurrent, distributed services. Rest assured that you'll get more details on OTP later.

You can check to see that Elixir and Erlang are working correctly, like this:

```
$ elixir -v
Elixir 1.1.0
```

Let's also install Hex, Elixir's package manager:

```
$ mix local.hex
* creating ~/.mix/archives/hex-0.10.4.ez
```

Elixir is working, and if you were building strictly a JSON API or a very simple application it would be enough. For this application, since you'll be building both front end and backend with Phoenix, you need to install the code that will help you manage assets. That means you'll have to install Node.js.

Ecto Needs PostgreSQL

Ecto uses the PostgreSQL[4] database adapter by default, and Phoenix adopts this default. It's the database engine we'll be using throughout the book, so you'll need version 9.2 or greater. You can check your local version like this:

```
$ psql --version
psql (PostgreSQL) 9.2.1
```

Node.js for Assets

Web development often requires web assets to be processed for deployment. Rather than reinvent the wheel, developers can optionally use Node.js tools for those services. Phoenix will use brunch.io to compile static assets such as

---

1. http://www.erlang.org
2. http://elixir-lang.org
3. http://elixir-lang.org/getting-started/introduction.html
4. http://www.postgresql.org/download/

JavaScript and CSS by default, and Brunch.io uses npm, the Node.js package manager, to install its dependencies. Once it's installed, Phoenix will rely on them for asset management. Follow the directions on the Node.js[5] site and make sure you have version 5.3.0 or greater. Test your installation like this:

```
$ node --version
v5.3.0
```

Phoenix has a feature called *live reloading*, which automatically reloads web pages as our assets and templates change. If you're running Linux, you're also going to need to install inotify[6] to support live reloading. Other operating systems are covered.

We're finally ready for Phoenix.

Phoenix

You're going to work in the Elixir language to write your code, so you'll use the Mix utility to run development tasks. Let's use Mix to install the Phoenix archive, and then to install Phoenix itself:

```
$ mix archive.install https://github.com/phoenixframework/archives/raw/
/master/phoenix_new.ez
* creating ~/.mix/archives/phoenix_new.ez
```

Now you're ready to roll!

Creating a Throwaway Project

Since C programmers wrote the first Hello, World examples in 1978, the first traditional program you write when learning almost any language has been Hello, World. So we don't break with tradition, we're going to create a Hello, World application as our first project. It will help you get your feet wet. When you're done, you'll get to see all of those layers we talked about in practice.

You now have a shiny new Phoenix installation. It's time to build a project. You're in a functional language, so you're going to spend all of your time writing functions. This common project structure will help you organize things so you don't have to reimagine it for each project.

In Elixir, repetitive tasks that manage the programming cycle will run in Mix. Each time you call this utility, you specify a *task*—an Elixir script—to run. Let's use a task now to create our first Phoenix project, like this:

---

5.   http://nodejs.org
6.   http://www.phoenixframework.org/docs/installation#section-inotify-tools-for-linux-users-

```
$ mix phoenix.new hello
* creating hello/config/config.exs
...

Fetch and install dependencies? [Yn] y
* running mix deps.get
* running npm install && node node_modules/brunch/bin/brunch build
```

We're all set! Run your Phoenix application:

```
$ cd hello
$ mix ecto.create
$ mix phoenix.server
```

If you receive database errors when running mix ecto.create, double-check your Hello.Repo username and password values in config/dev.exs and match your system settings where necessary.

You can also run your app inside Interactive Elixir (IEx) as:

```
$ iex -S mix phoenix.server
```

The phoenix.new Mix task created a project, including all of the files needed to compile and run it. You'll see how the basic tools work, and then what the directories are and where things go as we build the project. For now, we need to do a little bit more.

At the bottom of the mix phoenix.new output, you can see a few sentences that tell you what to do next. We'll skip the instructions related to ecto, since our application won't use a database for now. We want to start Phoenix, though. Change into the hello directory and run the Phoenix web server through Mix, which will start looking for requests on port 4000, like this:

```
$ cd hello
```

```
hello $ mix phoenix.server
[info] Running Hello.Endpoint with Cowboy on http://localhost:4000
```

```
$
```

You can see that the server started on port 4000. The [info] blocks tell you exactly where this server is running. Point your browser to http://localhost:4000/. You can see a simple Phoenix welcome page on page 22.

And we're live! There's no way we're going to get a million-dollar valuation with this product, though. Let's begin to change that by building our first feature.

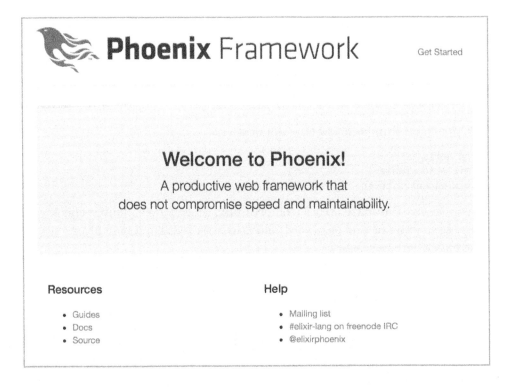

Building a Feature

Our first feature won't be complicated. It'll print a string when you load a specific URL. To build that feature, we're going to use a small fraction of the files that mix phoenix.new created. Don't worry. You'll get a tour of the whole tree a little later. For now, everything we need is in the web subdirectory. We'll edit router.ex to point a URL to our code. We'll also add a controller to the web/controllers subdirectory, a view to web/views, and a template to web/templates.

First things first. We want to map requests coming in to a specific URL to the code that satisfies our request. We'll tie a URL to a function on a controller, and that function to a view. You'll do so in the routing layer, as you would for other web frameworks. Routes in Phoenix go in web/router.ex by default. The .ex extension is for compiled Elixir files. Take a look at that file now. Scroll to the bottom, and you'll find a block that looks like this:

getting_started/listings/hello/web/router.ex

```
scope "/", Hello do
  pipe_through :browser

  get "/", PageController, :index
end
```

You can see a block of requests, scoped to /. That means that this group of routes will attempt to match all routes beginning with /. The pipe_through :browser macro handles some housekeeping for all common browser-style requests. You can see one route that takes requests that look like / and sends them to the :index action on the PageController. This looks like the right place to add our route. Add the following route *above the existing route*:

```
get "/hello", HelloController, :world
get "/", PageController, :index
```

This new code will match routes starting with /hello and send them to the :world function on the HelloController module. If you'd like, you can point your browser to localhost:4000/hello, but you'll get an error page because our controller module doesn't exist yet:

Let's fix that. All controllers in Phoenix are in web/controllers. Create a web/controllers/hello_controller.ex file that looks like this:

getting_started/listings/hello/web/controllers/hello_controller.ex

```
defmodule Hello.HelloController do
  use Hello.Web, :controller

  def world(conn, _params) do
    render conn, "world.html"
  end
end
```

This controller is simple. If you're new to Elixir, you'll often see use SomeModule to introduce specific functionality to a module. The use Hello.Web, :controller call prepares us to use the Phoenix Controller API, including making some functions available that we'll want to use later. The router will call the world action on our controller, passing all of the information we need. We call the functions invoked by the router on our controller's actions, but don't get confused. They're just functions.

Once again, you might point your browser to localhost:4000/hello, but you'd find that it's still not working. We have yet to create our view, so Phoenix reports:

```
undefined function: Hello.HelloView.render/2
    (module Hello.HelloView is not available)
```

That makes sense. Let's easily fix that problem by creating a view called web/views/hello_view.ex with the following contents:

getting_started/listings/hello/web/views/hello_view.ex

```
defmodule Hello.HelloView do
  use Hello.Web, :view
end
```

That file doesn't actually do any work beyond tying the view for world with some code to render a template. We'll rely on the defaults to render a template, which doesn't yet exist. One more time, you see an error when you point your browser to localhost:4000/hello:

```
Could not render "world.html" for Hello.HelloView, please define
    a clause for render/2 or define a template at "web/templates/hello".
    No templates were compiled for this module.
```

We're getting closer. Create the following template at web/templates/hello/world.html.eex, and we're done:

getting_started/listings/hello/web/templates/hello/world.html.eex

```
<h1>From template: Hello world!</h1>
```

As soon as you save your code, notice that the web page reloads! We have live reloading enabled, so whenever we touch templates or template assets, you'll see an automatic page reload.

The .eex extension denotes a template, which Phoenix will compile into a function. If you look closely, you can see that the page we loaded has a header. We're implicitly using the layout defined in the web/views/layout_view.ex view and the template defined in web/templates/layout/app.html.eex. We'll work more with views a little later. For now, it's enough for you to know it's there.

Enjoy the results. It's not a fully operational death star, but you're well on your way.

Using Routes and Params

Right now, there's no dynamic information in our route, and we don't need any *yet*, but later we'll need to grab dynamic data from the URL to look up data from our database. Let's use our sandbox to see how that works. We'll use dynamic routes closely with Elixir's pattern matching. First, let's revise our route. Replace the first route in web/router.ex with this one:

```
get "/hello/:name", HelloController, :world
```

Notice that we're matching a URL pattern—/hello, as before—but we also add /:name to the route. The : tells Phoenix to create a parameter called :name in our route and pass that name as a parameter to the controller. Change the world function on web/controllers/hello_controller.ex to look like this:

```
def world(conn, %{"name" => name}) do
  render conn, "world.html", name: name
end
```

Our new action uses the second argument, which is a map of inbound parameters. We match to capture the name key in the name variable, and pass the result to render in a keyword list. If you're new to Elixir, that function header looks a little different from what you might have seen before. Something special is happening, so let's look at it in a little more detail. If you already understand pattern matching, you can skip to the next section.

Pattern Matching in Functions

The Elixir language has an excellent feature called *pattern matching*. When Elixir encounters a = operator, it means "make the thing on the left match the thing on the right." You can use this feature in two different ways: to take data structures apart, or to test. Let's look at an example:

```
iex> {first, second, third} = {:lions, :tigers, :bears}
{:lions, :tigers, :bears}

iex> first
:lions

iex> {first, second, :bears} = {:lions, :tigers, :bears}
{:lions, :tigers, :bears}

iex> {first, second, :armadillos} = {:lions, :tigers, :bears}
** (MatchError) no match of right hand side value: {:lions, :tigers, :bears}
```

In the first statement, we're matching a 3-tuple to {:lions, :tigers, :bears}. Elixir tries to make the expression on the left match, and it can do so by assigning first to :lions, and second to :tigers. In this case, we're using the pattern match to pick off pieces of the inside of the data structure.

In the third or fourth statement, we're doing something different. We're matching to do a test. When the interpreter tries to match the two, it succeeds and passes on, or fails and throws an exception.

You can also use pattern-matching syntax within your function heads in both of these ways. Type the following into your console:

```
iex> austin = %{city: "Austin", state: "Tx"}
%{city: "Austin", state: "Tx"}

iex> defmodule Place do
...>    def city(%{city: city}), do: city
...>    def texas?(%{state: "Tx"}), do: true
...>    def texas?(_), do: false
...> end
```

This module uses pattern matching in two different ways. The first function uses pattern matching to destructure the data, or take it apart. We use it to extract the city. It grabs the value for the :city key from any map. Although this bit of destructuring is trivial, sometimes the data structures can be deep, and you can reach in and grab the attributes you need with a surgeon's precision.

The second function, texas?, is using a pattern match as a test. If the inbound map has a :state keyword that's set to Tx, it'll match. Otherwise, it'll fall through to the next function, returning false. If we wanted to, we could:

- Match all maps with a given key, as in has_state?(%{state: _}), where the underscore _ will match anything
- Use strings as keys instead of atoms, as in has_state?(%{"state" => "Tx"})
- Match a state, and assign the whole map to a variable, as in has_state?(%{"state" => "Tx"} = place)

The point is, pattern matching is a huge part of Elixir and Phoenix programming. We'll use it to grab only certain types of connections, and also to grab individual pieces of the connection, conveniently within the function heading.

With all of that in mind, let's look at our controller action again:

```
def world(conn, %{"name" => name}) do
  render conn, "world.html", name: name
end
```

That makes more sense now. We're grabbing the name field from the second argument, which contains the inbound parameters. Our controller then renders the world.html template, passing in the local data. The local data prepares a map of variables for use by the templates. Now our views can access the name variable we've specified.

Chris says:
Atom Keys vs. String Keys?

In the world action in our controllers, the external parameters have string keys, "name" => name, while internally we use name: name. That's a convention followed throughout Phoenix. External data can't safely be converted to atoms, because the atom table isn't garbage-collected. Instead, we explicitly match on the string keys, and then our application boundaries like controllers and channels will convert them into atom keys, which we'll rely on everywhere else inside Phoenix.

Using Assigns in Templates

Now, all that remains is to tweak our template in web/templates/hello/world.html.eex to make use of the value. You can access the name specified in the world action as @name, like this:

```
<h1>Hello <%= String.capitalize @name %>!</h1>
```

The <%= %> brackets surround the code we want to substitute into the rendered page. @name will have the value of the :name option that we passed to render. We've worked for this reward, so point your browser to localhost:4000/hello/phoenix. It's ALIVE!

We've done a lot in a short time. Some of this plumbing might seem like magic to you, but you'll find that Phoenix is marvelously explicit, so it's easy to understand exactly what's happening, when, for each request. It's time to make this magic more tangible.

Going Deeper: The Request Pipeline

When we created the hello project, Mix created a bunch of directories and files. It's time to take a more detailed look at what all of those files do and, by extension, how Phoenix helps you organize applications.

When you think about it, typical web applications are just big functions. Each web request is a function call taking a single formatted string—the URL—as an argument. That function returns a response that's nothing more than a formatted string. If you look at your application in this way, your goal is to understand how functions are composed to make the one big function call that handles each request. In some web frameworks, that task is easier said than done. Most frameworks have hidden functions that are only exposed to those with deep, intimate internal knowledge.

The Phoenix experience is different because it encourages breaking big functions down into smaller ones. Then, it provides a place to explicitly register each smaller function in a way that's easy to understand and replace. We'll tie all of these functions together with the Plug library.

Think of the Plug library as a specification for building applications that connect to the web. Each plug consumes and produces a common data structure called Plug.Conn. Remember, that struct represents *the whole universe for a given request*, because it has things that web applications need: the inbound request, the protocol, the parsed parameters, and so on.

Think of each individual plug as a function that takes a conn, does something small, and returns a slightly changed conn. The web server provides the initial data for our request, and then Phoenix calls one plug after another. Each plug can transform the conn in some small way until you eventually send a response back to the user.

Even responses are just transformations on the connection. When you hear words like *request* and *response*, you might be tempted to think that a request is a plug function call, and a response is the return value. That's not what happens. A response is just one more action on the connection, like this:

```
conn
|> ...
|> render_response
```

The whole Phoenix framework is made up of organizing functions that do something small to connections, *even rendering the result*. Said another way...

Plugs are functions.

Your web applications are pipelines of plugs.

Phoenix File Structure

If web applications in Phoenix are functions, the next logical step is to learn where to find those individual functions and how they fit together to build a coherent application. Let's work through the project directory structure, focusing on only the most important ones for now. Here's what your directories look like now:

```
...
├── config
├── lib
├── test
├── web
...
```

Phoenix configuration goes into config, your supervision trees and long-running processes go into lib, tests in test, and your web-related code—including models, views, templates, and controllers—goes in web.

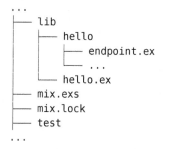

José says:

What Goes in web vs. lib?

Lots of people have asked me what goes in each directory, expecting a complicated answer. It's simple. When you have code reloading turned on, the code in web is reloaded, and the code in lib isn't, making lib the perfect place to put long-running services, like Phoenix's PubSub system, the database connection pool, or your own supervised processes.

In this section, you'll walk through each of these pieces, including the pieces you created and many other ones that Phoenix generated. To sleuth out the entire pipeline of functions for a full web request, you need to start at the beginning. You'll start with the basic code that Elixir and Erlang depend on.

Elixir Configuration

Since Phoenix projects are Elixir applications, they have the same structure as other Mix projects. Let's look at the basic files in the project:

```
...
├── lib
│   ├── hello
│   │   ├── endpoint.ex
│   │   └── ...
│   └── hello.ex
├── mix.exs
├── mix.lock
├── test
...
```

We've already encountered the .ex files, which are to be compiled to .beam files that run on the Erlang virtual machine. The .exs files are Elixir scripts. They're not compiled to .beam files. The compilation happens in memory, each time they are run. They're excellent for quick-changing scripts or stand-alone development-time tasks.

The project we created is a Mix project, named after the build tool that nearly all Elixir projects use. All Mix projects have a common structure. Each project has a configuration file, mix.exs, containing basic information about the project that supports tasks like compiling files, starting the server, and managing dependencies. When we add dependencies to our project, we'll need to make sure they show up here. Also, after we compile the project, mix.lock will include the specific versions of the libraries we depend on, so we guarantee that our production machines use exactly the same versions that we used during development and in our build servers.

Each Mix project also has a lib directory. Support for starting, stopping, and supervising each application is in lib/hello.ex.

Also, each Mix project has a test directory that hosts all tests. Phoenix adds some files to this test structure to support testing-specific files like controllers and views. We haven't yet written any tests, but when we do, they'll live in test.

Environments and Endpoints

Your application will run in an environment. The environment contains specific configuration that your web application needs. You can find that configuration in config:

```
. . .
├── config
│   ├── config.exs
│   ├── dev.exs
│   ├── prod.exs
│   ├── prod.secret.exs
│   └── test.exs
. . .
```

Phoenix supports a master configuration file plus an additional file for each environment you plan to run in. The environments supported by default are development (dev.exs), test (test.exs), and production (prod.exs), but you can add any others that you want.

You can see the three environment files, the master config.exs file containing application-wide configuration concerns, and a file that has secret production passwords that you'd likely want to keep out of version control. It's called prod.secret.exs. This file is usually populated by deployment tasks.

You switch between prod, dev, and test environments via the MIX_ENV environment variable. We'll spend most of our time in this book in dev and test modes. That'll be easy, because your Mix task will have you working in dev by default, and it'll shift to test when you run automated tests with mix.

The master configuration file, config/config.exs, initially contains information about logging, and *endpoints*. Remember when we said that your web applications were just functions? An endpoint is the boundary where the web server hands off the connection to our application code. Now, you'll see that config/config.exs contains a single endpoint called Hello.Endpoint. Open the file called config/config.exs in your editor:

```
use Mix.Config

# Configures the endpoint
config :hello, Hello.Endpoint,
  url: [host: "localhost"],
  root: Path.dirname(__DIR__),
  secret_key_base: "QNU... ...Oo/eLnw",
  render_errors: [accepts: ~w(html json)],
  pubsub: [name: Hello.PubSub,
          adapter: Phoenix.PubSub.PG2]
```

Even though you might not understand this entire block of code, you can see that this code has our endpoint, which is the beginning of our world. The config function call configures the Hello.Endpoint endpoint in our :hello application, giving a keyword list with configuration options. Let's look at that endpoint, which we find in lib/hello/endpoint.ex:

```
defmodule Hello.Endpoint do
  use Phoenix.Endpoint, otp_app: :hello

  plug Plug.Static, ...
  plug Plug.RequestId
  plug Plug.Logger

  plug Plug.Parsers, ...
  plug Plug.MethodOverride
  plug Plug.Head

  plug Plug.Session, ...
  plug Hello.Router
end
```

You can see that this chain of functions, or plugs, does the typical things that almost all production web servers need to do: deal with static content, log requests, parse parameters, and the like. Remember, you already know how to read this code. It'll translate to a pipeline of functions, like this:

```
connection
|> Plug.Static.call
|> Plug.RequestId.call
|> Plug.Logger.call
|> Plug.Parsers.call
|> Plug.MethodOverride.call
|> Plug.Head.call
|> Plug.Session.call
|> Hello.Router.call
```

That's an oversimplification, but the basic premise is correct. Endpoints are the chain of functions at the beginning of each request.

Now you can get a better sense of what's going on. Each request that comes in will be piped through this full list of functions. If you want to change the logging layer, you can change logging for all requests by specifying a different logging function here.

Summarizing what we have so far: an endpoint is a plug, one that's made up of other plugs. Your application is a series of plugs, beginning with an endpoint and ending with a controller:

```
connection
|> endpoint
|> plug
|> plug
...
|> router
|> HelloController
```

We know that the last plug in the endpoint is the router, and we know we can find that file in web/router.ex.

José says:
Can I Have More Than One Endpoint?

Although applications usually have a single endpoint, Phoenix doesn't limit the number of endpoints your application can have. For example, you could have your main application endpoint running on port 80 (HTTP) and 443 (HTTPS), as well as a specific admin endpoint running on a special port—let's say 8080 (HTTPS)—with specific characteristics and security constraints.

Even better, we could break those endpoints into separate applications but still run them side by side. You'll explore this later on when learning about umbrella projects in Chapter 11, *OTP*, on page 199.

The Router Flow

Now that you know what plugs are, let's take a fresh look at our router. Crack open web/router.ex. You can see that it's made up of two parts: pipelines and a route table. Here's the first part:

getting_started/listings/hello/web/router.ex

```
defmodule Hello.Router do
  use Hello.Web, :router

  pipeline :browser do
    plug :accepts, ["html"]
    plug :fetch_session
    plug :fetch_flash
    plug :protect_from_forgery
    plug :put_secure_browser_headers
  end

  pipeline :api do
    plug :accepts, ["json"]
  end
```

Sometimes, you'll want to perform a common set of tasks, or transformations, for some logical group of functions. Not surprisingly, you'll do each transformation step with a plug and group these plugs into pipelines. When you think about it, a pipeline is just a bigger plug that takes a conn struct and returns one too.

In router.ex, you can see two pipelines, both of which do reasonable things for a typical web application. The *browser pipeline* accepts only HTML. It provides some common services such as fetching the session and a user message system called the *flash*, used for brief user notifications. It also provides some security services, such as request forgery protection.

We'd use the second pipeline of functions for a typical JSON API. This stack only calls the function that accepts only JSON requests, so if you had the brilliant idea of converting the whole API site to accept only XML, you could do so by changing one plug in one place.

Our hello application uses the browser pipeline, like this:

getting_started/listings/hello/web/router.ex

```
scope "/", Hello do
  pipe_through :browser

  get "/", PageController, :index
end
```

Now you can tell exactly what the pipeline does. All of the routes after pipe_through :browser—all of the routes in our application—go through the browser pipeline. Then, the router triggers the controller.

In general, the router is the last plug in the endpoint. It gets a connection, calls a pipcline, and then calls a controller. When you break it down, every traditional Phoenix application looks like this:

```
connection
|> endpoint
|> router
|> pipeline
|> controller
```

- The endpoint has functions that happen for every request.

- The connection goes through a named pipeline, which has common functions for each major type of request.

- The controller invokes the model and renders a template through a view.

Let's look at the final piece of this pipeline, the controller.

Controllers, Views, and Templates

From the previous section, you know that a request comes through an end-point, through the router, through a pipeline, and into the controller. The controller is the gateway for the bulk of a traditional web application. Like a puppet master, your controller pulls the strings for this application, making data available in the connection for consumption by the view. It potentially fetches database data to stash in the connection and then redirects or renders a view. The view substitutes values for a template.

For Phoenix, your application code, including your HTML and JavaScript, goes mostly into the web directory. Right now, that directory looks like the figure on page 35.

You can see two top-level files, router.ex and web.ex. You've already seen router.ex, which tells Phoenix what to do with each inbound request. web.ex contains some glue code that defines the overall application structure.

The second part of this book will be dedicated to applications that use the channels directory, so let's skip that for now. You've already coded a simple controller, so you know what the basic structure looks like.

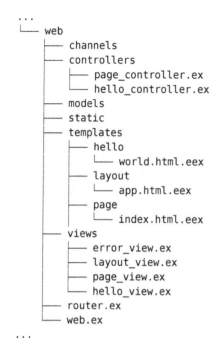

```
. . .
└── web
    ├── channels
    ├── controllers
    │   ├── page_controller.ex
    │   └── hello_controller.ex
    ├── models
    ├── static
    ├── templates
    │   ├── hello
    │   │   └── world.html.eex
    │   ├── layout
    │   │   └── app.html.eex
    │   ├── page
    │   │   └── index.html.eex
    ├── views
    │   ├── error_view.ex
    │   ├── layout_view.ex
    │   ├── page_view.ex
    │   └── hello_view.ex
    ├── router.ex
    └── web.ex

. . .
```

As you might expect for the support of old-style MVC applications, you can see that web contains directories for models, views, and controllers. There's also a directory for templates—because Phoenix separates the views from the templates themselves—as well as a directory for static content.

We've created code in the controller, views, and templates/hello directories, and we've added code to router.ex as well. This application is fairly complete. After all, it's handling plenty of production-level concerns for you:

- The Erlang virtual machine and OTP engine will help the application scale.

- The endpoint will filter out static requests and also parse the request into pieces, and trigger the router.

- The browser pipeline will honor Accept headers, fetch the session, and protect from attacks like Cross-Site Request Forgery (CSRF).

All of these features are quickly available to you for tailoring, but they're also conveniently stashed out of your way in a structure that's robust, fast, and easy to extend. In fact, there's no magic at all. You have a good picture of exactly which functions Phoenix calls on a request to /hello, and where that code lives within the code base:

```
connection              # Plug.Conn
|> endpoint             # lib/hello/endpoint.ex
|> browser              # web/router.ex
|> HelloController.world  # web/controllers/hello_controller.ex
|> HelloView.render(    # web/views/hello_view.ex
       "world.html")    # web/templates/hello/world.html.eex
```

It's easy to gloss over these details and go straight to the web directory, and entrust the rest of the details to Phoenix. We encourage you instead to stop and take a look at exactly what happens for each request, from top to bottom.

Wrapping Up

We've gotten off to a strong start. You've created a first project. Though all of the concepts might still be a bit hazy, you now have a high-level understanding of how Phoenix projects hang together. The core concepts are these:

- We installed Phoenix, which is built using Erlang and OTP for the service layer, Elixir for the language, and Node.js for packaging static assets.

- We used the Elixir build tool mix to create a new project and start our server.

- Web applications in Phoenix are pipelines of plugs.

- The basic flow of traditional applications is endpoint, router, pipeline, controller.

- Routers distribute requests.

- Controllers call services and set up intermediate data for views.

In the next chapter, we're going to build a more hardy controller. You'll see how data flows through Phoenix, from the controller all the way into templates. You'll learn about concepts like layouts along the way. Let's get cracking!

## CHAPTER 3

Controllers, Views, and Templates

By now, you should have a loose grasp of how Phoenix applications work. You know that a typical request starts at an endpoint, flows through a router, and then flows into a controller. You should be starting to appreciate that web programming is a functional problem, and that it's natural to represent it using a functional language.

As we promised, we're going to abandon our brief Hello, World application. For the rest of the book, we're going to work in a new project, and we'll continue developing it through to the end. Before we get started, though, let's take a deeper look at how controllers work.

The Controller

In this chapter, we focus on building the controllers, views, and templates. Though Phoenix has generators that could generate much of a simple web app from scratch, we're going to build part of it by hand so we can appreciate how the parts fit together. Before we fire up the generators, let's talk about how the controller hangs together.

Our application will be called rumbl. When we're all done, the application will allow us to take videos (hosted elsewhere) and attach comments to them *in real time* and play them back alongside the comments of other users. Think of it as *Mystery Science Theater 3000* meets Twitter: At scale, this application will be tremendously demanding because each user will record and play back comments that must be saved and served quickly so that the content stays relevant:

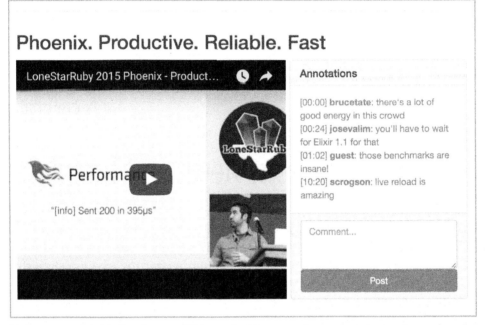

Before we get to the heavy lifting of videos and comments, we're going to handle users so you can get fully grounded in basic concepts first. Initially, we'll focus on a controller that handles our users. Let's talk about what we want to happen when a request for our user controller comes in via a browser:

```
connection
|> endpoint
|> router
|> browser_pipeline
|> UserController
```

A request enters through the endpoint (lib/rumbl/endpoint.ex) and then goes into the router (web/router.ex). The router matches the URL pattern and dispatches the connection through the browser pipeline, which then calls UserController. Let's break that last part down a little further, assuming that the request invokes the index action:

```
connection
|> UserController.index
|> UserView.render("index.html")
```

We need to build the controller to do the work for our individual request, the view to render our template, and the template. We also need to connect the route.

We need to do one more bit of housekeeping. Controller actions can do many different kinds of tasks. Often, that work consists of connecting to some kind of data source, like another website or a database. In this chapter, most of our actions will need access to users. For example, the UserController.index function will need to read users from a database. But first, we're going to retrieve our users from a hand-coded bucket called a *repository*. We're choosing this strategy because it helps us separate the data itself from the ceremony surrounding how it's saved. Ecto, the database library, uses a similar pattern. That way, we won't have to overwhelm you with Ecto's features as you're learning about controllers. When the time is right, we'll simply replace our basic repository with something more fully functional.

With the theory out of the way, it's time to do some real work. Let's get started.

Creating the Project

Let's go ahead and create a new application, called rumbl, with mix phoenix.new:

```
$ mix phoenix.new rumbl

Fetch and install dependencies? [Yn] y
* running mix deps.get
* running npm install && node node_modules/brunch/bin/brunch build

We are all set! Run your Phoenix application:

    $ cd rumbl
    $ mix phoenix.server

You can also run your app inside IEx:

    $ iex -S mix phoenix.server

Before moving on, configure your database in `config/dev.exs` and run:

    $ mix ecto.create

$
```

First, run mix ecto.create to prep your database for later use. Next, start the app up with mix phoenix.server to make sure it's working, and point your browser to http://localhost:4000/. You see the familiar Phoenix home page. That's not exactly what we're looking for. We can steal some of that goodness to build our own messaging.

A Simple Home Page

The default web page is a simple template that has HTML. For now, we can use it to form the foundation of our home page. Let's start to tweak it right now. Make your web/templates/page/index.html.eex look like this:

controllers_views_templates/listings/rumbl/web/templates/page/index.html.eex

```
<div class="jumbotron">
  <h2>Welcome to Rumbl.io!</h2>
  <p class="lead">Rumble out loud.</p>
</div>
```

Now we have a home page started. Notice that your browser has already changed:

Now that we have a home page, more or less, we can start to think about what to do about our users.

Creating Some Users

Rather than bog down in a digression on databases, data libraries, and related concerns, let's agree to keep things simple in the beginning. We'll start with a few hard-coded users. This strategy will help us in the long run too, because it'll allow us to test our actions, views, and templates quickly, without needing to create a full database underneath.

Let's define a Rumbl.User module with the fields id, name, username, and password:

controllers_views_templates/listings/rumbl/web/models/user.ex

```
defmodule Rumbl.User do
  defstruct [:id, :name, :username, :password]
end
```

The User module defines an Elixir struct, which is Elixir's main abstraction for working with structured data.

Elixir Structs

Elixir structs are built on top of maps. You've already seen maps in use. Sometimes, we have maps with clearly defined keys. Let's say we have a map for users. Run iex -S mix to start an interactive Elixir within our application but without running the Phoenix server:

```
iex> alias Rumbl.User
iex> user = %{usernmae: "jose", password: "elixir"}
%{password: "elixir", usernmae: "jose"}
iex> user.username
** (KeyError) key :username not found in: %{password: "elixir", usernmae: "jose"}
```

You may have noticed that we misspelled username as usernmae. A limitation of maps is that they offer protection for bad keys only at runtime, when we effectively access the key. However, many times we'd like to know about such errors as soon as possible, often at compilation time. Structs solve this exact problem. Let's try again but this time using our newly defined Rumbl.User struct:

```
iex> jose = %User{name: "Jose Valim"}
%User{id: nil, name: "Jose Valim", username: nil, password: nil}

iex> jose.name
"Jose Valim"
```

One of the first things to notice is default values. Even though we specified only the :name field when creating the struct, Elixir conveniently filled in the remaining ones. Now, if we misspell a key, we're protected:

```
iex> chris = %User{nmae: "chris"}
** (CompileError) iex:3: unknown key :nmae for struct User
    ...
```

We misspelled the name: key and got an error. Nice.

Notice that the syntax for structs and maps is nearly identical, except for the name of the struct. There's a good reason for that. A struct *is* a map that has a __struct__ key:

```
iex> jose.__struct__
Rumbl.User
```

It's time to stub out a cheap and dirty database. We'll package those users into an API that follows a pattern called a *repository*.

Working with Repositories

A repository is an API for holding things. Let's build a data interface that'll make it easy to snap in a quick stub that's fast and backed by hardcoded data for the short term. This interface should allow us to rapidly test the application as we build it, and also to test our views and templates with simple hardcoded maps. Later, we can replace our hardcoded implementation with a full database-backed repository. Said another way, we want to separate the concerns of the *data* from concerns of the *database*. We can hack our homegrown repository together in Elixir using a few quick lines of code.

Replace the default repository implementation in lib/rumbl/repo.ex with this shell:

```elixir
defmodule Rumbl.Repo do

  @moduledoc """
  In memory repository.
  """

end
```

At the bottom, before the trailing end, we want to add a function to get all of our users:

controllers_views_templates/listings/rumbl/lib/rumbl/repo.ex

```elixir
def all(Rumbl.User) do
  [%Rumbl.User{id: "1", name: "José", username: "josevalim", password: "elixir"},
   %Rumbl.User{id: "2", name: "Bruce", username: "redrapids", password: "7langs"},
   %Rumbl.User{id: "3", name: "Chris", username: "chrismccord", password: "phx"}]
end
def all(_module), do: []
```

Let's also add a couple of functions to get a user by id, or by a custom attribute:

controllers_views_templates/listings/rumbl/lib/rumbl/repo.ex

```elixir
def get(module, id) do
  Enum.find all(module), fn map -> map.id == id end
end

def get_by(module, params) do
  Enum.find all(module), fn map ->
    Enum.all?(params, fn {key, val} -> Map.get(map, key) == val end)
  end
end
```

Now, our Repo is complete. We need to do a little housekeeping. Right now, the application tries to start the Rumbl.Repo by default. Since our file is no longer an Ecto repository, we should comment that out. In lib/rumbl.ex, comment out the line that starts the repository:

```elixir
# Start the Ecto repository
# supervisor(Rumbl.Repo, []),
```

Now, our application has an interface that looks like a read-only database from the outside but is a dumb list of maps from the inside. Let's take it for a spin. Start the console with iex -S mix:

```
iex> alias Rumbl.User
iex> alias Rumbl.Repo

iex> Repo.all User
[%Rumbl.User{id: "1", name: "José", password: "elixir", username: "josevalim"},
 %Rumbl.User{id: "3", name: "Chris", password: "phoenix", username: "cmccord"},
 %Rumbl.User{id: "2", name: "Bruce", password: "7langs", username: "redrapids"}]

iex> Repo.all Rumbl.Other
[]

iex> Repo.get User, "1"
%Rumbl.User{id: "1", name: "José", password: "elixir", username: "josevalim"}

iex> Repo.get_by User, name: "Bruce"
%Rumbl.User{id: "2", name: "Bruce", password: "7langs", username: "redrapids"}
```

And presto, we have a working fake repository. Our controller will work fine. In fact, *our tests will work fine with a repository stub as well.* With some minor tweaks, this strategy will serve us well as we take the controller through its paces.

Now that we have users, we can move ahead to the actual code that fetches and renders them.

Building a Controller

You've already built a simple controller, so you know the drill. At this point, we could create all of the routes needed by a user automatically, but we're going to play the boring community lifeguard that yells "Walk!" If you understand how a single route works, it'll be much easier to explore the powerful shortcuts later. Specifically, we need two routes. UserController.index will show a list of users, and UserController.show will show a single user. As always, create the routes in router.ex:

controllers_views_templates/listings/rumbl/web/router.ex

```
scope "/", Rumbl do
  pipe_through :browser
  get "/users",     UserController, :index
  get "/users/:id", UserController, :show
  get "/", PageController, :index
end
```

Notice that we have our two new routes and the default route for /. Our two new routes use the new UserController, which doesn't yet exist, with the :show and :index actions. The names and URLs we've chosen for these actions aren't random. The :show, :index, :new, :create, :edit, :update, and :delete actions are all frequently used in Phoenix. For now, follow along strictly, and you'll learn the shortcuts later.

Let's take a closer look at the :index route:

```
get "/users", UserController, :index
```

You've seen the get macro before. The route matches HTTP GET requests to a URL that looks like /users and sends them to the UserController, calling the index action. That route stores :index—the action we intend to invoke—in the conn and then calls the right pipeline.

Now, restart your server and point your browser to http://localhost:4000/users. You get some debugging information, but you don't have to go beyond the title to find this message:

```
UndefinedFunctionError at GET /users

undefined function: Rumbl.UserController.init/1
  (module Rumbl.UserController is not available)
```

That makes sense; we haven't written the controller yet. Let's create a controller in web/controllers/user_controller.ex and include one function, called index, which will find :users from our repository:

controllers_views_templates/listings/rumbl/web/controllers/user_controller.ex
```
defmodule Rumbl.UserController do
  use Rumbl.Web, :controller

  def index(conn, _params) do
    users = Repo.all(Rumbl.User)
    render conn, "index.html", users: users
  end
end
```

Let's take that code apart. There's a little bit of ceremony at the top of the file that defines our module and announces that we're going to use the :controller API. Right now, the only action is index.

If you access the users page again, you can see that we're getting an error message, but we've traded up:

```
UndefinedFunctionError at GET /users

undefined function: Rumbl.UserView.render/2
  (module Rumbl.UserView is not available)
```

Progress! Next, we need to code a view.

Coding Views

This is your second pass through this process. The first time, you built a Hello, World style feature, one with a controller, view, and template. Now it's time for the more detailed explanation that you were promised earlier. In many other web frameworks, the terms *view* and *template* are often used synonymously. It's enough for users to know that when a controller finishes a task, a view is somehow rendered.

In Phoenix, the terminology is a little more explicit. A *view* is a module containing rendering functions that convert data into a format the end user will consume, like HTML or JSON. You can write such functions as you would any other Elixir function. Those rendering functions can also be defined from templates. A *template* is a function on that module, compiled from a file containing a raw markup language and embedded Elixir code to process substitutions and loops. The separation of the view and template concepts makes it easy to render data any way you want, be it with a raw function, an embedded Elixir engine, or any other template engine.

In short, views are modules responsible for rendering. Templates are web pages or fragments that allow both static markup and native code to build response pages, compiled into a function. In Phoenix, you eventually compile both to functions. Let's build a view in web/views/user_view.ex:

controllers_views_templates/listings/rumbl/web/views/user_view.ex

```elixir
defmodule Rumbl.UserView do
  use Rumbl.Web, :view
  alias Rumbl.User

  def first_name(%User{name: name}) do
    name
    |> String.split(" ")
    |> Enum.at(0)
  end
end
```

We add a simple first_name function to parse a user's first name from that user's name field. Next, in web/templates, we create a user directory and a new index template in web/templates/user/index.html.eex:

controllers_views_templates/listings/rumbl/web/templates/user/index.html.eex

```eex
<h1>Listing Users</h1>

<table class="table">
  <%= for user <- @users do %>
    <tr>
      <td><b><%= first_name(user) %></b> (<%= user.id %>)</td>
```

```
    <td><%= link "View", to: user_path(@conn, :show, user.id) %></td>
  </tr>
<% end %>
</table>
```

That's mostly HTML markup, with a little Elixir mixed in. At runtime, Phoenix will translate this template to a function, but think of it this way. EEx executes Elixir code that's within <%= %> tags, injecting the result into the template. EEx evaluates code within <% %> tags without injecting the result. We'll try to use code without side effects in views wherever possible, so we'll use mostly the <%= %> form. You've seen template code before, but you'll walk through it anyway.

The expression for user <- @users walks through the users, rendering each user using the template code inside the do block, and rolling up the result into the template. Remember, we've already populated @users within our index action.

Each user is a map. We render the name field, the id field, and a link. That link comes from a helper function.

> ### Chris says:
> # Why Are Templates So Fast in Phoenix?
>
> After compilation, templates are functions. Since Phoenix builds templates using linked lists rather than string concatenation the way many imperative languages do, one of the traditional bottlenecks of many web frameworks goes away. Phoenix doesn't have to make huge copies of giant strings.
>
> Since Elixir has only a single copy of the largest and most frequently used strings in your application, the hardware caching features of most CPUs can come into play. The book's introduction talked about the performance of the routing layer. The performance of the view layer is just as important.

Using Helpers

That link function packs a surprising amount of punch into a small package. Phoenix helpers provide a convenient way to drop common HTML structures onto your view. There's nothing special about them. Helpers are simply Elixir functions. For example, you can call the functions directly in IEx:

```
$ iex -S mix

iex> Phoenix.HTML.Link.link("Home", to: "/")
{:safe, ["<a href=\"/\">", "Home", "</a>"]}

iex> Phoenix.HTML.Link.link("Delete", to: "/", method: "delete")
```

```
{:safe,
 [["<form action=\"/\" class=\"link\" method=\"post\">",
   "<input name=\"_method\" type=\"hidden\" value=\"delete\">
    <input name=\"_csrf_token\" type=\"hidden\" value=\"UhdjBFUcOh...\">"],
  ["<a data-submit=\"parent\" href=\"#\">", "[x]", "</a>"], "</form>"]}
```

The second argument to our link function is a keyword list, with the to: argument specifying the target. We use a path that's automatically created for our :show route to specify the link target. Now you can see that our list has the three users we fetched from our repository:

Listing Users

José (1)	View
Bruce (2)	View
Chris (3)	View

At this point you may be wondering where the HTML helpers come from. At the top of each view, you can find the following definition: use Rumbl.Web, :view. This code snippet is the one responsible for setting up our view modules, importing all required functionality. Open up web/web.ex to see exactly what's imported into each view:

controllers_views_templates/rumbl/web/web.ex

```elixir
def view do
  quote do
    use Phoenix.View, root: "web/templates"

    # Import convenience functions from controllers
    import Phoenix.Controller, only: [get_csrf_token: 0,
                                      get_flash: 2,
                                      view_module: 1]

    # Use all HTML functionality (forms, tags, etc)
    use Phoenix.HTML

    import Rumbl.Router.Helpers
    import Rumbl.ErrorHelpers
    import Rumbl.Gettext
  end
end
```

Phoenix.HTML is responsible for the HTML functionality in views, from generating links to working with forms. Phoenix.HTML also provides HTML safety: *by default, applications are safe from cross-site scripting (XSS) attacks,* because only the markup generated by Phoenix.HTML functions is considered safe. That's why the link function returns a tuple. The first element of the tuple—the :safe atom—indicates that the content in the second element is known to be safe.

To learn about existing HTML helpers, visit the Phoenix.HTML documentation.[1]

Keep in mind that the web.ex file is not a place to attach your own functions. You want to keep this file skinny and easy to understand. For example, the contents of the view function will be macro-expanded *to each and every view*! So remember, in web.ex, prefer import statements to defining your own functions.

That's a good amount of progress so far. Let's create one more action, and the corresponding template, to round out our actions.

Showing a User

Now that we've created the code to show a list of users, we can work on showing a single user. To refresh your memory, let's look at the route we created earlier:

```
get "/users/:id", UserController, :show
```

That's easy enough. On a request to /users/:id, where :id is part of the inbound URL, the router will add at least two things we'll need to conn, including the :id that's part of the URL, and the action name, :show. Then, the router will call the plugs in our pipeline, and then the UserController. To show a single user using this request, we need a controller action, which we add to web/controllers/user_controller.ex:

controllers_views_templates/listings/rumbl/web/controllers/user_controller.change1.ex
```
def show(conn, %{"id" => id}) do
  user = Repo.get(Rumbl.User, id)
  render conn, "show.html", user: user
end
```

Now, you can see why Plug breaks out the params part of the inbound conn. We can use params to extract the individual elements our action needs. In this case, we're matching on the "id" key to populate the id variable. We then use that to fetch a record from Repo, and use that to render the result.

When you point the browser to localhost:4000/users/1, predictably, Phoenix screams at you. You've not yet built the template.

Add that to web/templates/user/show.html.eex:

controllers_views_templates/listings/rumbl/web/templates/user/show.html.eex
```
<h1>Showing User</h1>
<b><%= first_name(@user) %></b> (<%= @user.id %>)
```

---

1. http://hexdocs.pm/phoenix_html

Point your browser to /users/1. You can see the first user, with the dynamic content piped in as we require.

Naming Conventions

When Phoenix renders templates from a controller, it infers the name of the view module, Rumbl.UserView, from the name of the controller module, Rumbl.User-Controller. The view modules infer their template locations from the view module name. In our example, our Rumbl.UserView would look for templates in the web/templates/user/ directory. Phoenix uses singular names throughout, avoiding confusing pluralization rules and naming inconsistencies.

You'll see how to customize these conventions later. For now, know that you can let Phoenix save you some time by letting the good old computer do the work for you. Break the rules if you have to, but if you're smart about it, you'll save some tedious ceremony along the way.

Nesting Templates

Often there's a need to reduce duplication in the templates themselves. For example, both of our templates have common code that renders a user. Take the common code and create a user template in web/templates/user/user.html.eex:

```
<b><%= first_name(@user) %></b> (<%= @user.id %>)
```

We create another template to render a user. Then, whenever we build tables or listings of users in many different contexts, we can share the code that we update only once. Now, change your show.html.eex template to render it:

```
<h1>Showing User</h1>
<%= render "user.html", user: @user %>
```

Also, change your index.html.eex template to render it:

```
<tr>
  <td><%= render "user.html", user: user %></td>
  <td><%= link "View", to: user_path(@conn, :show, user.id) %></td>
</tr>
```

At this point, it's worth emphasizing that a view in Phoenix is just a module, and templates are just functions. When we add a template named web/templates/user/user.html.eex, the view extracts the template from the filesystem and makes it a function in the view itself. That's why we need the view in the first place. Let's build on this thought inside iex -S mix:

```
iex> user = Rumbl.Repo.get Rumbl.User, "1"
%Rumbl.User{...}
```

```
iex> view = Rumbl.UserView.render("user.html", user: user)
{:safe, [[[["" | "<b>"] | "José"] | "</b> ("] | "1"] | ")\n"]}
```

```
iex> Phoenix.HTML.safe_to_string(view)
"<b>José</b> (1)\n"
```

We fetch a user from the repository and then render the template directly.
Because Phoenix has the notion of HTML safety, render returns a tuple, tagged
as :safe, and the contents are stored in a list for performance. We convert this
safe and fast representation into a string by calling Phoenix.HTML.safe_to_string.

Each template in our application becomes a render(template_name, assigns) clause
in its respective view. So, rendering a template is a combination of pattern
matching on the template name and executing the function. Because the
rendering contract is so simple, nothing is stopping developers from defining
render clauses directly on the view module, skipping the whole template. This
is the technique used in Rumbl.ErrorView, a view invoked by Phoenix whenever
our application contains errors:

controllers_views_templates/rumbl/web/views/error_view.ex

```
def render("404.html", _assigns) do
  "Page not found"
end
```

```
def render("500.html", _assigns) do
  "Server internal error"
end
```

The Phoenix.View module—the one used to define the views themselves—also
provides functions for rendering views, including a function to render and
convert the rendered template into a string in one pass:

```
iex> user = Rumbl.Repo.get Rumbl.User, "1"
%Rumbl.User{...}
```

```
iex> Phoenix.View.render(Rumbl.UserView, "user.html", user: user)
{:safe, [[[["" | "<b>"] | "José"] | "</b> ("] | "1"] | ")\n"]}
```

```
iex> Phoenix.View.render_to_string(Rumbl.UserView, "user.html", user: user)
"<b>José</b> (1)\n"
```

Behind the scenes, Phoenix.View calls render in the given view and adds some
small conveniences, like wrapping our templates in layouts whenever one is
available. Let's find out how.

Layouts

When we call render in our controller, instead of rendering the desired view
directly, the controller first renders the layout view, which then renders the

actual template in a predefined markup. This allows developers to provide a consistent markup across all pages without duplicating it over and over again.

Since layouts are regular views with templates, all the knowledge that you've gained so far applies to them. In particular, each template receives a couple of special assigns when rendering, namely @view_module and @view_template. You can see these in web/templates/layout/app.html.eex:

```
controllers_views_templates/rumbl/web/templates/layout/app.html.eex
  <p class="alert alert-info" role="alert"><%= get_flash(@conn, :info) %></p>
  <p class="alert alert-danger" role="alert"><%= get_flash(@conn, :error) %></p>

  <%= render @view_module, @view_template, assigns %>
</div> <!-- /container -->
<script src="<%= static_path(@conn, "/js/app.js") %>"></script>
```

It's just pure HTML with a render call of render @view_module, @view_template, assigns, but it doesn't need to be restricted to HTML. As in any other template, the connection is also available in layouts as @conn, giving you access to any other helper in Phoenix. When you call render in your controller, you're actually rendering with the :layout option set by default. This allows you to render the view and template for your controller action in the layout with a plain render function call. No magic is happening here.

We can tweak the existing layout to be a little more friendly to our application. Rather than slog through a bunch of CSS and HTML here, we'll let you work out your own design. If you choose to do so, replace the layout you find at web/templates/layout/app.html.eex with one you like better. As always, you'll see your browser autoupdate.

We're just about done here. By now, our growing company valuation is somewhere north of, well, the tree house you built in the third grade. Don't worry, though: things will pick up in a hurry. You're going to go deeper faster than you thought possible.

Wrapping Up

We packed a ton into this chapter. Let's summarize what you've done:

- We created a simple repository. We did so to simplify your plunge into the world of controllers and views.

- We created actions, which serve as the main point of control for each request.

- We created views, which exist to render templates.

- We created templates, which generate HTML for our users.

- We employed helpers, which are simple Phoenix functions used in templates.

- We used layouts, which are HTML templates that embed an action's HTML.

In the next chapter, we're going to replace our homegrown repository with a database-backed one using Ecto. By the time we're done, we'll be reading our users from the database and entering new users with forms.

Don't stop now! Things are just getting interesting.

## CHAPTER 4

Ecto and Changesets

Up to now, we've been focusing on our application's presentation layer with views and templates, and controlling those views with controllers. Our backend uses a simple in-memory repository instead of a real database. There's a method to our madness, though. That repository uses the same API as Ecto, the Elixir framework for persistence. In this chapter, we'll convert our application to use a real Ecto repository backed by a Postgres database. By the time you're done, your repository will be able to save users and search for them using an advanced query API.

Understanding Ecto

If you've used persistence frameworks like LINQ in .NET or Active Record in Rails, you'll see some common threads in Ecto but also some significant differences. Ecto is a wrapper that's primarily intended for relational databases, allowing developers to read and persist data to underlying storage such as PostgreSQL. It has an encapsulated query language that you can use to build layered queries that can then be composed into more-sophisticated ones.

Ecto also has a feature called *changesets* that holds all changes you want to perform on the database. It encapsulates the whole process of receiving external data, casting and validating it before writing it to the database.

In this chapter, we'll start with a basic database-backed repository. We'll then move on to creating data and managing updates with changesets, saving most of the query language for later.

Ecto is likely going to be a little different from many of the persistence layers you've used before. If you want Ecto to get something, you have to explicitly ask for it. This feature will probably seem a little tedious to you at first, but it's the only way to guarantee that your application has predictable performance when the amount of data grows.

We're going to use Ecto's first-ever implementation, PostgreSQL. Install PostgreSQL, consulting the Postgres homepage[1] for details if necessary.

When we set up our in-memory repository, we briefly changed lib/rumbl/repo.ex to remove the default Ecto repository. Let's change it back to what Phoenix included by default, like this:

ecto/listings/rumbl/lib/rumbl/repo.ex

```
defmodule Rumbl.Repo do
  use Ecto.Repo, otp_app: :rumbl
end
```

We also disabled the Ecto Repo supervisor in our supervision tree. Let's reenable it by uncommenting the supervisor in lib/rumbl.ex:

ecto/listings/rumbl/lib/rumbl.change1.ex

```
supervisor(Rumbl.Endpoint, []),
# Start the Ecto repository
supervisor(Rumbl.Repo, []),
```

Ecto is an Elixir library, and it's configured like any other application. You can find the development configuration in config/dev.exs:

ecto/rumbl/config/dev.exs

```
config :rumbl, Rumbl.Repo,
  adapter: Ecto.Adapters.Postgres,
  username: "postgres",
  password: "postgres",
  database: "rumbl_dev",
  hostname: "localhost",
  pool_size: 10
```

We specify the default repository for our application and also the database adapter it'll use. We also tell Ecto to use our Postgres database, and we specify the username, password, and database parameters. You need to replace those with your own database username and password. We'll use the Postgres adapter, which is included by Phoenix. If you'd like, you can configure Ecto with MySQL, MSSQL, SQLite, and more. You can expect this list to grow.

Now it's time to create a real database-backed Ecto repository. When you type the following command, Ecto creates the underlying database, if it's not already there:

---

1. http://www.postgresql.org/

```
$ mix ecto.create
The database for Rumbl.Repo has been created.
```

As yet, we haven't done the heavy lifting to specify our users. We've only tied
Phoenix to this Postgres database. Let's create some schemas and tie those
tables to code.

Defining the User Schema and Migration

Ecto has a DSL that specifies the fields in a struct and the mapping between
those fields and the database tables. Let's use that now. To define our schema,
replace the contents in web/models/user.ex with the following:

ecto/listings/rumbl/web/models/user.ex

```
defmodule Rumbl.User do
  use Rumbl.Web, :model

  schema "users" do
    field :name, :string
    field :username, :string
    field :password, :string, virtual: true
    field :password_hash, :string

    timestamps
  end
end
```

This DSL is built with Elixir macros. The schema and field macros let us specify
both the underlying database table and the Elixir struct. Each field corresponds
to both a field in the database and a field in our local User struct. The primary
key is automatically defined and defaults to :id. We also add a virtual field for
our password, since we need an intermediate field before hashing the password
in the password_hash field. Virtual fields are not persisted to the database. After
the schema definition, Ecto defines an Elixir struct for us, which we can create
by calling %Rumbl.User{} as we did before.

Finally, our schema uses use Rumbl.Web, :model at the top. Take a look at web/web.ex
to see everything it injects into our Rumbl.User module:

ecto/rumbl/web/web.ex

```
def model do
  quote do
    use Ecto.Schema

    import Ecto
    import Ecto.Changeset
    import Ecto.Query, only: [from: 1, from: 2]
  end
end
```

For now, it only uses Ecto.Schema and imports functions to work with changesets and queries, but this function serves as an extension point that'll let us explicitly alias, import, or use the various libraries our model layer might need. With Ecto, you needn't worry about plugins and external packages adding or removing functionality behind the scenes.

We've treated our code with care, and we should give our database *at least* the same level of respect. Now that we have our Repo and User schema configured, we need to make the database reflect the structure of our application. Phoenix uses *migrations* for that purpose. A migration changes a database to match the structure our application needs. For our new feature, we need to add a migration to create our users table with columns matching our User schema.

```
$ mix ecto.gen.migration create_user
* creating priv/repo/migrations
* creating priv/repo/migrations/20150916023702_create_user.exs
```

The mix ecto.gen.migration creates a migration file for us with a special timestamp to ensure ordering of our database migrations. Note that your migration file-name is different from ours because Ecto prepends a timestamp to maintain the ordering of migrations. Key in these changes within your empty change function:

ecto/listings/rumbl/priv/repo/migrations/20150916023702_create_user.exs

```
defmodule Rumbl.Repo.Migrations.CreateUser do
  use Ecto.Migration

  def change do
    create table(:users) do
      add :name, :string
      add :username, :string, null: false
      add :password_hash, :string

      timestamps
    end

    create unique_index(:users, [:username])
  end
end
```

In the dark days of persistence frameworks, before migrations were commonplace, changes to the database weren't versioned with the source code. Often, those changes weren't even automated. That strategy was fine if new code worked the first time, but it opened the door for problems:

- When deploying new code, programmers often introduced errors when changing the database.

> ## What Is a Model?
>
> At this point, you may be asking yourself, "What is a model?" In Phoenix, models, controllers, and views are layers of functions. Just as a controller is a layer to transform requests and responses according to a communication protocol, the model is nothing more than a group of functions to transform data according to our business requirements.
>
> In this book, we use the word *schema* to describe the native form of the data, and the word *struct* to refer to the data itself, but *structs are not models*. In fact, many functions from our model layer might not deal with our application's structs at all. They can manipulate other structures such as changesets and queries. The important thing to understand is that the model is the layer of functions that supports our business rules rather than the data that flows through those functions.

- The high stress of code rollbacks led to frequent mistakes when changes were rolled back under pressure.
- Building a fresh development environment was tough because the schema history was too fragmented.

In general, migrating a database, both up for a successful deploy and down for an unsuccessful deploy, should be an automated and repeatable process. The Ecto.Migration API[2] provides several functions to create, remove, and change database tables, fields, and indexes. These functions also have counterparts to do the reverse. Here, we used the create, add, and timestamps macros to build our users table and matched the fields with our User schema. For example, add creates a new field, and timestamps creates a couple of fields for us, inserted_at and updated_at.

Now all that's left is to migrate up our database:

```
$ mix ecto.migrate
[info] == Running Rumbl.Repo.Migrations.CreateUser.change/0 forward
[info] create table users
[info] create index users_username_index
[info] == Migrated in 0.3s
```

Be careful. The ecto.migrate task will migrate the database *for your current environment*. So far, we've been running the dev environment. To change the environment, you'd set the MIX_ENV operating-system environment variable.

Now, our database is configured, and the schema exists. Phoenix is built on top of OTP, a layer for reliably managing services. We can use OTP to start key services like Ecto repositories in a supervised process so that Ecto and

---

2. http://hexdocs.pm/ecto/Ecto.Migration.html

Phoenix can do the right thing in case our repository crashes. The process that manages all this is called Rumbl.Repo, and we start it in our application's supervision tree in lib/rumbl.ex, like this:

```
children = [
  ...
  # Start the Ecto repository
  supervisor(Rumbl.Repo, []),
  ...
]
```

Now that our configuration is established, let's take it for a spin.

Using the Repository to Add Data

With our database ready, we can begin to persist our User structs. Let's hop into an IEx shell and create the users that we previously hard-coded in our in-memory repository. We'll worry about hashing the password later.

This Is a Bad Idea

You don't want to store plain-text passwords into your database! We'll temporarily save plain-text passwords *only as an intermediate step* toward a more sophisticated user authentication system.

Spin up your console with iex -S mix, and insert some data:

```
iex> alias Rumbl.Repo
iex> alias Rumbl.User

iex> Repo.insert(%User{
...>   name: "José", username: "josevalim", password_hash: "<3<3elixir"
...> })
[debug] INSERT INTO "users" ("inserted_at", "name", "password_hash", ...
{:ok,
 %Rumbl.User{__meta__: #Ecto.Schema.Metadata<:loaded>, id: 1,
   inserted_at: #Ecto.DateTime<2015-09-23T03:23:32Z>, name: "José",
   password: nil, password_hash: "<3<3elixir",
   updated_at: #Ecto.DateTime<2015-09-23T03:23:32Z>,
   username: "josevalim"}}

iex> Repo.insert(%User{
...>   name: "Bruce", username: "redrapids", password_hash: "7langs"
...> })
  ...
iex> Repo.insert(%User{
...>   name: "Chris", username: "cmccord", password_hash: "phoenix"
...> })
```

And we're up! You can see that Ecto is creating the id field and populating our timestamps for us. You might be curious to see whether we can use it the same way we used our UserController to find users. Let's take a look:

```
iex> Repo.all(User)
[debug] SELECT u0."id", u0."name", u0."username", u0."password_hash",
  u0."inserted_at", u0."updated_at" FROM "users" AS u0 [] OK query=229.4ms)
[%Rumbl.User{__meta__: #Ecto.Schema.Metadata<:loaded>,
  id: 1, ..., name: "José", password_hash: "<3<3elixir", ... },
 %Rumbl.User{__meta__: #Ecto.Schema.Metadata<:loaded>,
   id: 2, ..., name: "Bruce", password_hash: "7langs", ... },
 %Rumbl.User{__meta__: #Ecto.Schema.Metadata<:loaded>,
  id: 3, ..., name: "Chris", password_hash: "phoenix",...}]
iex> Repo.get(User, 1)
[debug] SELECT u0."id", u0."name", u0."username",
              u0."password_hash", u0."inserted_at",
              u0."updated_at" FROM "users"
              AS u0
              WHERE (u0."id" = $1) [1] OK query=136.6ms queue=20.0ms

%Rumbl.User{__meta__: #Ecto.Schema.Metadata<:loaded>,
 id: 1, ..., name: "José", password_hash: "<3<3elixir", ... }
```

We haven't touched the controller at all, but you'll find that our changes are already working for us. Our Repo API remains exactly the same, but we're fetching records from the database instead. That's one of the strengths of repositories. One interface can have many different implementations, and even configurations. Visit our users page and view the logs to see the inserted records:

```
$ mix phoenix.server
[info] Running Hello.Endpoint with Cowboy on http://localhost:4000
```

Now visit http://localhost:4000/users as before, but watch the logs to see Ecto's SQL statements being executed:

```
[info] GET /users
[debug] Processing by Rumbl.UserController.index/2
  Parameters: %{}
  Pipelines: [:browser]
[debug] SELECT u0."id", u0."name", u0."username", u0."password_hash",
        u0."inserted_at", u0."updated_at" FROM "users" AS u0 [] (3.6ms)
[info] Sent 200 in 1ms
```

You can see that we're fetching data from the database instead of the in-memory store. We're making plenty of progress here, but there's still work to do. Let's build some forms to create new users via a web interface.

Building Forms

Now that we have a database-backed repository, let's add the ability to create new users in our system. We're going to use Phoenix's form builders for that purpose. First, open up your controller at web/controllers/user_controller.ex and set up a new user record for our new template, like this:

ecto/listings/rumbl/web/controllers/user_controller.change1.ex

```
alias Rumbl.User

def new(conn, _params) do
  changeset = User.changeset(%User{})
  render conn, "new.html", changeset: changeset
end
```

Notice the User.changeset function. This function receives a struct and the controller parameter, and returns an Ecto.Changeset. Changesets let Ecto manage record changes, cast parameters, and perform validations. We use a changeset to build a customized strategy for dealing with each specific kind of change, such as creating a user or updating sensitive information. Let's add a changeset function to our User module in web/models/user.ex with some essential validations:

ecto/listings/rumbl/web/models/user.change1.ex

```
def changeset(model, params \\ :empty) do
  model
  |> cast(params, ~w(name username), [])
  |> validate_length(:username, min: 1, max: 20)
end
```

Our changeset accepts a User struct and parameters. We then pass the cast function a list of words to tell Ecto that name and username are required, and there are no optional fields. cast makes sure we provide all necessary required fields. Then, it casts all required and optional values to their schema types, rejecting everything else.

We pipe cast, which returns an Ecto.Changeset, into validate_length to validate the username length. Ecto.Changeset defines both cast and validate_length, so we import it as part of the model function in web/web.ex.

For now, because we haven't listed password as either a required or optional field, our changeset ignores it. This is superb, given that our password-hashing system still isn't in place, and storing passwords in clear text would be dangerous.

Chris says:
Why Is the Second Parameter :empty?

If no parameters are specified, we can't just default to an empty map, because that would be indistinguishable from a blank form submission. Instead, we default params to the :empty atom. By convention, Ecto will produce an invalid changeset, with empty parameters.

At this point, you might wonder why Ecto adds this little bit of complexity through changesets. You may have seen other frameworks that add validations directly to the schema. We could simply write a set of one-size-fits-all validations and then pass a set of updated attributes to the create or update API.

When conventional persistence frameworks allow one-size-fits-all validations, they're forced to work harder and manage change across multiple concerns. Here's the problem. Imagine that your boss lays down the requirement of logging into your application through Facebook. That update requires a different kind of password validation, and a different kind of enforcement for password rules, so you build a custom validation and tweak your model layer in clever ways to trigger the right password rules at the right time. Then, your increasingly irritating boss asks for a JSON API, and your JSON programmers aren't content with the cute "Oops, we broke something" error messages that seemed to work fine for end users. You dig deeply into the persistence API and decide that the error reporting no longer works for you. Your stomach sinks as it does for that first roller coaster drop while you hope against hope that the car will rise again, but you instinctively know that this ride is at its zenith. It's always downhill from here.

One size does not fit all when it comes to update strategies. Validations, error reporting, security, and the like can change. When they do, if your single update policy is tightly coupled to a schema, it'll *hurt*. The changeset lets Ecto decouple update policy from the schema, and that's a good thing because you can handle each update policy in its own separate changeset function. You'll see a good example of this policy segregation when your learn about authentication.

Now that we've updated our models and controllers to handle new users, we need to add the new action to our router. Replace your main router scope with the following code:

ecto/listings/rumbl/web/router.change1.ex

```
scope "/", Rumbl do
  pipe_through :browser

  get "/", PageController, :index
  resources "/users", UserController, only: [:index, :show, :new, :create]
end
```

resources is a shorthand implementation for a common set of actions that follow a convention called REST. In general, REST allows users to use the web almost like a database, using create, read, update, and delete operations to access *resources* via simple HTTP verbs. We use the resources macro to add a bunch of common routes that we'd otherwise need to write by hand. Since index and show already followed this convention, we remove the two get macros for the :index and :show actions, and we replace them with the resources macro. Since we don't need the edit or delete actions, we pass the :only option to explicitly list the routes we want generated. The following would be equivalent to a resources "/users", UserController declaration:

```
get "/users", UserController, :index
get "/users/:id/edit", UserController, :edit
get "/users/new", UserController, :new
get "/users/:id", UserController, :show
post "/users", UserController, :create
patch "/users/:id", UserController, :update
put "/users/:id", UserController, :update
delete "/users/:id", UserController, :delete
```

Sure, the resources macro has been known to reduce carpal tunnel syndrome almost as much as an ergonomic workspace, but it's more than a keystroke saver. By keeping to these conventions where you can, you're also communicating in a language that other programmers also understand. Creating these routes also makes additional functions available. You can use routes by name to build links, HTML elements, and the like.

If at any time you want to see all available routes, you can run the phoenix.routes Mix task, like this:

```
$ mix phoenix.routes
  page_path  GET   /            Rumbl.PageController :index
  user_path  GET   /users       Rumbl.UserController :index
  user_path  GET   /users/new   Rumbl.UserController :new
  user_path  GET   /users/:id   Rumbl.UserController :show
  user_path  POST  /users       Rumbl.UserController :create
```

With the route behind us, let's move on to the template. Now create a new file named web/templates/user/new.html.eex and add this:

ecto/listings/rumbl/web/templates/user/new.html.eex

```
<h1>New User</h1>

<%= form_for @changeset, user_path(@conn, :create), fn f -> %>
  <div class="form-group">
    <%= text_input f, :name, placeholder: "Name", class: "form-control" %>
  </div>
  <div class="form-group">
    <%= text_input f, :username, placeholder: "Username", class: "form-control" %>
  </div>
  <div class="form-group">
    <%= password_input f, :password, placeholder: "Password", class: "form-control" %>
  </div>
  <%= submit "Create User", class: "btn btn-primary" %>
<% end %>
```

Use a helper function, rather than HTML tags, to build the form, giving it an anonymous function. form_for provides conveniences like security, UTF-8 encoding, and more. The function takes three arguments: a changeset, a path, and an anonymous function. That function takes one argument, the form data we're labeling f. We're asking the template engine to build a function returning everything in the template between fn f -> and end. You can see the additional helpers in play as well. These build three input fields and a submit tag. Similar to link, all those helpers are documented in the Phoenix.HTML library.[3]

If we visit http://localhost:4000/users/new in our browser to inspect the generated HTML, we see the following markup:

```
<form accept-charset="UTF-8" action="/users" method="post">
  <input name="_csrf_token"
         type="hidden"
         value="MFgTPhAieHUgGzJ2OiRDXXw3Luc7wV7h/reiiA==">
  <input name="_utf8" type="hidden" value="✓">
  <div class="form-group">
    <input class="form-control"
           id="user_name"
           name="user[name]"
           placeholder="Name"
           type="text">
  </div>
  <div class="form-group">
    <input class="form-control"
           id="user_username"
           name="user[username]"
           placeholder="Username"
           type="text">
  </div>
```

---

3. http://hexdocs.pm/phoenix_html

```
<div class="form-group">
  <input class="form-control"
         id="user_password"
         name="user[password]"
         placeholder="Password"
         type="password">
</div>
<input class="btn btn-primary" type="submit" value="Create User">
</form>
```

You can see all of the work the form_for tag and the other helper functions are doing for you. The special _csrf_token hidden parameter was injected for us, and it makes sure that a user's requests are hard to spoof across sites. Also, though we didn't specify the name user with each of our text fields, the parameter names like user[name] and user[password] were pulled from our changeset.

> **José says:**
> ## How Does Phoenix Know Which Data to Show in the Form?
>
> Our application passes a changeset from Ecto to the form_for helper. The Phoenix team had a problem. How should we make the changes in the changeset available to the form? We could have hard-coded form_for to directly use Ecto.Changeset, but we weren't happy with that choice. It would be brittle and hard to extend.
>
> Imagine that your company decides to build an in-house data abstraction for some new technology and you want to integrate it with Phoenix. With forms tightly coupled to changesets, you'd be lost. You'd have to either rewrite forms or fork Phoenix. We needed a contract. Elixir protocols are the perfect solution to this problem.
>
> To solve the form_for coupling problem, we defined a protocol named Phoenix.HTML.Form-Data, which separates the *interface* from the *implementation*. Ecto.Changeset implements this protocol to convert its internal data to the structure required by Phoenix forms, all properly documented in the Phoenix.HTML.FormData contract.

You can probably guess where the data will go. The form will send a POST request to "/users", but we haven't yet created the action for it. Let's do that now.

Creating Resources

Recall our changes to the router.ex file, when we added the resources "/users" macro to router.ex to build a set of conventional routes. One new route maps posts to "/users" to the UserController.create action. Add a create function to UserController:

ecto/listings/rumbl/web/controllers/user_controller.change2.ex

```
def create(conn, %{"user" => user_params}) do
  changeset = User.changeset(%User{}, user_params)
  {:ok, user} = Repo.insert(changeset)

  conn
  |> put_flash(:info, "#{user.name} created!")
  |> redirect(to: user_path(conn, :index))
end
```

This pattern of code should be getting familiar to you by now. We keep piping functions together until the conn has the final result that we want. Each function does an isolated transform step. We do the backend code first, creating the changeset and then inserting it into the repository. Then, we take the connection and transform it twice, adding a flash message with the put_flash function, and then add a redirect instruction with the redirect function. Both of these are simple plug functions that we use to transform the connection, one step at a time.

Now let's try it out by visiting http://localhost:4000/users/new:

New User

Jackie

jackie

Password

Create User

And when we click Create User, we should be sent back to the users index page to see our inserted user:

Jackie created!

Listing Users

José (1)   View

Bruce (2)   View

Chris (3)   View

Jackie (4)   View

We still have work to do, though. Type a username that's too long, and you're greeted with Phoenix's debug error page with the error "no match of right hand side value."

We were expecting a result of the shape {:ok, user} but got {:error, changeset}. Our validations failed, and we got a result indicating so. To fix this problem, let's check for both outcomes, showing relevant validation errors upon failure. First we need to update our UserController to react to an invalid changeset:

ecto/listings/rumbl/web/controllers/user_controller.change3.ex

```
def create(conn, %{"user" => user_params}) do
  changeset = User.changeset(%User{}, user_params)
  case Repo.insert(changeset) do
    {:ok, user} ->
      conn
      |> put_flash(:info, "#{user.name} created!")
      |> redirect(to: user_path(conn, :index))
    {:error, changeset} ->
      render(conn, "new.html", changeset: changeset)
  end
end
```

We insert the new user record and then match on the return code. On success, we add a flash message to the conn and then redirect to the user_path, which takes us to the index action. On error, we simply render the new.html template, passing the conn and the changeset with the failed validations.

Next, let's show the validation errors for each form input field in web/templates/user/new.html.eex:

ecto/listings/rumbl/web/templates/user/new.change1.html.eex

```
<%= if @changeset.action do %>
  <div class="alert alert-danger">
    <p>Oops, something went wrong! Please check the errors below.</p>
  </div>
<% end %>

<div class="form-group">
  <%= text_input f, :name, placeholder: "Name", class: "form-control" %>
  <%= error_tag f, :name %>
</div>
<div class="form-group">
  <%= text_input f, :username, placeholder: "Username", class: "form-control" %>
  <%= error_tag f, :username %>
</div>
<div class="form-group">
  <%= password_input f, :password, placeholder: "Password", class: "form-control" %>
  <%= error_tag f, :password %>
</div>
```

The :action field of a changeset indicates an action we tried to perform on it, such as :insert in this case. By default it's nil when we build a new changeset, so if our form is rendered with any truthy action, we know validation errors have occurred. In our code, we first check for the existence of @changeset.action. If it's present, we show a validation notice at the top of the form. Next, we use the error_tag helper defined in web/views/error_helpers.ex to display an error tag next to each form input with the validation error for each field.

Now try again to submit your form with invalid fields:

New User

Oops, something went wrong! Please check the errors below.

Name

Username

should be at least 1 character(s)

Password

Create User

Presto!

If you've not yet appreciated the Ecto strategy for changesets, this code should help. The changeset had all validation errors because the Ecto changeset carries the validations and stores this information for later use. In addition to validation errors, the changesets also *track changes*!

Let's see how that works. Crack open IEx:

```
iex> changeset = Rumbl.User.changeset(%Rumbl.User{username: "eric"})
%Ecto.Changeset{changes: %{}, ...}

iex> import Ecto.Changeset
nil

iex> changeset = put_change(changeset, :username, "ericmj")
%Ecto.Changeset{changes: %{username: "ericmj"}, ...}

iex> changeset.changes
%{username: "ericmj"}

iex> get_change(changeset, :username)
"ericmj"
```

Now you have a more complete picture. Ecto is using changesets as a bucket to hold everything related to a database change, before and after persistence. You can use this information to do more than see what changed. Ecto lets you write code to do the minimal required database operation to update a record. If a particular change must be checked against a database constraint, such as a unique index, changesets do that. If Ecto can enforce validations without hitting the database, you can do that too. You'll explore the broader changeset API, validations, and strategies as we build out the rest of our application.

Wrapping Up

It's a good time to pause and take stock of what we've done. It's been a busy chapter.

- We began the chapter by introducing Ecto and announcing our intention to replace the in-memory repository with a database-backed repository using Ecto.

- We configured our new database and connected it to OTP, so that Elixir could do the right thing in the event of a Phoenix or Ecto crash.

- We created a schema, complete with information about each necessary field.

- We created a migration, to help us specify our database tables and auto-mate doing and undoing any database changes.

- We created a changeset so Ecto could efficiently track and manage each change requested by our application.

- We integrated this change into our application.

We've already come a long way, and we're only a few chapters in. We're ready to handle some more-sophisticated application features. Let's get rolling. In the next chapter, you'll use some of these new features to authenticate a user.

## CHAPTER 5

Authenticating Users

We have something that is starting to look like an application. Our database-backed repository is wired to our controller using changesets and forms. Let's ramp up the sophistication with real login forms, sessions, and password hashing. Rather than use something off the shelf, we can build it ourselves. Along the way you'll learn more about Ecto changesets and plugs, and we'll introduce session handling.

As you've seen, Phoenix makes it easy to add functionality to your application from bottom to top. Authentication forms the foundation for your whole application's security system, though, so we're going to be sure each decision is right.

Preparing for Authentication

Authentication is one of those features that can make or break your whole application experience. Programmers need to be able to easily layer on the right services and to direct requests where they need to go. Administrators need to trust the underlying policies, and also to configure the password constraints. Initially, we'll plan our approach and install the necessary dependencies.

Our approach to authentication will be a conventional one. Users will provide credentials when registering. We'll store those in the database in a secure way. A user starting a session will need to provide the credentials, and we'll check those against our database. We'll mark each user as authenticated in the session, so that users are granted access until their sessions expire or they log out.

Above all else, we want this system to be secure. We won't write the dicey parts ourselves, and we'll make sure that we use approaches that are well understood to be secure. We'll use as much as we can from Phoenix, and we'll rely on the comeonin package to handle the critical hashing piece.

We're going to start with the hashing of the user's password. We'll use comeonin because it uses up-to-date and secure hashing schemes. Like the best tools, it's also easy to use, so there's less to break. Add :comeonin to your mix.exs dependencies to handle password hashing, like this:

```
defp deps do
  [...,
   {:comeonin, "~> 2.0"}]
end
```

Next, add :comeonin to your applications list so it's started with your app:

authentication/listings/rumbl/mix.change1.exs

```
def application do
  [mod: {Rumbl, []},
   applications: [:phoenix, :phoenix_html, :cowboy, :logger, :gettext,
                  :phoenix_ecto, :postgrex, :comeonin]]
end
```

An application is what you think it is: a collection of modules that work together and can be managed as a whole. They generally handle critical services, like the ones in the list in mix.change1.exs. So far, our application relies on :phoenix and :phoenix_ecto, as you'd expect, but also :logger for logging services, the :postgrex database driver, :gettext for internationalization, and now :comeonin for managing our password hashing.

Now run mix deps.get to fetch your new dependencies, like this:

```
$ mix deps.get
```

When you're done, the :comeonin application library is in the deps directory, and it's started before your own :rumbl application is started. Now that our preparations are out of the way, we're ready to begin the implementation.

Managing Registration Changesets

You've already seen a changeset for creating a new user—the one that handles the name and username. Let's review that now:

authentication/rumbl/web/models/user.ex

```
def changeset(model, params \\ :empty) do
  model
  |> cast(params, ~w(name username), [])
  |> validate_length(:username, min: 1, max: 20)
end
```

The Ecto.Changeset.cast function converts that naked map to a changeset and, for security purposes, limits the inbound parameters to the ones you specify. Then, we fire a validation limiting the length of valid usernames to one to twenty characters. Remember, we need to supply :empty parameters instead of an empty map so Ecto can distinguish our blank new changeset from an empty form submission and skip validations. A failing validation sets errors in the changeset that we can then display to the user.

We use the preceding changeset to handle all of the attributes except the password, so we can use it for updating nonsensitive information, as a user would do on that user's profile page. The next changeset manages our password, like this:

authentication/listings/rumbl/web/models/user.change1.ex

```elixir
def registration_changeset(model, params) do
  model
  |> changeset(params)
  |> cast(params, ~w(password), [])
  |> validate_length(:password, min: 6, max: 100)
  |> put_pass_hash()
end
```

We need to convert the password to a more secure hashed value for the database. That changeset calls the first changeset, casts it to accept the password parameter, validates the length of our password, and then calls a private function to hash our password and add it to the results.

Here you can see how easy it is to compose with changesets. We used our base changeset function to apply the required parameters to the username validation. Then we validated our virtual password field. Notice that it's trivial to validate our virtual password field, though we're not actually storing that value in the database! Persistence is not strongly coupled to our change policies.

Next, we pipe to a put_pass_hash function that performs our password hashing. Let's see how that works:

authentication/listings/rumbl/web/models/user.change1.ex

```elixir
defp put_pass_hash(changeset) do
  case changeset do
    %Ecto.Changeset{valid?: true, changes: %{password: pass}} ->
      put_change(changeset, :password_hash, Comeonin.Bcrypt.hashpwsalt(pass))
    _ ->
      changeset
  end
end
```

We first check if the changeset is valid so we won't waste time hashing an invalid or missing password. Then, we use comeonin to hash our password, following the instructions in the readme file. Finally, we put the result into the changeset as password_hash. If the changeset is invalid, we simply return it to the caller.

The changesets make our code slightly more complex for trivial cases. Rather than marking the schema with specific validations that all callers must use, we must specify independent changesets. In the long run, we bet that changes from multiple clients with different validation and tracking requirements will make our application much simpler. If our experience with past applications is any indication, it's a pretty safe bet.

Let's take it for a spin:

```
iex> alias Rumbl.User
iex> changeset = User.registration_changeset(%User{}, %{
...>   username: "max", name: "Max", password: "123"
... })
%Ecto.Changeset{action: nil,
 changes: %{name: "Max", password: "123", username: "max"}, constraints: [],
 errors: [password: {"should be at least %{count} character(s)", [count: ...

iex> changeset.valid?
false

iex> changeset.changes
%{name: "Max", password: "123", username: "max"}
```

As we expected, creating a user with our registration changeset and a bad password results in an invalid changeset. When we inspect the changeset.changes, we can see that password_hash is missing because we didn't bother hashing a password we knew to be invalid. Let's continue and see what happens when we create a valid registration changeset:

```
iex> changeset = User.registration_changeset(%User{}, %{
...>   username: "max", name: "Max", password: "123 super secret"
...> })
%Ecto.Changeset{action: nil,
 changes: %{name: "Max", password: "123 super secret",
   password_hash: "$2b$12$UM7/YxK02GSwumyIoHtnIH8J4iHKLOXyim",
  username: "max"}, constraints: [], errors: [], filters: %{}, ...

iex> changeset.valid?
true

iex> changeset.changes
%{name: "Max", password: "123 super secret",
   password_hash: "$2b$12$UM7/YxK02GSwUIQl1M5QK.57IpucPnmumyIoHtnIH8J4iHKLOXyim",
  username: "max"}
```

When given a valid password, our changeset applies the put_pass_hash function and puts a change for our password_hash field, but we now have an issue. The users we inserted up to this point all have plain-text passwords, which won't be valid with the system's new password-hashing behavior. Let's fix that now by updating our existing users with properly hashed passwords. Key this into your IEx session:

```
iex>
for u <- Rumbl.Repo.all(User) do
  Rumbl.Repo.update!(User.registration_changeset(u, %{
    password: u.password_hash || "temppass"
  }))
end
```

Now our new and existing users alike will have valid, secure passwords. The readers with a strong security background can now exhale. We're no longer storing passwords in the clear in our database. There's no longer any danger that this toxic early prototype could escape from the lab. Now that things are working more safely, let's integrate that new code into our controller.

Creating Users

The create action in the UserController must now use our new registration_changeset, like this:

authentication/listings/rumbl/web/controllers/user_controller.change1.ex

```
def create(conn, %{"user" => user_params}) do
  changeset = User.registration_changeset(%User{}, user_params)
  case Repo.insert(changeset) do
    {:ok, user} ->
      conn
      |> put_flash(:info, "#{user.name} created!")
      |> redirect(to: user_path(conn, :index))
    {:error, changeset} ->
      render(conn, "new.html", changeset: changeset)
  end
end
```

We use pattern matching to pick off the user_params from the inbound form. We create a registration changeset, and if it's valid, we insert it and present the result to the user. If not, we simply render the new template again, with the changeset, which now has the errors from our failed validations.

You should be smiling now. Our changeset insulates our controller from the change policies encoded in our model layer while keeping the model free of side effects. Similar to connection pipelines, validations are a pipeline of functions that transform the changeset. The changeset is a data structure that explicitly tracks changes and their validity. The actual change happens only when we call the repository in the controller.

Now we should be able to visit http://localhost:4000/users/new and create new users with our registration changeset. We have a problem, though. Newly registered users are not automatically logged in, and users still can't log in or log out at will.

We need to create an authentication service and make it available throughout our system. You've used plugs created by others, but for this job it's time you learn to create your own. We'll implement authentication as a plug. That way we can add it to a pipeline in our router so other controllers can use it as needed.

The Anatomy of a Plug

Before we build our plug, let's take a deep dive into the Plug library and learn how plugs work from the inside. There are two kinds of plugs: *module plugs* and *function plugs*. A function plug is a single function. A module plug is a module that provides two functions with some configuration details. Either way, they work the same.

We have seen both kinds of plugs in use. From the endpoint module in lib/rumbl/endpoint.ex, you can see an example of a module plug:

```
plug Plug.Logger
```

You specify a module plug by providing the module name. In the router, you can see an example of a function plug:

```
plug :protect_from_forgery
```

You specify a function plug with the name of the function as an atom. Because a module is just a collection of functions, it strengthens the idea that plugs are just functions.

For our first plug, we'll write a module plug that encapsulates all the authentication logic in one place.

Module Plugs

Sometimes you might want to share a plug across more than one module. In that case, you can use a module plug. To satisfy the Plug specification, a module plug must have two functions, named init and call.

The simplest possible module plug returns the given options on init and the given connection on call. This plug does nothing:

```elixir
defmodule NothingPlug do
  def init(opts) do
    opts
  end

  def call(conn, _opts) do
    conn
  end
end
```

Remember, a typical plug transforms a connection. The main work of a module plug happens in call. In our NothingPlug, we simply pass the connection through without changes. The call will happen *at runtime*.

Sometimes, you might want to let the programmer change the behavior of a plug. We can do that work in the second argument to call, options. In our NothingPlug, we don't need any more information to do our job, so we ignore the options.

Sometimes, you might need Phoenix to do some heavy lifting to transform options. That's the job of the init function. init will happen at *compile time*. Plug uses the result of init as the second argument to call. Because init is called at compilation time, it's the perfect place to validate options and prepare some of the work. That way, call can be as fast as possible. Since call is the workhorse, we want it to do as little work as possible.

For both module and function plugs, the request interface is the same. conn, the first argument, is the data we pass through every plug. It has the details for any request, and we morph it in tiny steps until we eventually send a response. All plugs take a conn and return a conn.

You'll see piped functions using a common data structure over and over in Elixir. The trick that makes this tactic work is having the right common data structure. Since Plug works with web APIs, our data structure will specify the typical details of the web server's domain.

In Phoenix, you'll see connections, usually abbreviated conn, literally everywhere. At the end of the day, the conn is only a Plug.Conn struct, and it forms the foundation for Plug.

Plug.Conn Fields

You can find great online documentation for Plug.Conn.[1] This structure has the various fields that web applications need to understand about web requests and responses. Let's look at some of the supported fields.

---

1. http://hexdocs.pm/plug/Plug.Conn.html

Request fields contain information about the inbound request. They're parsed by the adapter for the web server you're using. Cowboy is the default web server that Phoenix uses, but you can also choose to plug in your own. These fields contain strings, except where otherwise specified:

host

> The requested host. For example, www.pragprog.com.

method

> The request method. For example, GET or POST.

path_info

> The path, split into a List of segments. For example, ["admin", "users"].

req_headers

> A list of request headers. For example, [{"content-type", "text/plain"}].

scheme

> The request protocol as an atom. For example, :https.

You can get other information as well, such as the query string, the remote IP address, the port, and the like. For Phoenix, if a web request's information is available from the web server's adapter, it's in Plug.Conn.

Next comes a set of *fetchable fields*. A fetchable field is empty until you explicitly request it. These fields require a little time to process, so they're left out of the connection by default until you want to explicitly fetch them:

cookies

> These are the request cookies with the response cookies.

params

> These are the request parameters. Some plugs help to parse these parameters from the query string, or from the request body.

Next are a series of fields that are used to process web requests. These fields help to encrypt cookies, process user-defined functions, and the like. Here are some of the fields you'll encounter:

assigns

> This user-defined map contains anything you want to put in it.

halted

> Sometimes a connection must be halted, such as a failed authorization. In this case, the halting plug sets this flag.

state

> This field contains the state of the connection. You can know if a response has been :set, :sent, or more by introspecting it.

You can also find a secret_key_base for everything related to encryption.

Since the Plug framework handles the whole life cycle of a request, including both the request and the response, Plug.Conn provides fields for the response:

resp_body

> Initially an empty string, the response body will contain the HTTP response string when it's available.

resp_cookies

> The resp_cookies has the outbound cookies for the response.

resp_headers

> These headers follow the HTTP specification and contain information such as the response type and caching rules.

status

> The response code generally contains 200–299 for success, 300–399 for redirects, 400–499 for not-found, and 500+ for errors.

Finally, Plug supports some private fields reserved for the adapter and frameworks:

adapter

> Information about the adapter is created here.

private

> This field has a map for the private use of frameworks.

Initially, a conn comes in almost blank and is filled out progressively by different plugs in the pipeline. For example, the endpoint may parse parameters, and the application developer will set fields primarily in assigns. Functions that render set the response fields such as status, change the state, and so on.

Plug.Conn also defines many functions that directly manipulate those fields, which makes abstracting the work of doing more complex operations such as managing cookies or sending files straightforward.

Now that you have a little more knowledge, we're ready to transform the connection by writing our first plug.

Writing an Authentication Plug

The authentication process works in two stages. First, we'll store the user ID in the session every time a new user registers or a user logs in. Second, we'll check if there's a new user in the session and store it in conn.assigns for every incoming request, so it can be accessed in our controllers and views. Let's start with the second part because it's a little easier to follow.

Create a file called web/controllers/auth.ex that looks like this:

authentication/listings/rumbl/web/controllers/auth.ex

```
defmodule Rumbl.Auth do
  import Plug.Conn

  def init(opts) do
    Keyword.fetch!(opts, :repo)
  end

  def call(conn, repo) do
    user_id = get_session(conn, :user_id)
    user    = user_id && repo.get(Rumbl.User, user_id)
    assign(conn, :current_user, user)
  end
end
```

In the init function, we take the given options, extracting the repository. Keyword.fetch! raises an exception if the given key doesn't exist, so Rumbl.Auth always requires the :repo option.

call receives the repository from init and then checks if a :user_id is stored in the session. If one exists, we look it up and assign the result in the connection. assign is a function imported from Plug.Conn that slightly transforms the connection—in this case, storing the user (or nil) in conn.assigns. That way, the :current_user will be available in all downstream functions including controllers and views.

Let's add our plug to the router, at the end of the browser pipeline:

authentication/listings/rumbl/web/router.change1.ex

```
pipeline :browser do
  plug :accepts, ["html"]
  plug :fetch_session
  plug :fetch_flash
  plug :protect_from_forgery
  plug :put_secure_browser_headers
  plug Rumbl.Auth, repo: Rumbl.Repo
end
```

With our plug in place, we can begin to use this information downstream.

Restricting Access

The Rumbl.Auth plug processes the request information and transforms the conn, adding :current_user to conn.assigns. Now, downstream plugs can use it to find out if a user is logged in.

We'll use this information to restrict access to pages where we list or show user information. Specifically, we don't want to allow users to access the :index and :show actions of Rumbl.UserController unless they're logged in.

Open up Rumbl.UserController and add the following function:

authentication/listings/rumbl/web/controllers/user_controller.change2.ex

```
defp authenticate(conn) do
  if conn.assigns.current_user do
    conn
  else
    conn
    |> put_flash(:error, "You must be logged in to access that page")
    |> redirect(to: page_path(conn, :index))
    |> halt()
  end
end
```

If there's a current user, we return the connection unchanged. Otherwise we store a flash message and redirect back to our application root. We use halt(conn) to stop any downstream transformations.

Let's invoke the authenticate function from index to try it out:

authentication/listings/rumbl/web/controllers/user_controller.change2.ex

```
def index(conn, _params) do
  case authenticate(conn) do
    %Plug.Conn{halted: true} = conn ->
      conn
    conn ->
      users = Repo.all(User)
      render conn, "index.html", users: users
  end
end
```

Now visit http://localhost:4000/users, where we're redirected back to the root with a message telling us to log in, as shown in the screenshot on page 80.

We could make the same changes to the show action, invoking our plug and honoring halt. And we could do the same thing every time we require authentication. We'd also have code that's repetitive, ugly, and error prone. We need to *plug* the authenticate function for the actions to be protected. Let's do that.

Like endpoints and routers, controllers also have their own plug pipeline. Each plug in the controller pipeline is executed in order, before the action is invoked. The controller pipeline lets us explicitly choose which actions fire any given plug.

To plug the authenticate function, we must first make it a function plug. A function plug is any function that receives two arguments—the connection and a set of options—and returns the connection. With a minor tweak, we can satisfy that contract. You need only add an options variable, which you'll ignore:

authentication/listings/rumbl/web/controllers/user_controller.change3.ex

```
defp authenticate(conn, _opts) do
  if conn.assigns.current_user do
    conn
  else
    conn
    |> put_flash(:error, "You must be logged in to access that page")
    |> redirect(to: page_path(conn, :index))
    |> halt()
  end
end
```

Now let's plug it in our controller, right after use Rumbl.Web:

authentication/listings/rumbl/web/controllers/user_controller.change3.ex

```
plug :authenticate when action in [:index, :show]
```

Then, change the index action back to its previous state, like this:

authentication/listings/rumbl/web/controllers/user_controller.change3.ex

```
def index(conn, _params) do
  users = Repo.all(Rumbl.User)
  render conn, "index.html", users: users
end
```

Visit http://localhost:4000/users to see our plug in action. We redirect, exactly as we should.

Let's take a minute to appreciate the code we've written so far. A small change to our authentication lets us plug it before every action. We can also share it with any other controllers or even move it to a router pipeline, restricting whole sections of our application with minor changes. None of these features relies on magical inheritance mechanisms, only our explicit lists of functions in our plug pipelines.

At this point, you may also be wondering what happened with halt. When we changed the index action, we had to explicitly check if the connection halted or not, before acting on it. Plug pipelines explicitly check for halted: true between every plug invocation, so the halting concern is neatly solved by Plug.

In fact, you're seeing Elixir macro expansion in action. Let's take an arbitrary example. Suppose you write code like this:

```
plug :one
plug Two
plug :three, some: :option
```

It would compile to:

```
case one(conn, []) do
  %{halted: true} = conn -> conn
  conn ->
    case Two.call(conn, Two.init([])) do
      %{halted: true} = conn -> conn
      conn ->
        case three(conn, some: :option) do
          %{halted: true} = conn -> conn
          conn -> conn
        end
    end
end
```

Elixir macros and macro expansion are beyond the scope of this book. What you need to know is that at some point in the compile process, Elixir would translate the first example to the second. Conceptually, not much is happening here, and that's exactly the beauty behind Plug. For each plug, we invoke it with the given options, check if the returned connection halted, and move forward if it didn't. It's a simple abstraction that allows us to express and compose both simple and complex functionality.

With all that said, we already have a mechanism for loading data from the session and using it to restrict user access. But we still don't have a mechanism to log the users in.

Logging In

Let's add a tiny function to Rumbl.Auth that receives the connection and the user, and stores the user ID in the session:

authentication/listings/rumbl/web/controllers/auth.change1.ex

```
def login(conn, user) do
  conn
  |> assign(:current_user, user)
  |> put_session(:user_id, user.id)
  |> configure_session(renew: true)
end
```

As you recall, the Plug.Conn struct has a field called assigns. We call setting a value in that structure an *assign*. Our function stores the given user as the :current_user assign, puts the user ID in the session, and finally configures the session, setting the :renew option to true. The last step is extremely important and it protects us from session fixation attacks. It tells Plug to send the session cookie back to the client with a different identifier, in case an attacker knew, by any chance, the previous one.

Let's go back to the Rumbl.UserController.create action and change it to call the login function after we insert the user in the database:

authentication/listings/rumbl/web/controllers/user_controller.change2.ex

```
def create(conn, %{"user" => user_params}) do
  changeset = User.registration_changeset(%User{}, user_params)
  case Repo.insert(changeset) do
    {:ok, user} ->
      conn
      |> Rumbl.Auth.login(user)
      |> put_flash(:info, "#{user.name} created!")
      |> redirect(to: user_path(conn, :index))
    {:error, changeset} ->
      render(conn, "new.html", changeset: changeset)
  end
end
```

Now visit http://localhost:4000/users/new, register a new user, and try to access the pages that we restricted previously. As you can see, the user can finally access them.

Implementing Login and Logout

We made great progress in the last section. We created a module plug that loads information from the session, used this information to restrict user access and then created the functionality that allows us to finally store users in the session.

We're almost done with our authentication feature. We need to implement both login and logout functionality, as well as change the layout to include links to those pages.

First things first. We need to add some new routes to web/router.ex:

authentication/listings/rumbl/web/router.change2.ex

```
scope "/", Rumbl do
  pipe_through :browser # Use the default browser stack

  get "/", PageController, :index
  resources "/users", UserController, only: [:index, :show, :new, :create]
  resources "/sessions", SessionController, only: [:new, :create, :delete]
end
```

We add three of the prepackaged REST routes for /sessions. We use the REST routes for GET /sessions/new to show a new session login form, POST /sessions to log in, and DELETE /sessions/:id to log out.

Next, we need a SessionController to handle those actions. Create a web/controllers/session_controller.ex, like this:

authentication/listings/rumbl/web/controllers/session_controller.ex

```
defmodule Rumbl.SessionController do
  use Rumbl.Web, :controller

  def new(conn, _) do
    render conn, "new.html"
  end
end
```

The new action simply renders our login form. We need a second action, create, to handle the form submission, like this:

authentication/listings/rumbl/web/controllers/session_controller.change1.ex

```
def create(conn, %{"session" => %{"username" => user, "password" =>
                                  pass}}) do
  case Rumbl.Auth.login_by_username_and_pass(conn, user, pass, repo:
                                             Repo) do
    {:ok, conn} ->
      conn
      |> put_flash(:info, "Welcome back!")
      |> redirect(to: page_path(conn, :index))
    {:error, _reason, conn} ->
      conn
      |> put_flash(:error, "Invalid username/password combination")
      |> render("new.html")
  end
end
```

That create action picks off the inbound arguments for username as user, and for password as pass. Then, we call an as-yet-undefined helper function called Rumbl.Auth.login_by_username_and_pass. On success, we report a success flash message to the user and redirect to page_path. Otherwise, we report a failure message to our user and render new again.

Let's implement Rumbl.Auth.login_by_username_and_pass next, alongside the remaining authentication logic:

authentication/listings/rumbl/web/controllers/auth.change2.ex

```
import Comeonin.Bcrypt, only: [checkpw: 2, dummy_checkpw: 0]

def login_by_username_and_pass(conn, username, given_pass, opts) do
  repo = Keyword.fetch!(opts, :repo)
  user = repo.get_by(Rumbl.User, username: username)

  cond do
    user && checkpw(given_pass, user.password_hash) ->
      {:ok, login(conn, user)}
    user ->
      {:error, :unauthorized, conn}
    true ->
      dummy_checkpw()
      {:error, :not_found, conn}
  end
end
```

We fetch the repository from the given opts and look up a user with the specified username. If we find a matching user, we log in, setting up the proper assigns and updating the session. If the password doesn't match but a user exists, we return :unauthorized; otherwise we return :not_found. When a user isn't found, we use comeonin's dummy_checkpw() function to simulate a password check with variable timing. This hardens our authentication layer against timing attacks,[2] which is crucial to keeping our application secure.

We still need to create our view and template. Create a new web/views/session_view.ex file that looks like this:

authentication/listings/rumbl/web/views/session_view.ex

```
defmodule Rumbl.SessionView do
  use Rumbl.Web, :view
end
```

Next, we need a session directory for our new view, so create a web/templates/session/new.html.eex with our new login form, like this:

authentication/listings/rumbl/web/templates/session/new.html.eex

```
<h1>Login</h1>

<%= form_for @conn, session_path(@conn, :create), [as: :session], fn f -> %>
  <div class="form-group">
    <%= text_input f, :username, placeholder: "Username", class: "form-control" %>
  </div>
  <div class="form-group">
    <%= password_input f, :password, placeholder: "Password", class: "form-control" %>
  </div>
  <%= submit "Log in", class: "btn btn-primary" %>
<% end %>
```

We use form_for as in our new-user forms, but instead of passing a changeset, we pass the %Plug.Conn{} struct. This technique is useful when you're creating forms that aren't backed by a changeset, such as a login or search form. Let's visit /sessions/new in our browser and try some login attempts.

With a bad login, we see an error flash notice and our template rerendered:

---

2. https://en.wikipedia.org/wiki/Timing_attack

Now let's try a good login:

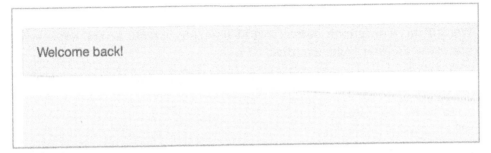

It works!

Presenting User Account Links

We've come a long way. We can now authenticate a user in a secure way. We're using a single function that we can reliably share across each feature of the application that needs it. Now, we can turn our attention to showing customized headers in our layout based on a user's authentication status. Let's start with a welcome message and a logout link.

We want to change the layout of the application to handle the new user features so that other views can also take advantage of these features. Let's update the layout in web/templates/layout/app.html.eex. Change it to look like this:

authentication/listings/rumbl/web/templates/layout/app.change1.html.eex

```
<div class="header">
  <ol class="breadcrumb text-right">
    <%= if @current_user do %>
      <li><%= @current_user.username %></li>
      <li>
        <%= link "Log out", to: session_path(@conn, :delete, @current_user),
                      method: "delete" %>
      </li>
    <% else %>
      <li><%= link "Register", to: user_path(@conn, :new) %></li>
      <li><%= link "Log in", to: session_path(@conn, :new) %></li>
    <% end %>
  </ol>
  <span class="logo"></span>
</div>
```

You can see our strategy. We test whether the user is authenticated by checking if the @current_user is present. Because the user is stored in conn.assigns.current_user, it's automatically available as @current_user in our views. To put it more broadly, everything in conn.assigns is available in our views.

If the user is available, we show the name, followed by a logout link. Otherwise, we allow users to register themselves or log in. If you're watching closely, you can see that this template uses the session_path twice when building the login and logout links. Each link function uses it a little differently, as you'll see when we break it down.

The code uses the Phoenix helpers to build a link:

```
link "Log out",
  to:     session_path(@conn, :delete, @current_user),
  method: "delete"
```

The link:

- Has the text Log out

- Links to the session_path path with the @conn connection, the :delete action, and the @current_user argument

- Uses the HTTP delete method

By passing the :method option to link, Phoenix generates a form tag instead of an anchor tag. Links without a specified HTTP method will default to GET, and Phoenix will render a simple link.

Let's head back to our browser and try it out. When we visit http://localhost:4000, we see the Log in link in the header:

Now sign in with one of the accounts you created earlier:

And it works.

Now that we have a working dynamic header with a Log out link, we need to implement the delete action in our SessionController and handle clearing the user's session in our auth module. That's nearly trivial to do.

First let's do the work to delete the session in Rumbl.Auth:

authentication/listings/rumbl/web/controllers/auth.change2.ex

```
def logout(conn) do
  configure_session(conn, drop: true)
end
```

This time we're invoking configure_session and setting :drop to true, which will drop the whole session at the end of the request. If you want to keep the session around, you could also delete only the user ID information by calling delete_session(conn, :user_id).

Now, we need only add the controller action. In web/controllers/session_controller.ex, add the delete action, like this:

authentication/listings/rumbl/web/controllers/session_controller.change2.ex

```
def delete(conn, _) do
  conn
  |> Rumbl.Auth.logout()
  |> redirect(to: page_path(conn, :index))
end
```

Following the link in our layout will now clear out the session and redirect us to the root.

Wrapping Up

This chapter has been challenging, but we've come a long way. Let's take stock:

- We added the comeonin dependency to our project.

- We built our own authentication layer.

- We built the associated changesets to handle validation of passwords.

- We implemented a module plug that loads the user from the session and made it part of our browser pipeline.

- We implemented a function plug and used it alongside some specific actions in our controller pipeline.

In the next chapter, you'll dive deeper into Ecto's waters by exploring relationships. We'll also begin to flesh out our application, using code generators to speed us along.

## CHAPTER 6

Generators and Relationships

So far, our look at Ecto has been pretty basic. We've fetched and written data to the repository, but we still haven't connected any models together. Relational databases like Postgres are named that way for a reason. Dealing with related data is the defining characteristic of that whole family of databases, so management of relationships is the feature that makes or breaks any persistence layer. This chapter takes you on a deeper dive into Ecto by exploring how to tie our schemas together in the database. We'll use code generators to accelerate the process, and you'll walk through what these generators do for us.

When you're through, you'll know how to take greater advantage of some of the code generators in Phoenix, and you'll have a better understanding of Ecto relationships.

Using Generators

To dig into Ecto, we're going to have to define relationships, and for that we need to extend the domain of our application. That's great, because our application is going to need those features. Let's define our problem in a little more detail.

Adding Videos and Annotations

The rumbl application will let users choose a video. Then, they can attach their comments, in real time. Users can play back these videos with comments over time. See what it looks like in the figure on page 92.

Users create videos. Then, users can create annotations on those videos. If you've ever seen *Mystery Science Theater 3000*, you know exactly what we're going for. In that show, some robots sat on the bottom of the screen, throwing in their opinions about bad science fiction.

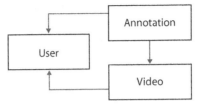

Here's how it's going to work. Rather than building everything by hand as we did with the User model, we're going to use generators to build the skeleton—including the migration, controllers, and templates to bootstrap the process for us. It's going to happen fast, and we're going to move through the boilerplate quickly, so be sure to follow closely.

Generating Resources

Phoenix includes two Mix tasks to bootstrap applications. phoenix.gen.html creates a simple HTTP scaffold with HTML pages, and phoenix.gen.json does the same for a REST-based API using JSON. They give you a simple scaffold for a traditional web-based application with CRUD (create, read, update, and delete) operations. You get migrations, controllers, and templates for basic CRUD operations of a resource, as well as tests so you can hit the ground running. You won't write all your Phoenix code this way, but the generators are a great way to get up and running quickly. They can also help new users learn how the Phoenix layers fit together in the context of a working application.

Our application will need videos. We'll start with a few fields, including:

- An associated User
- A creation time for the video
- A URL of the video location
- A title
- The type of the video

Later, our application will let users decorate these videos with annotations. But first, we need users to be able to create and show their videos. Let's use the phoenix.gen.html Mix task to generate our resource, like this:

```
$ mix phoenix.gen.html Video videos user_id:references:users \
url:string title:string description:text

* creating priv/repo/migrations/20150826023759_create_video.exs
* creating web/models/video.ex
* creating test/models/video_test.exs
* creating web/controllers/video_controller.ex
* creating web/templates/video/edit.html.eex
* creating web/templates/video/form.html.eex
```

```
* creating web/templates/video/index.html.eex
* creating web/templates/video/new.html.eex
* creating web/templates/video/show.html.eex
* creating web/views/video_view.ex
* creating test/controllers/video_controller_test.exs
```

Add the resource to your browser scope in web/router.ex:

```
    resources "/videos", VideoController
```

Remember to update your repository by running migrations:

```
    $ mix ecto.migrate
```

All of the preceding files should look familiar to you, because you wrote a similar stack of code for the user layer. Let's break that command down. Following the mix phoenix.gen.html command, we have:

- The name of the module that defines the model
- The plural form of the model name
- Each field, with some type information

This mix command may be more verbose than you've seen elsewhere. In some frameworks, you might use simple one-time generator commands, which leave it up to the framework to inflect plural and singular forms as requests come and go. At the end of the day, it ends up adding complexity to the framework—and, indirectly, to your application—only to save a few keystrokes every once in a while.

This is a place where it pays to be explicit. For all things internal, Phoenix frees you from memorizing unnecessary singular and plural conventions by consistently using singular forms in models, controllers, and views. In your application boundaries, such as URLs and table names, you provide a bit more information, because you can use pluralized names. Since creating plural forms is imperfect and rife with exceptions, the generator command is the perfect place to tell Phoenix exactly what we need.

It's time to follow up on the remaining instructions printed by the generator. First, we need to add the route to web/router.ex:

```
resources "/videos", VideoController
```

The question is: in which pipeline? Let's review what we know and come back to that question shortly.

Our Video is a REST resource, and these routes work just like the ones we created for User. As with the index and show actions in UserController, we also want to restrict the video actions to logged-in users. We've already written the code for authentication in the user controller. Let's recap that now:

authentication/listings/rumbl/web/controllers/user_controller.change3.ex

```
defp authenticate(conn, _opts) do
  if conn.assigns.current_user do
    conn
  else
    conn
    |> put_flash(:error, "You must be logged in to access that page")
    |> redirect(to: page_path(conn, :index))
    |> halt()
  end
end
```

To share this function between routers and controllers, move it to Rumbl.Auth,
call it authenticate_user for clarity, make it public (use def instead of defp), import
our controller functions for put_flash and redirect, and alias our router helpers:

relationships/listings/rumbl/web/controllers/auth.change1.ex

```
import Phoenix.Controller
alias Rumbl.Router.Helpers

def authenticate_user(conn, _opts) do
  if conn.assigns.current_user do
    conn
  else
    conn
    |> put_flash(:error, "You must be logged in to access that page")
    |> redirect(to: Helpers.page_path(conn, :index))
    |> halt()
  end
end
```

You could be tempted to also import the router helpers, but we want to use
Rumbl.Auth in our router, so that would lead to a circular dependency between
the router and the auth module. An alias will suffice. Save the auth.ex file and
open up web/web.ex. Let's share our new function across all controllers:

relationships/listings/rumbl/web/web.change1.ex

```
def controller do
  quote do
    use Phoenix.Controller

    alias Rumbl.Repo
    import Ecto
    import Ecto.Query, only: [from: 1, from: 2]

    import Rumbl.Router.Helpers
    import Rumbl.Gettext
    import Rumbl.Auth, only: [authenticate_user: 2] # New import
  end
end
```

And let's share it with the router:

relationships/listings/rumbl/web/web.change1.ex

```elixir
def router do
  quote do
    use Phoenix.Router

    import Rumbl.Auth, only: [authenticate_user: 2] # New import
  end
end
```

Next, we need to rename the :authenticate plug to :authenticate_user in our UserController so it uses the newly imported function:

relationships/listings/rumbl/web/controllers/user_controller.change1.ex

```elixir
plug :authenticate_user when action in [:index, :show]
```

Now, back to the router. Let's define a new scope called /manage containing the video resources. This scope pipes through the browser pipeline and our newly imported authenticate_user function, like this:

relationships/listings/rumbl/web/router.change1.ex

```elixir
scope "/manage", Rumbl do
  pipe_through [:browser, :authenticate_user]

  resources "/videos", VideoController
end
```

pipe_through works with a single pipeline, and it also supports a list of them. Furthermore, because pipelines are also plugs, nothing is stopping us from giving a plug, like authenticate_user, to pipe_through.

We now have a whole group of actions that allow the users to manage content. In a business application, many of those groups of tasks would have a policy, or checklist. Our combination of plugs with pipe_through allows developers to mix and match those policies at will. Applications can use as many plugs and pipelines as they need to do a job, organizing them in scopes.

We're almost ready to give the generated code a try. Let's run the last instruction from the generator and update the database by running migrations:

```
$ mix ecto.migrate
Generated rumbl app
00:23:35.119 [info]  == Running
    Rumbl.Repo.Migrations.CreateVideo.change/0 forward
00:23:35.119 [info]  create table videos
00:23:35.132 [info]  create index videos_user_id_index
00:23:35.135 [info]  == Migrated in 0.1s
```

Next start your server:

```
$ mix phoenix.server
```

And we're all set. Head over to your browser and visit http://localhost:4000/manage/videos as a logged-in user. We see an empty list of videos:

Now let's click New video to create a video. We see the generated form for a new video:

Fill out the form and click Submit. You see a list of your new videos, just as you should. We're not yet scoping those to a given user, but we still have a great start. We know that code generators like this one aren't unique, that dozens of other tools and languages do the same. Still, it's a useful exercise that can rapidly ramp up your understanding of Phoenix and even Elixir. Let's take a quick glance at what was generated.

Examining the Generated Controller and View

The generated controller is complete: it contains all REST actions, where both create and update manipulate changesets before inserting or updating the respective entry in the database.

The VideoController, like any other controller, also has a pipeline, and the Phoenix generator plugs a function called scrub_params for the create and update actions:

```
plug :scrub_params, "video" when action in [:create, :update]
```

HTML forms don't have the concept of nil, so every time blank input is sent through the form, it arrives as an empty string to our Phoenix application. If we didn't scrub those empty strings out, they would leak throughout our whole application, forcing us to differentiate between nil and blank strings everywhere.

Instead, we can use the scrub_params function, letting us deal with that problem right at the boundary. scrub_params checks and transforms any empty string into nil for any data inside the video parameter, allowing us to treat our data in a much more uniform way.

Finally, the view looks like an empty module, but at this point we know that it'll pick all templates in web/templates/video and transform them into functions, such as render("index.html", assigns):

relationships/listings/rumbl/web/views/video_view.ex

```
defmodule Rumbl.VideoView do
  use Rumbl.Web, :view
end
```

Take some time and read through the template files in web/templates/video/ to see how Phoenix uses forms, links, and other HTML helpers. Next, you'll read about Ecto relationships, starting with the generated migration.

Generated Migrations

Let's open up the video migration in priv/repo/migrations:

relationships/listings/rumbl/priv/repo/migrations/20150918023013_create_video.exs

```
def change do
  create table(:videos) do
    add :url, :string
    add :title, :string
    add :description, :text
    add :user_id, references(:users, on_delete: :nothing)
    timestamps
  end

  create index(:videos, [:user_id])
end
```

Phoenix generates a migration for all the fields that we passed on the command line, like the migration we created by hand for our users table. You can see that our generator made effective use of the type hints we provided. In relational databases, *primary keys*, such as our automatically generated id field, identify rows. *Foreign keys*, such as our user_id field, point from one table to the primary key in another one. At the database level, this foreign key lets the database get in on the act of maintaining consistency across our two relationships. Ecto is helping us to do the right thing.

The change function handles two database changes: one for migrating up and one for migrating down. A migration up applies a migration, and a migration down reverts it. This way, if you make a mistake and need to move a single migration up or down, you can do so.

For example, let's say you meant to add a view_count field to your generated create_video migration before you migrated the database up. You could create a new migration that adds your new field. Since you haven't pushed your changes upstream yet, you can roll back, make your changes, and then migrate up again. First, you'd roll back your changes:

```
$ mix ecto.rollback
02:46:54.058 [info]  == Running
Rumbl.Repo.Migrations.CreateVideo.change/0 backward
02:46:54.059 [info]  drop index videos_user_id_index
02:46:54.060 [info]  drop table videos
02:46:54.065 [info]  == Migrated in 0.0s
$
```

We verify that our database was fully migrated up. Then we run mix ecto.rollback to undo our CreateVideo migration. At this point, we could add our missing view_count field. We don't need a view_count at the moment, so let's migrate back up and carry on:

```
$ mix ecto.migrate
02:50:21.714 [info]  == Running
Rumbl.Repo.Migrations.CreateVideo.change/0 forward
02:50:21.715 [info]  create table videos
02:50:21.724 [info]  create index videos_user_id_index
02:50:21.729 [info]  == Migrated in 0.1s
```

The migration sets up the basic relationships between our tables and—now that we've migrated back up—we're ready to leverage those relationships in our schemas.

Building Relationships

After the migration, Ecto generated a schema. This file is responsible for identifying the fields in a way that ties in to both the database table and the Elixir struct. Now let's take a look at the schema in web/models/video.ex:

relationships/listings/rumbl/web/models/video.ex

```
schema "videos" do
  field :url, :string
  field :title, :string
  field :description, :string
  belongs_to :user, Rumbl.User

  timestamps
end
```

Our schema sets up a belongs_to association, defining a :user_id field of type :integer and an association field. Our migration defines a :user_id foreign key. Ecto will use these elements to build the right association between our models.

The video module also includes a changeset function, similar to the one that we defined for User. The only difference is between the required and optional fields in two module attributes, making it easier for us to reuse them later:

relationships/listings/rumbl/web/models/video.ex

```
@required_fields ~w(url title description)
@optional_fields ~w()

def changeset(model, params \\ :empty) do
  model
  |> cast(params, @required_fields, @optional_fields)
end
```

The :user_id field is neither required nor optional in the previous example, because many times the field doesn't come from external data such as forms but, rather, directly from the application. That's exactly our case. We'll make sure to associate the current user from the session to each new video.

To do so, let's make sure our relationship goes both ways in our schemas. If a video belongs to a user, we should add a has_many relationship to our User schema in web/models/user.ex, like this:

relationships/listings/rumbl/web/models/user.change1.ex

```
schema "users" do
  field :name, :string
  field :username, :string
  field :password, :string, virtual: true
  field :password_hash, :string
  has_many :videos, Rumbl.Video

  timestamps
end
```

With the has_many statement, we now have a complete one-to-many association. Now a user effectively has many videos. By defining these relationships, we can now use Ecto's association features. Fire up a new iex -S mix session, and let's fetch a user from the database and grab that user's videos:

```
iex> alias Rumbl.Repo
iex> alias Rumbl.User
iex> import Ecto.Query

iex> user = Repo.get_by!(User, username: "josevalim")
%Rumbl.User{...}

iex> user.videos
#Ecto.Association.NotLoaded<association :videos is not loaded>
```

Ecto associations are explicit! When you want Ecto to fetch some records, you need to ask. When you don't ask, you can be sure that you won't get them. This decision may seem tedious at first, but it's useful. One of the most time-consuming things about dealing with persistence frameworks is that they can often fetch rows you don't need or fetch in inefficient ways. When these kinds of changes cascade, you can quickly run up a tab that you're unable to pay.

Digging deeper, you can see that referencing videos returns Ecto.Assocation.NotLoaded. Let's load some videos, like this:

```
iex> user = Repo.preload(user, :videos)
%Rumbl.User{...},

iex> user.videos
[]
```

That's the ticket. Repo.preload accepts one or a collection of association names, and it can fetch all associated data—in this case, :videos. After Ecto fetches the association, we can reference the user.videos. To make this more meaningful, we need some associated data. Let's create a video for one of our users:

```
iex> user = Repo.get_by!(User, username: "josevalim")
%Rumbl.User{...}

iex> attrs = %{title: "hi", description: "says hi", url: "example.com"}
iex> video = Ecto.build_assoc(user, :videos, attrs)
%Rumbl.Video{...}

iex> video = Repo.insert!(video)
%Rumbl.Video{...}
```

Ecto.build_assoc allows us to build a struct, with the proper relationship fields already set. In this case, calling build_assoc is equivalent to this:

```
iex> %Rumbl.Video{user_id: user.id, title: "hi",
...>              description: "says hi", url: "example.com"}
%Rumbl.Video{...}
```

Now that our user has at least one video, let's try preload again:

```
iex> user = Repo.get_by!(User, username: "josevalim")
%Rumbl.User{...}

iex> user = Repo.preload(user, :videos)
%Rumbl.User{...}

iex> user.videos
[%Rumbl.Video{...}]
```

Preload is great for bundling data. Other times we want to fetch the videos associated with a user, without storing them in the user struct, like this:

```
iex> query = Ecto.assoc(user, :videos)
#Ecto.Query<...>

iex> Repo.all(query)
[%Rumbl.Video{...}]
```

assoc is another convenient function from Ecto that returns an Ecto.Query with all videos scoped to the given user, or to a list of users. We convert this query into data by calling Repo.all. As you'll learn in the next chapter, we'll be able to further manipulate this query, allowing us to slice the data in any way we want. For now, let's dig deeper into related data.

Managing Related Data

Our generated video controller gave us the CRUD basics, but as with any generated code, we're going to need to tailor it to our needs. We want to link videos with users for this social platform. To do so, we need to grab the current user from the connection and scope our operations against the user. Open up your web/controllers/video_controller.ex, and let's take a look at the new action:

```
def new(conn, _params) do
  changeset = Video.changeset(%Video{})
  render(conn, "new.html", changeset: changeset)
end
```

We need to change it so the video is built with the user_id pointing to the id of the user currently stored in the connection at conn.assigns.current_user. We know that the build_assoc function in Ecto does that and, if we look at web/web.ex, we see that all controllers import Ecto, so the function is already available. Let's rewrite the action:

```
def new(conn, _params) do
  changeset =
    conn.assigns.current_user
    |> build_assoc(:videos)
    |> Video.changeset()

  render(conn, "new.html", changeset: changeset)
end
```

This gives us what we want, mostly. We could move conn.assigns.current_user to a private function and use it in all other actions in our controller, but let's explore a different solution. Since all actions depend on the current_user, Phoenix allows us to make this dependency clearer while also removing the boilerplate with a custom action function in the controller:

relationships/listings/rumbl/web/controllers/video_controller.change1.ex

```
def action(conn, _) do
  apply(__MODULE__, action_name(conn),
        [conn, conn.params, conn.assigns.current_user])
end
```

Every controller has its own default action function. It's a plug that dispatches to the proper action at the end of the controller pipeline. We're replacing it because we want to change the API for our controller actions. It's easy enough. We call apply to call our action the way we want. The apply function takes the module, the action name, and the arguments. Rather than explicitly using the name of our module, we use the __MODULE__ directive, which expands to the current module, in atom form. Now, if our module name changes, we don't have to change our code along with it. The arguments are now the connection, the parameters, and the current user.

Let's tweak new and create actions to receive all three parameters:

relationships/listings/rumbl/web/controllers/video_controller.change1.ex

```elixir
def new(conn, _params, user) do
  changeset =
    user
    |> build_assoc(:videos)
    |> Video.changeset()

  render(conn, "new.html", changeset: changeset)
end

def create(conn, %{"video" => video_params}, user) do
  changeset =
    user
    |> build_assoc(:videos)
    |> Video.changeset(video_params)

  case Repo.insert(changeset) do
    {:ok, _video} ->
      conn
      |> put_flash(:info, "Video created successfully.")
      |> redirect(to: video_path(conn, :index))
    {:error, changeset} ->
      render(conn, "new.html", changeset: changeset)
  end
end
```

The preceding changes guarantee that every video created is properly associated to the current user. For the remaining actions, let's allow users to access and manipulate only their videos. For such, we need a function to look up all videos for a user:

relationships/listings/rumbl/web/controllers/video_controller.change1.ex

```elixir
defp user_videos(user) do
  assoc(user, :videos)
end
```

We use the assoc function, also imported from Ecto, to return a query of all videos scoped to the given user. Next, we use the new user_videos function in the index and show actions:

relationships/listings/rumbl/web/controllers/video_controller.change1.ex

```elixir
def index(conn, _params, user) do
  videos = Repo.all(user_videos(user))
  render(conn, "index.html", videos: videos)
end

def show(conn, %{"id" => id}, user) do
  video = Repo.get!(user_videos(user), id)
  render(conn, "show.html", video: video)
end
```

The only difference is that we're using our new query instead of the default one that returns all videos. Notice that we're using user_videos even in the show action that fetches videos by ID. This guarantees that users can only access the information from videos they own. If the ID of a video the user doesn't own is given, Ecto raises an error saying that the record couldn't be found. Let's do the same change to edit and update to ensure that they can only change videos coming from the association:

relationships/listings/rumbl/web/controllers/video_controller.change1.ex

```
def edit(conn, %{"id" => id}, user) do
  video = Repo.get!(user_videos(user), id)
  changeset = Video.changeset(video)
  render(conn, "edit.html", video: video, changeset: changeset)
end

def update(conn, %{"id" => id, "video" => video_params}, user) do
  video = Repo.get!(user_videos(user), id)
  changeset = Video.changeset(video, video_params)

  case Repo.update(changeset) do
    {:ok, video} ->
      conn
      |> put_flash(:info, "Video updated successfully.")
      |> redirect(to: video_path(conn, :show, video))
    {:error, changeset} ->
      render(conn, "edit.html", video: video, changeset: changeset)
  end
end
```

Finally, we need to do the same for delete:

relationships/listings/rumbl/web/controllers/video_controller.change1.ex

```
def delete(conn, %{"id" => id}, user) do
  video = Repo.get!(user_videos(user), id)
  Repo.delete!(video)

  conn
  |> put_flash(:info, "Video deleted successfully.")
  |> redirect(to: video_path(conn, :index))
end
```

Once again, we fetch a video from the scoped list of user videos. After those changes, our users have a panel for managing their videos in a safe way. Using Ecto.assoc, we built a simple authorization rule restricting deletes and updates to the video's owner.

Wrapping Up

In this chapter, we generated a Video resource with a relationship to User and made changes to the generated code, learning a lot along the way:

- We converted a private plug into a public function and shared it with our controllers and routers.

- You learned how to migrate and roll back changes to the database.

- We defined relationships between User and Video schemas and used functions from Ecto to build and retrieve associated data.

- You learned that Ecto uses strictly explicit semantics to determine if a relationship is loaded or not.

The next chapter will take everything up a notch by exploring Ecto queries and leveraging the database constraints. When we're done, you'll be able to ensure data uniqueness and use the database to maintain data integrity. Turn the page, and let's get started!

## CHAPTER 7

Ecto Queries and Constraints

In the last chapter, we extended our application domain by associating videos to users. Now we'll let users organize their videos with categories. We want our users to select which category a video belongs to upon video creation. To build this feature, you'll need to learn more about Ecto queries and the different ways you can retrieve data from the database.

We want to build our feature safely so that corrupt data can't creep into our database, so we'll spend some time working with database constraints. Database engines like Postgres are called *relational* for a reason. A tremendous amount of time and effort has gone into tools and features that help developers define and enforce the relationships between tables. Instead of treating the database as pure dumb storage, Ecto uses the strengths of the database to help keep the data consistent. You'll learn about error-reporting strategies so you'll know when to report an error and when to let it crash, letting other application layers handle the problem.

Let's get started.

Adding Categories

In this section, we're going to add some categories. We'll use many of the same techniques we discovered in our user-to-video relationship to manage the relationships between videos and categories. A video optionally belongs to a category, one chosen by the end user. First, let's generate the model and migration, using phoenix.gen.model, like this:

```
$ mix phoenix.gen.model Category categories name:string
* creating priv/repo/migrations/20150829145417_create_category.exs
* creating web/models/category.ex
* creating test/models/category_test.exs
```

This generator will build the model with a schema and migration for us.

Generating Category Migrations

Next let's edit our migration to mark the name field as NOT NULL and create an unique index for it:

queries/listings/rumbl/priv/repo/migrations/20150918041601_create_category.exs

```
defmodule Rumbl.Repo.Migrations.CreateCategory do
  use Ecto.Migration

  def change do
    create table(:categories) do
      add :name, :string, null: false

      timestamps
    end

    create unique_index(:categories, [:name])
  end
end
```

Next, we add the referential constraints to our Video schema, like this:

queries/listings/rumbl/web/models/video.change1.ex

```
Line 1  schema "videos" do
   -      field :url, :string
   -      field :title, :string
   -      field :description, :string
   5      belongs_to :user, Rumbl.User
   -      belongs_to :category, Rumbl.Category
   -
   -      timestamps
   -    end
   10
   -    @required_fields ~w(url title description)
   -    @optional_fields ~w(category_id)
```

On lines 6 and 12, we create a simple belongs-to relationship and make a new category_id field optional.

Let's use mix ecto.gen.migration to build a migration that adds category_id to video:

```
$ mix ecto.gen.migration add_category_id_to_video
* creating priv/repo/migrations
* creating
priv/repo/migrations/20150829190252_add_category_id_to_video.exs
```

This relationship allows us to add a new category ID to our existing videos. Now open up your new priv/repo/migrations/20150829190252_add_category_id_to_video.exs and key this in:

queries/listings/rumbl/priv/repo/migrations/20150918042635_add_category_id_to_video.exs

```
def change do
  alter table(:videos) do
    add :category_id, references(:categories)
  end
end
```

This code means that we want the database to enforce a constraint between videos and categories. The database will help make sure that the category_id specified in the video exists, similar to what we've done between videos and users. Finally, migrate your database with your two new migrations:

```
$ mix ecto.migrate
15:05:52.249 [info]  ==
   Running Rumbl.Repo.Migrations.CreateCategory.change/0 forward

15:05:52.249 [info]  create table categories

15:05:52.494 [info]  == Migrated in 2.4s

15:05:52.573 [info]  ==
   Running Rumbl.Repo.Migrations.AddCategoryIdToVideo.change/0 forward

15:05:52.573 [info]  alter table videos

15:05:52.587 [info]  == Migrated in 0.1s
```

We migrated our categories and added the proper foreign keys. The database will maintain the database integrity, regardless of what we do on the Phoenix side. It's time to populate our database with some categories.

Setting Up Category Seed Data

We expect our categories to be fixed. After we define a few of them, we don't expect them to change. For this reason, we don't need to create a controller with a view and templates to manage them. Instead, let's create one small script that we can run every time we need to insert data in the database.

Phoenix already defines a convention for seeding data. Open up priv/repo/seeds.exs and read the comments Phoenix generated for us. Phoenix will make sure that our database is appropriately populated. We only need to drop in a script that uses our repository to directly add the data we want. Then, we'll be able to run Mix commands when it's time to create the data.

Let's add the following to the end of the seeds file:

queries/listings/rumbl/priv/repo/seeds.change1.exs

```
alias Rumbl.Repo
alias Rumbl.Category

for category <- ~w(Action Drama Romance Comedy Sci-fi) do
  Repo.insert!(%Category{name: category})
end
```

We set up some aliases and then traverse a list of category names, writing them to the database. Let's run the seeds file with mix run:

```
$ mix run priv/repo/seeds.exs
```

Presto! We have categories. Before we move on, let's look at a potential error condition here. We've all been in situations where small developer mistakes snowballed, creating bigger problems. Consider the case in which a developer accidentally adds our categories twice. Then, before the developer discovers the mistake, *an end user uses two different categories of the same name.* Then, the developer mistakenly deletes a category with user data, and our snowball rolls on, picking up destructive mass and speed.

Let's check to see what happens if someone runs the seeds file twice:

```
$ mix run priv/repo/seeds.exs
** (Ecto.ConstraintError) constraint error when attempting to insert
model:

    * unique: categories_name_index
```

One of the constraints we added to the database was a unique constraint for the name column. When we try to insert an existing category, the database refuses and Ecto throws an exception, *as it should.* Our developer's snowball is snuffed out from the very beginning, before the tiny mistake has any chance to grow. We can do better, though. Let's prevent an error in the first place by simply checking if the category exists before creating it:

queries/listings/rumbl/priv/repo/seeds.change2.exs

```
alias Rumbl.Repo
alias Rumbl.Category

for category <- ~w(Action Drama Romance Comedy Sci-fi) do
  Repo.get_by(Category, name: category) ||
    Repo.insert!(%Category{name: category})
end
```

For a script, that's an adequate solution. We're not going to run it that often, and we're likely to be able to address any problems quickly. However, for production code—which might process thousands of requests per second—we need a more robust error strategy that works with the protections we've built into the database. You'll explore such strategies later on in this chapter when you read about constraints.

Associating Videos and Categories

Now that we've populated our database with categories, we want to allow users to choose a category when creating or editing a video. To do so, we'll do all of the following:

- Fetch all categories names and IDs from the database
- Sort them by the name
- Pass them into the view as part of a select input

To build this feature, we want to write a query. Let's spend a little time with Ecto exploring queries a little more deeply. Fire up your project in IEx, and let's warm up with some queries:

```
iex> import Ecto.Query
iex> alias Rumbl.Repo
iex> alias Rumbl.Category

iex> Repo.all from c in Category,
...>          select: c.name
```

The Repo.all function takes an Ecto query, and we've passed it a basic one. In this case:

- Repo.all means return all rows.
- from is a macro that builds a query.
- c in Category means we're pulling rows (labeled c) from the Category schema.
- select: c.name means we're going to return only the name field.

And Ecto returns a few debugging lines that contain the exact SQL query we're sending to the database, and the resulting five category names:

```
[debug] SELECT c0."name" FROM "categories" AS c0 [] OK query=0.7ms
["Action", "Drama", "Romance", "Comedy", "Sci-fi"]
```

We can order category names alphabetically by passing the :order_by option to our query. We can also return a tuple from both the id and name fields. Let's give it another try:

```
iex> Repo.all from c in Category,
...>          order_by: c.name,
...>          select: {c.name, c.id}
[{"Action", 1}, {"Comedy", 4}, {"Drama", 2},
 {"Romance", 3}, {"Sci-fi", 5}]
```

However, we rarely need to define the whole query at once. Ecto queries are *composable*, which means you can define the query bit by bit:

```
iex> query = Category
Category
iex> query = from c in query, order_by: c.name
#Ecto.Query<>
iex> query = from c in query, select: {c.name, c.id}
#Ecto.Query<>
iex> Repo.all query
[{"Action", 1}, {"Comedy", 4}, {"Drama", 2},
 {"Romance", 3}, {"Sci-fi", 5}]
```

This time, instead of building the whole query at once, we write it in small steps, adding a little more information along the way. This strategy works because Ecto defines something called the queryable protocol. from receives a queryable, and you can use any queryable as a base for a new query. A queryable is an Elixir protocol. Recall that protocols like Enumerable (for Enum) define APIs for specific language features. This one defines the API for something that can be queried.

That's also why we can call Repo.all either as Repo.all(Category) or Repo.all(query): because both Category and query implement the so-called Ecto.Queryable protocol. By abiding by the protocol, you can quickly layer together sophisticated queries with Ecto.Query, maintaining clear boundaries between your layers and adding sophistication without complexity.

Use what you've learned to associate videos and categories in our application. As with changesets, add code that builds and transforms queries to models while all interaction with the repository belongs to the controller—because the controller is the place we want complex interactions to live.

Let's add two functions to our Category module, one that sorts the results and another that fetches names and IDs:

queries/listings/rumbl/web/models/category.change1.ex

```
def alphabetical(query) do
  from c in query, order_by: c.name
end

def names_and_ids(query) do
  from c in query, select: {c.name, c.id}
end
```

Those functions receive queries, or more precisely, queryables, and return queryables. With our functions in place, you can now load all categories in VideoController:

queries/listings/rumbl/web/controllers/video_controller.change1.ex

```
alias Rumbl.Category

plug :load_categories when action in [:new, :create, :edit, :update]

defp load_categories(conn, _) do
  query =
    Category
    |> Category.alphabetical
    |> Category.names_and_ids
  categories = Repo.all query
  assign(conn, :categories, categories)
end
```

We define a plug that builds a query by composing multiple functions that
we define in our Category model. Once the query is built, we hand it off to the
repository, which fetches the names and IDs tuples and assigns them to the
connection. Now, those names and IDs are available as @categories in our
templates for the actions we specify in our when clause. We'll use the name as
the label for each option in a select and the id as the option value.

Let's change the video form template at web/templates/video/form.html.eex to include
a new select field:

queries/listings/rumbl/web/templates/video/form.change1.html.eex

```
<div class="form-group">
  <%= label f, :category_id, "Category", class: "control-label" %>
  <%= select f, :category_id, @categories, class: "form-control",
                              prompt: "Choose a category" %>
</div>
```

And change video/new.html.eex to pass the @categories in conn.assigns when rendering
the form:

queries/listings/rumbl/web/templates/video/new.change1.html.eex

```
<h2>New video</h2>

<%= render "form.html", changeset: @changeset, categories: @categories,
                        action: video_path(@conn, :create) %>

<%= link "Back", to: video_path(@conn, :index) %>
```

Also change video/edit.html.eex:

queries/listings/rumbl/web/templates/video/edit.change1.html.eex

```
<h2>Edit video</h2>

<%= render "form.html", changeset: @changeset, categories: @categories,
                        action: video_path(@conn, :update, @video) %>

<%= link "Back", to: video_path(@conn, :index) %>
```

That's it. Now we can create videos with optional categories. We're doing so with query logic that lives in its own module so we'll be able to better test and extend those features. Try it out by visiting http://localhost:4000/manage/videos/new:

New video

Url

Category

✓ Choose a category
Action
Comedy
Drama
Romance
Sci-fi

Description

Submit

Before we finish this chapter, we'll add the proper mechanisms to ensure that the category sent by the user is valid. But first, let's take this opportunity to explore Ecto queries a little more deeply.

Diving Deeper into Ecto Queries

So far, you know Ecto queries like a YouTube dog knows how to ride a bike. We've written our first query and we know that queries compose, but we still haven't explored many concepts. It's time to take off the training wheels and see more-advanced examples.

Open up IEx once more, and let's retrieve a single user:

```
iex> import Ecto.Query
iex> alias Rumbl.Repo
iex> alias Rumbl.User

iex> username = "josevalim"
"josevalim"

iex> Repo.one(from u in User, where: u.username == ^username)
...
%Rumbl.User{username: "josevalim", ...}
```

We're using the same concepts you learned before:

- Repo.one means return one row.

- from u in User means we're reading from the User schema.

- where: u.username == ^username means return the row where u.username == ^username. Remember, the ^ operator (called the pin operator) means we want to keep ^username the same.

- When the select part is omitted, the whole struct is returned, as if we'd written select: u.

Repo.one doesn't mean "return the first result." It means "one result is expected, so if there's more, fail." This query language is a little different from what you may have seen before. This API is not just a composition of strings. By relying on Elixir macros, Ecto knows where user-defined variables are located, so it's easier to protect the user from security flaws like SQL-injection attacks.

Ecto queries also do a good part of the query normalization at compile time, so you'll see better performance while leveraging the information in our schemas for casting values at runtime. Let's see some of these concepts in action by using an incorrect type in a query:

```
iex> username = 123
123

iex> Repo.all(from u in User, where: u.username == ^username)
** (Ecto.CastError) iex:4: value `123` in `where`
   cannot be cast to type :string in query:
     from u in Rumbl.User,
     where: u.username == ^123
```

The ^ operator interpolates values into our queries where Ecto can scrub them and safely put them to use, without the risk of SQL injection. Armed with our schema definition, Ecto is able to cast the values properly for us and match up Elixir types with the expected database types.

In other words, we define the repository and schemas and let Ecto changesets and queries tie them up together. This strategy gives developers the proper level of isolation because we mostly work with data, which is straightforward, and leave all complex operations to the repository.

You already know a bit about the differences between traditional MVC and Phoenix's tweak from the perspective of controllers. More explicitly, we'd like to keep functions with side effects—the ones that change the world around us—in the *controller* while the *model* and *view* layers remain side effect free. Since Ecto splits the responsibilities between the repository and its data API, it fits our world view perfectly. This figure shows how it all fits together:

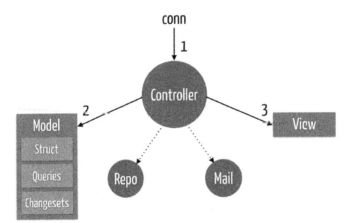

When a request comes in, the controller is invoked. The controller might read data from the socket (a side effect) and parse it into data structures, like the params map. When we have the parsed data, we send it to the model, which transforms those parameters into changesets or queries.

Elixir structs, Ecto changesets, and queries are just data. We can build or transform any of them by passing them from function to function, slightly modifying the data on each step. When we've molded the data to the shape of our business-model requirements, we invoke the entities that can change the world around us, like the repository (Repo) or the system responsible for delivering emails (Mail). Finally, we can invoke the view. The view converts the model data, such as changesets and structs, into view data, such as JSON maps or HTML strings, which is then written to the socket via the controller—another side effect.

Because the controller already encapsulates side effects by reading and writing to the socket, it's the perfect place to put interactions with the repository, while the model and view layers are kept free of side effects. When you get the layers of an application right, you often see that these kinds of benefits come in bunches. The same strategy that improves the manageability of our code will also make our code easier to test.

The Query API

So far, we've used only the == operator in queries, but Ecto supports a wide range of them:

- Comparison operators: ==, !=, <=, >=, <, >
- Boolean operators: and, or, not
- Inclusion operator: in
- Search functions: like and ilike

- Null check functions: is_nil
- Aggregates: count, avg, sum, min, max
- Date/time intervals: datetime_add, date_add
- General: fragment, field, and type

In short, you can use many of the same comparison, inclusion, search, and aggregate operations for a typical query that you'd use in Elixir. You can see documentation and examples for many of them in the Ecto.Query.API documentation.[1] Those are the basic features you're going to use as you build queries. You'll use them from two APIs: keywords syntax and pipe syntax. Let's see what each API looks like.

Writing Queries with Keywords Syntax

The first syntax expresses different parts of the query by using a keyword list. For example, take a look at this code for counting all users with usernames starting with j or c. You can see keys for both :select and :where:

```
iex> Repo.one from u in User,
...>          select: count(u.id),
...>          where: ilike(u.username, ^"j%") or
...>                 ilike(u.username, ^"c%")

2
```

The u variable is bound as part of Ecto's from macro. Throughout the query, it represents entries from the User schema. If you attempt to access u.unknown or match against an invalid type, Ecto raises an error. Bindings are useful when our queries need to join across multiple schemas. Each join in a query gets a specific binding.

Let's also build a query to count all users:

```
iex> users_count = from u in User, select: count(u.id)

 #Ecto.Query<from u in Rumbl.User, select: count(u.id)>
```

Simple enough. We use from to build a query, selecting count(u.id). Now, let's say that we want to take advantage of this fantastic count feature to build some more-complex queries. Since the best usernames have a j, let's count the users that match a case-insensitive search for j, like this:

```
iex> j_users = from u in users_count, where: ilike(u.username, ^"%j%")
 #Ecto.Query<from u in Rumbl.User, where: ilike(u.username, ^"%j%"),
 select: count(u.id)>
```

---

1. http://hexdocs.pm/ecto/Ecto.Query.API.html

Beautiful. You've built a new query, based on the old one. Although we've used the same binding as before, u, we didn't have to. You're free to name your query variables however you like, because Ecto doesn't use their names. The following query is equivalent to the previous one:

```
iex> j_users = from q in users_count, where: ilike(q.username, ^"%j%")
 #Ecto.Query<from u in Rumbl.User, where: ilike(u.username, ^"%j%"),
 select: count(u.id)>
```

You can use that composition wherever you have a query, be it written with the keyword syntax or the pipe syntax that you'll learn next.

Using Queries with the Pipe Syntax

Let's look at some other expressions. For example, let's build some queries with the Elixir pipe.

You've seen different query expressions constructed with key-value pairs. You can also build queries by piping through query macros.

Most often, you'll want to import from to build up a query against a queryable, but you can also use other query macros such as where and select where it makes sense. Each takes a queryable and returns a queryable, so you can pipe them together like this:

```
iex> User |>
     select([u], count(u.id)) |>
     where([u], ilike(u.username, ^"j%") or ilike(u.username, ^"c%")) |>
     Repo.one()

[debug] SELECT count(u0.id)
  FROM "users" AS u0
  WHERE (u0."username" ILIKE $1 OR u0."username" ILIKE $2) ["j%", "c%"]
OK query=0.9ms
2
```

Because each query is independent of others, we need to specify the binding manually for each one as part of a list. This binding is conceptually the same as the one we used in from u in User. We have a single binding, so we use a list with a single element, but we could use a longer list with more bindings if our query had joins.

The query syntax you choose depends on your taste and the problems you're trying to solve. The former syntax is probably more convenient for pulling together ad-hoc queries and solving one-off problems. The latter is probably better for building an application's unique complex layered query API. Each approach has its advantages.

Fragments

A poorly designed API will break down if it doesn't provide every feature that you need from the underlying storage you're trying to access. If Ecto gives you everything you need from the database layer beneath, that's great. If not, you don't have to panic and fork Ecto to build your own mapping layer. Since we can't represent all possible queries in Elixir's syntax, we need a backup plan.

A programming truism is that the best abstractions offer an escape hatch, one that exposes the user to one deeper level of abstraction on demand. Ecto has such a feature, called the *query fragment*. A query fragment sends part of a query directly to the database but allows you to construct the query string in a safe way.

Imagine that you want to look up the user by username in a case-insensitive way. Though Ecto doesn't give us everything we need, you can access that feature by using an Ecto SQL fragment, like this:

```
from(u in User,
    where: fragment("lower(username) = ?",
                    ^String.downcase(uname)))
```

Using a fragment allows us to construct a fragment of SQL for the query but safely interpolate the String.downcase(uname) code using a prepared statement. Whether the interpolated values are Ecto query expressions or Postgres SQL fragments, Ecto safely escapes all interpolated values.

When everything else fails and even fragments aren't enough, you can always run direct SQL with Ecto.Adapters.SQL.query:

```
iex> Ecto.Adapters.SQL.query(Rumbl.Repo, "SELECT power($1, $2)", [2, 10])
[debug] SELECT power($1, $2) [2, 10] OK query=2.5ms
{:ok, %{columns: ["power"], command: :select, num_rows: 1, rows: [[1024.0]]}}
```

From the query result, you can fetch all kinds of information, such as the returned columns, the number of rows, and the result set itself. It's best to stick to Ecto query expressions wherever possible, but you have a safe escape hatch when you need it.

Querying Relationships

Ecto queries also offer support for associations. When working with relationships, you learned that Ecto associations are explicit, and we used Repo.preload to fetch associated data. Let's recap:

```
iex> user = Repo.one from(u in User, limit: 1)
%Rumbl.User{...}

iex> user.videos
#Ecto.Association.NotLoaded<association :videos is not loaded>

iex> user = Repo.preload(user, :videos)
%Rumbl.User{...}

iex> user.videos
[]
```

However, we don't always need to preload associations as a separate step. Ecto allows us to preload associations directly as part of a query, like this:

```
iex> user = Repo.one from(u in User, limit: 1, preload: [:videos])
%Rumbl.User{...}

iex> user.videos
[]
```

Ecto also allows us to join on associations inside queries, filtering them in any way that makes sense:

```
iex> Repo.all from u in User,
...>          join: v in assoc(u, :videos),
...>          join: c in assoc(v, :category),
...>         where: c.name == "Comedy",
...>        select: {u, v}
[{%Rumbl.User{...}, %Rumbl.Video{...}}]
```

This time, Ecto returns users and videos side by side as long as the video belongs to the Comedy category. We use a tuple in select, but we could also return each entry in a list, or even a map.

We expect that you'll find plenty of joy when you work with Ecto queries. They're flexible but also extremely readable. They're composable enough to flex but also rigid enough to offer type support and security when it comes to interacting with tainted external data. However, not all problems can be solved with queries. Sometimes, you'll need to use the underlying database to help manage database integrity. For those cases, Ecto provides *constraints*.

Constraints

Constraints allow us to use underlying relational database features to help us maintain database integrity. For example, let's validate our categories. When we create a video, we need to make sure that our category exists. We might be tempted to solve this problem by simply performing a query, but such an approach would be unsafe due to race conditions. In most cases, we would expect it to work like this:

1. The user sends a category ID through the form.

2. We perform a query to check if the category ID exists in the database.

3. If the category ID does exist in the database, we add the video with the category ID to the database.

However, someone could delete the category between steps 2 and 3, allowing us to ultimately insert a video without an existing category in the database. In any sufficiently busy application, that approach *will lead to inconsistent data* over time. Ecto has relentlessly pushed us to define references and indexes in our database because sometimes, doing a query won't be enough and we'll need to rely on database constraints.

In Phoenix, we use constraints to manage change in a way that combines the harsh protections of the database with Ecto's gentle guiding hand to report errors without crashing. Let's firm up some terminology before we get too far:

constraint
   An explicit database constraint. This might be a uniqueness constraint on an index, or an integrity constraint between primary and foreign keys.

constraint error
   The Ecto.ConstraintError, which you saw when we tried to add a category twice.

changeset constraint
   A constraint annotation added to the changeset that allows Ecto to convert constraint errors into changeset error messages.

changeset error messages
   Beautiful error messages for the consumption of humans.

Relational databases deal with relationships between tables. A database constraint is a mechanism for restricting data in a table based on the needs of an application. For example, a given user_id must exist as the id field in a users table, or an email field must be unique. Ensuring data is consistent across records is a critical job that all database-backed applications need to handle.

You have three approaches to solving this problem, and all have trade-offs. First, you might decide to let the application (and the web framework) manage relationships for you. This approach, adopted by frameworks like Rails, leads to simpler code and database layers that are much more portable, but at a cost. At best, the integration and error reporting is likely to suffer. At worst, these features won't be available or get used at all, leading to race conditions and inconsistent data.

Second, you could let the database manage all code that touches data. Through the use of layers such as stored procedures, this extreme approach will lead to excellent database integrity but is difficult to maintain and harder to code. This approach was famous just before the turn of the century, but not many people advocate using it any more.

The third approach is a hybrid approach whereby the application layer (and web server) use database services like referential integrity and transactions to strike a balance between the needs of the application layer and the needs of the database. This is the approach of Ecto and also most database layers.

Ecto allows developers to enjoy many of the guarantees databases offer in terms of data integrity. In fact, Ecto rewards developers for doing exactly this, both in the short term, by transforming constraint errors into user feedback, and in the long term by guaranteeing you won't be awake at 3:00 a.m. fixing bugs caused by inconsistent data. In the remainder of this chapter, we're going to walk you through how Ecto manages constraints.

Validating Unique Data

When we created the users table, we edited the migration to index the username field as unique:

```
create unique_index(:users, [:username])
```

Let's see what happens if we try to create a user with an existing username:

Oops. Our application blows up with a constraint error, similar to the one we saw when creating duplicated categories. If we inspect the error message in the terminal, or in the browser, we see:

```
[error] #PID<0.848.0> running Rumbl.Endpoint terminated
Server: localhost:4000 (http)
Request: POST /users
** (exit) an exception was raised:
    ** (Ecto.ConstraintError) constraint error when attempting to insert struct:
    * unique: users_username_index
```

If you would like to convert this constraint into an error, please
call unique_constraint/3 in your changeset and define the proper
constraint name. The changeset has not defined any constraint.

The error message has everything we need to do in order to move on. It says
our application failed because the unique constraint on the users_username_index
was violated. It also mentions we can convert the constraint error into a
changeset error message by calling unique_constraint in the changeset.

Let's do that. Open up web/models/user.ex and change the changeset function:

queries/listings/rumbl/web/models/user.change1.ex
```
def changeset(model, params \\ :empty) do
  model
  |> cast(params, ~w(name username), [])
  |> validate_length(:username, min: 1, max: 20)
  |> unique_constraint(:username)
end
```

We pipe the changeset into unique_constraint. By default, Ecto infers the constraint
name for us, but it can also be given with the :name option. Calling unique_con-
straint won't perform any validation on the spot. Instead, it stores all the relevant information in the changeset. When it's time, the repository can convert
those constraints into a human-readable error.

Let's try creating a user with an existing username once again.

New User

Oops, something went wrong! Please check the errors below.

Chris

cmccord

has already been taken

Password

Create User

Excellent, this is exactly what we expected: a nice, beautiful, human-readable
error. unique_constraint is only one of the different constraint mappings that
changesets offer. The next kind of constraint is a foreign-key check.

Validating Foreign Keys

After taking some time to appreciate our unique_constraint, let's continue with our category relationship. When the user picks a category for the video, we could provide some meaningful feedback if the operation fails. Let's update our Video changeset, like this:

queries/listings/rumbl/web/models/video.change2.ex

```
def changeset(model, params \\ :empty) do
  model
  |> cast(params, @required_fields, @optional_fields)
  |> assoc_constraint(:category)
end
```

That assoc_constraint converts foreign-key constraint errors into human-readable error messages and guarantees that a video is created only if the category exists in the database. Taking it for a spin, let's load some data inside iex -S mix:

```
iex> alias Rumbl.Category
iex> alias Rumbl.Video
iex> alias Rumbl.Repo
iex> import Ecto.Query

iex> category = Repo.get_by Category, name: "Drama"
%Rumbl.Category{...}
iex> video = Repo.one(from v in Video, limit: 1)
...
%Rumbl.Video{...}
```

Now let's use the video changeset to associate the video with the category:

```
iex> changeset = Video.changeset(video, %{category_id:
category.id})
iex> Repo.update(changeset)
...
{:ok, %Rumbl.Video{...}}
```

We updated our video with a category that exists. The update works, but suppose tried to update a video with a bad category:

```
iex> changeset = Video.changeset(video, %{category_id: 12345})
iex> Repo.update(changeset)
...
{:error, %Ecto.Changeset{}}
```

Oops. We couldn't update the video. Let's inspect the returned changeset further. IEx allows us to fetch a previous value by using v(n), where n is the number of the expression. You can also pass a negative value to grab the last n[th] expression:

```
iex> {:error, changeset} = v(-1)
iex> changeset.errors
[category: "does not exist"]
```

As with unique_constraint, when we set up assoc_constraint, we no longer get Ecto.ConstraintError. Instead, they're converted into changeset error messages.

You can try to reproduce this constraint error via our web application in a couple of ways. For example, you could load the page, then remove the category from the database and submit the form after choosing the removed category. If you feel a bit more sneaky, you can fiddle the select options in the browser console, changing their value and then submitting the form.

As we move forward, you'll see how changesets are an essential part of Ecto. *Each changeset encapsulates the whole change policy*, including allowed fields, detecting change, validations, and messaging the user.

On Delete

Our constraints have helped us insert and update database data safely. They should also apply when we remove data. Let's open up IEx once more:

```
iex> alias Rumbl.Repo
iex> category = Repo.get_by Rumbl.Category, name: "Drama"
%Rumbl.Category{...}
iex> Repo.delete category
** (Ecto.ConstraintError) constraint error when attempting to delete
struct
```

We pick the Drama category because we added a video to it in the previous section. A video is tied to the category, so we can't delete the category because it would leave orphaned records.

We could solve this problem in several ways, described briefly here, that you can explore further on your own. The first one is to use changeset constraints. Like insert and update, Repo.delete also accepts a changeset, and you can use foreign_key_constraint to ensure that no associated videos exist when a category is deleted; otherwise you get a nice error message. The foreign_key_constraint function is like the assoc_constraint we used earlier, except it doesn't inflect the foreign key from the relationship. This is particularly useful when you want to show the user why you can't delete the category:

```
iex> import Ecto.Changeset
iex> changeset = Ecto.Changeset.change(category)
iex> changeset = foreign_key_constraint(changeset, :videos,
  name: :videos_category_id_fkey, message: "still exist")
iex> Repo.delete changeset
{:error, changeset}
```

This time, we had to be a bit more explicit in the foreign_key_constraint call, because the foreign key has been set in the videos table. If needed, we could also add no_assoc_constraint to do the dirty work of lifting up the foreign-key name and setting a good error message. Check the Ecto docs for more information on no_assoc_constraint and other changeset constraint mappings.

Second, you could configure the database references to either cascade the deletions or simply make the videos.category_id columns NULL on delete. Let's open up the add_category_id_to_video migration:

```
add :category_id, references(:categories)
```

The references function accepts the :on_delete option with one of the following:

:nothing
    The default.

:delete_all
    When the category is deleted, all videos in that category are deleted.

:nilify_all
    When a category is deleted, the category_id of all associated videos is set to NULL.

There's no best option here. For the category, which supports a has_many :videos relationship, :nilify_all seems like a good choice, because the category isn't an essential part of the video. However, when deleting a user, you likely want to delete all the videos created by that user, purging all of the user's data.

The final choice is to set up :on_delete when configuring has_many or belongs_to relationships in your schema, moving the logic effectively to the application domain. This choice, however, is only recommended when you can't perform one of the preceding operations. After all, *the work best suited to the database must be done in the database.*

Let It Crash

You might be expecting us to proceed to add *_constraint functions to all of our changesets, ensuring that all failed constraint checks are converted into human-readable error messages.

We're not going to do so, and we shouldn't. When we added a foreign_key_constraint to the video belongs_to :category relationship, we knew we wanted to allow the user to choose the video category later on. If a category is removed at some point between the user loading the page and submitting the request to publish the video, setting the changeset constraint allows us to show a nice error message telling the user to pick something else.

This isn't so uncommon. Maybe you've started to publish a new video on Friday at 5:00 p.m. but decide to finish the process next Monday. Someone has the whole weekend to remove a category, making your form data outdated.

On the other hand, let's take the user has_many :videos relationship. Our application is the one responsible for setting up the relationship between videos and users. If a constraint is violated, it can only be a bug in our application or a data-integrity issue.

In such cases, *the user can do nothing to fix the error*, so crashing is the best option. Something unexpected really happened. But that's OK. We know Elixir was designed to handle failures, and Phoenix allows us to convert them into nice status pages. Furthermore, we also recommend setting up a notification system that aggregates and emails errors coming from your application, so you can discover and act on potential bugs when your software is running in production.

Putting it another way: the *_constraint changeset functions are useful when the constraint being mapped is triggered by external data, often as part of the user request. *Using changeset constraints only makes sense if the error message can be something the user can take action on.*

Wrapping Up

In this chapter, we pushed Ecto a little harder. We started with queries and went deep into the query API. We explored constraints and how Ecto integrates with the database, ensuring that our data is kept clean and consistent. We also built a category layer. Along the way, you learned many things about the Phoenix philosophy:

- We used Ecto's query API, which is independent of the repository API, to do some basic queries.

- We used two forms of queries, a keyword list–based syntax and a pipe-based syntax.

- We used fragments to pass SQL commands through the query API unchanged.

- We explored the different ways Ecto queries work with relationships, beyond data preloading.

- We wrote constraint-style validations for unique indexes and foreign-key violations.

- We learned how to choose between letting constraint errors go and when to report them to the user.

Next, you'll learn how to test everything we've seen so far.

## CHAPTER 8

Testing MVC

After reading through so many chapters, you might be wondering, "Where are all of the tests?" We strongly believe in writing tests as you go, but such an approach could be repetitive, awkward, and distracting in a book. Rather than present tests as we go, we decided to focus on presenting one concept at a time and save the tests for the end of each part. In this chapter, you'll see us use techniques to test everything we built in the first part of the book. We might not test every single line of code we've written so far, but we'll cover all of the concepts you'll need to test everything.

Regardless of what you're building or the language that you're using, many testing principles remain the same. Let's look at some of the principles we'd like to emphasize:

- Fast – We're going to make sure our tests run quickly and can run concurrently wherever possible.

- Isolated – We want to have the right level of isolation in our tests. Tests that are too isolated won't have enough context to be useful. Tests that aren't isolated enough will be difficult to understand and maintain.

- DRY (Don't Repeat Yourself) – We want to eliminate unnecessary repetition in our tests.

- Repeatable – We want the same test on the same code to always yield the same result.

You can probably already tell that the decisions made throughout the Phoenix platform make testing a joy. Clean contracts between layers of the application make it easy to get to the right level of isolation. The focus on immutability, concurrency, and speed will help our tests run quickly. Functional programming will help keep our tests DRY and repeatable.

Before we go too much further, let's settle on some common terminology, since different testing terms mean different things depending on which framework or language you're using.

A *unit test* exercises a function for one layer of your application. For example, if you're testing a web calculator, unit tests would exercise the Calculator module supporting your arithmetic. You might dedicate one or more tests to the add function on your calculator module.

An *integration test* focuses on the way different layers of an application fit together. Our integration tests in this chapter will generally do a request to a controller to use the things we've created so far. A single test will begin at our endpoint, run through our pipelines, read from the database, and render templates through views just as Phoenix requests would.

You may also encounter types of tests that we don't cover here. For a larger project, you'd also possibly want to test how multiple actions work together. For example, a single *acceptance test case* might sign the user on, perform several calculations that might build on each other, and then sign off. You might also consider *performance testing* to see how your application performs under load. In this book, we focus strictly on unit and integration tests.

Enough background! We're going to work through the various layers of our application. We'll start with some of the tools we can use to run tests and shape the tests we write. Next, we'll work through some integration tests and then focus on unit-testing the individual components.

Let's get started.

Understanding ExUnit

When you're testing with Phoenix, the framework builds default tests for you that help you keep the basic structure of your tests straight. Those templates even go a long way toward showing you how to build tests to cover your MVC code. Still, it's best to start at the beginning: a walkthrough of using ExUnit, Elixir's testing framework. Let's take a look at a basic Elixir test, one without Phoenix involved at all.

ExUnit has three main macros. The setup macro specifies some setup code that runs once before each test. The test macro defines a single isolated test. The assert macro specifies something we believe to be true about our code. If the assertion is true, the test passes. If it's false, the test fails. Either way, ExUnit reports the results, accumulating a list of failures and exceptions. Let's use these three macros in a simple test:

```elixir
defmodule MyTest do
  use ExUnit.Case, async: true

  setup do
    # run some tedious setup code
    :ok
  end

  test "pass" do
    assert true
  end

  test "fail" do
    assert false
  end
end
```

This code runs two tests. The first runs the setup function and then the pass test. The second again runs the setup function and the then fail test. The output will include a passing test and a failing test.

If you need to know more about Elixir tests, excellent online resources exist, such as the ExUnit documentation.[1] For now, let's move on to specifically testing Phoenix functions.

Using Mix to Run Phoenix Tests

Whether you knew it or not, Phoenix has already been generating default tests for you, such as test/controllers/video_controller_test.exs. We can go ahead and remove that file since it's built for generic REST actions, not the features we've specifically built into our controller. We've added user authentication, validations, and the like to our videos, so we'll start fresh with our VideoController tests. Delete the test/controllers/video_controller_test.exs file now, and then let's see where our test suite stands:

```
$ mix test
...
  1) test GET / (Rumbl.PageControllerTest)
     test/controllers/page_controller_test.exs:4
     Assertion with =~ failed
     code: html_response(conn, 200) =~ "Welcome to Phoenix!"
     lhs:  "<!DOCTYPE html>\n<html lang=\"en\">\n ..."
     rhs:  "Welcome to Phoenix!"
     stacktrace:
       test/controllers/page_controller_test.exs:6
....
Finished in 0.5 seconds (0.5s on load, 0.05s on tests)
8 tests, 1 failure
```

---

1. http://elixir-lang.org/docs/stable/ex_unit/ExUnit.Case.html

We have one basic test that was generated along with the standard Phoenix installation. Since our controller has some changes, the tests fail. Let's open this file and take a look:

testing_mvc/rumbl/test/controllers/page_controller_test.exs

```
defmodule Rumbl.PageControllerTest do
  use Rumbl.ConnCase

  test "GET /", %{conn: conn} do
    conn = get conn, "/"
    assert html_response(conn, 200) =~ "Welcome to Phoenix!"
  end
end
```

This test is pretty sparse, but let's see what we can glean. Notice Rumbl.ConnCase. Phoenix adds a test/support/conn_case.ex file to each new project. That file extends Phoenix.ConnTest to provide services to your test suite, such as support for setting up connections and calling your endpoint with specific routes. Open that module to see what's provided by default in the Rumbl.ConnCase module:

testing_mvc/rumbl/test/support/conn_case.ex

```
defmodule Rumbl.ConnCase do
  @moduledoc """
  This module defines the test case to be used by tests that require setting up
  a connection.

  Such tests rely on `Phoenix.ConnTest` and also imports other functionality to
  make it easier to build and query models.

  Finally, if the test case interacts with the database, it cannot be async. For
  this reason, every test runs inside a transaction which is reset at the
  beginning of the test unless the test case is marked as async.
  """

  use ExUnit.CaseTemplate

  using do
    quote do
      # Import conveniences for testing with connections
      use Phoenix.ConnTest

      alias Rumbl.Repo
      import Ecto
      import Ecto.Changeset
      import Ecto.Query, only: [from: 1, from: 2]

      import Rumbl.Router.Helpers

      # The default endpoint for testing
      @endpoint Rumbl.Endpoint
    end
  end
```

```
  setup tags do
    unless tags[:async] do
      Ecto.Adapters.SQL.restart_test_transaction(Rumbl.Repo, [])
    end

    {:ok, conn: Phoenix.ConnTest.conn()}
  end
end
```

As you'd expect, we use Phoenix.ConnTest to set up that API. Next, it imports convenient aliases we'll use throughout our tests. Finally, it sets the @endpoint module attribute, which is required for Phoenix.ConnTest. This attribute lets Phoenix know which endpoint to call when you directly call a route in your tests.

Also notice our setup block. It receives the test tags as arguments alongside any test metadata. If a given test isn't asynchronous, we assume that the test needs the database and restart the database transaction to guarantee that it'll run on clean slate. Then setup places a base conn into our test metadata and returns a new context with this connection, which flows into our page_controller_test as an optional second argument to the test macro. Using the ConnCase, you can call your controller code through your endpoints, using all of the relevant pipelines, just as the Phoenix framework would.

For example, in your page_controller_test, we called our controller with get conn, "/" rather than calling the index action on our controller directly. This practice gives us the *right level of isolation* because we're using the controller the same way Phoenix does.

Phoenix also gives us some helpers to test responses and keep our tests clean, such as the assertion from page_controller_test:

```
assert html_response(conn, 200) =~ "Welcome to Phoenix!"
```

These functions pack a lot of punch in a single function call. The simple statement html_response(conn, 200) does the following:

- Asserts that the conn's response was 200
- Asserts that the response content-type was text/html
- Returns the response body, allowing us to match on the contents

If our request had been a JSON response, we could have used another response assertion called json_response to match on any field of a response body. For example, you might write a json_response assertion like this:

```
assert %{user_id: user.id} = json_response(conn, 200)
```

Rumbl.ConnCase is just a foundation. You can personalize it to your own application. Now let's address our failing test. It looks like we were expecting our "Welcome to Phoenix!" message to exist, but we've changed that message along the way. Let's update the test:

testing_mvc/listings/rumbl/test/controllers/page_controller_test.change1.exs

```
test "GET /", %{conn: conn} do
  conn = get conn, "/"
  assert html_response(conn, 200) =~ "Welcome to Rumbl.io!"
end
```

Now you can run your test with a better result. This time, let's run a single test, like this:

```
$ mix test test/controllers/page_controller_test.exs:4
```
.

It passes! The page test we just fixed is an integration test. Let's learn more about them by writing our own VideoController integration tests from scratch.

Integration Tests

One of our basic principles for testing is isolation, but that doesn't mean that the most extreme isolation is always the right answer. The interactions among parts of your software are the very things that make it interesting. When you test your Phoenix applications, getting the right level of isolation is critical. Sometimes, a function is the perfect level of isolation. Sometimes, though, you'll want to run a test that encompasses multiple layers of your application. This is the realm of the integration test.

Fortunately, we have a natural architectural barrier that enforces the perfect balance. We're going to fully test the route through the endpoint, as a real web request will do. That way, we'll execute each plug and pick up all of the little transformations that occur along the way. We won't have to do any complex test setup, and we won't have any mismatch between the ways the tests and production server use our application. To top it off, testing through the endpoint is superfast, so we pay virtually no penalty.

Creating Test Data

We're going to focus on implementing tests for our video controller. To do so, we need to be able to rapidly create video and user records to support our tests. Let's create some persistence helpers for creating users and videos. Create a test/support/test_helpers.ex file and key this in:

testing_mvc/listings/rumbl/test/support/test_helpers.ex

```
defmodule Rumbl.TestHelpers do
  alias Rumbl.Repo

  def insert_user(attrs \\ %{}) do
    changes = Dict.merge(%{
      name: "Some User",
      username: "user#{Base.encode16(:crypto.rand_bytes(8))}",
      password: "supersecret",
    }, attrs)

    %Rumbl.User{}
    |> Rumbl.User.registration_changeset(changes)
    |> Repo.insert!()
  end

  def insert_video(user, attrs \\ %{}) do
    user
    |> Ecto.build_assoc(:videos, attrs)
    |> Repo.insert!()
  end
end
```

We add an insert_user function that accepts a set of attributes and creates a persistent user with them. Then, we do the same with a function called insert_video. That function must also take the user that created the video. We'll use this file as a convenient base for common helpers like this.

You might be tempted to automatically reach for complex factory libraries, as you would in other languages, or approaches that let you specify fixtures. For simple data with a few well-defined relationships and mostly static attributes, you might find that simple functions work better. For applications like ours, such an approach has much less ceremony and will serve perfectly well.

Keep in mind, though, that absolutes of any kind can get you into trouble. A contract exists between your tests and your test data, whether you choose to make it explicit or not. The best approach is to start slowly with functions. Later, as your needs—such as unique sequences and faked unique data—grow, you can decide to adopt a library based on the specific needs of your application. Libraries are like macros. Don't use one when a simple function will do the job.

Testing Logged-Out Users

With that warning out of the way, it's time to add our factory helpers to our application. You can add import Rumbl.TestHelpers to your ConnCase using block so we bring in our helpers in all our connection-related tests, like this:

testing_mvc/listings/rumbl/test/support/conn_case.change1.ex

```
using do
  quote do
    # Import conveniences for testing with connections
    use Phoenix.ConnTest

    alias Rumbl.Repo
    import Ecto
    import Ecto.Changeset
    import Ecto.Query, only: [from: 1, from: 2]

    import Rumbl.Router.Helpers
    import Rumbl.TestHelpers

    # The default endpoint for testing
    @endpoint Rumbl.Endpoint
  end
end
```

On line 12, we import our test helpers. We can now use our new insert_user and insert_video functions to create our test data as needed.

We're finally ready to start testing our VideoController. Create a file called test/controllers/video_controller_test.exs and make it look like this:

testing_mvc/listings/rumbl/test/controllers/video_controller_test.exs

```
defmodule Rumbl.VideoControllerTest do
  use Rumbl.ConnCase

  test "requires user authentication on all actions", %{conn: conn} do
    Enum.each([
      get(conn, video_path(conn, :new)),
      get(conn, video_path(conn, :index)),
      get(conn, video_path(conn, :show, "123")),
      get(conn, video_path(conn, :edit, "123")),
      put(conn, video_path(conn, :update, "123", %{})),
      post(conn, video_path(conn, :create, %{})),
      delete(conn, video_path(conn, :delete, "123")),
    ], fn conn ->
      assert html_response(conn, 302)
      assert conn.halted
    end)
  end
end
```

Since our video controller is locked behind user authentication, we want to make sure that every action is halted. Since all of those tests are the same except for the routes, we use Enum.each to iterate over all of the routes we want, and we make the same assertion for each response. Since we're verifying a halted connection that kicks logged out visitors back to the home page, we assert a html_response of 302.

Let's try our tests out:

```
$ mix test
.........

Finished in 0.6 seconds (0.5s on load, 0.1s on tests)
9 tests, 0 failures
```

And they pass. Now we need to test the actions with a logged-in user.

Preparing for Logged-In Users

You might be tempted to place the user_id in the session for the Auth plug to pick up:

```
conn()
|> fetch_session()
|> put_session(:user_id, user.id)
|> get("/videos")
```

This approach is a little messy. We don't want to store anything directly in the session, because we don't want to leak implementation details. Alternatively, we could do a direct request to the session controller. However, this would quickly become expensive, because most tests will require a logged-in user.

Instead, we choose to test our login mechanism in isolation and build a bypass mechanism for the rest of our test cases. We simply pass any user through in our conn.assigns as a pass-through for our Auth plug. Update your web/controllers/auth.ex, like this:

testing_mvc/listings/rumbl/web/controllers/auth.change1.ex

```
def call(conn, repo) do
  user_id = get_session(conn, :user_id)

  cond do
    user = conn.assigns[:current_user] ->
      conn
    user = user_id && repo.get(Rumbl.User, user_id) ->
      assign(conn, :current_user, user)
    true ->
      assign(conn, :current_user, nil)
  end
end
```

We've rewritten our call function using cond to check for multiple conditions, with our new condition at the top. Its sole job is to match on the current_user already in place in the assigns. If we see that we already have a current_user, we return the connection as is.

Let's be clear. What we're doing here is controversial. We're adding this code to make our implementation more testable. We think the trade-off is worth it. We're *improving the contract*. If a user is in the conn.assigns, we honor it, no matter how it got there. We have an improved testing story that doesn't require us to write mocks or any other elaborate scaffolding.

Now, all of our tests for logged-in users will be much cleaner.

Testing Logged-In Users

Now, we're free to add tests. We add a new test for the /videos route to test/controllers/video_controller_test.exs, like this:

```
testing_mvc/listings/rumbl/test/controllers/video_controller_test.change1.exs
setup do
  user = insert_user(username: "max")
  conn = assign(conn(), :current_user, user)
  {:ok, conn: conn, user: user}
end

test "lists all user's videos on index", %{conn: conn, user: user} do
  user_video  = insert_video(user, title: "funny cats")
  other_video = insert_video(insert_user(username: "other"), title: "another video")

  conn = get conn, video_path(conn, :index)
  assert html_response(conn, 200) =~ ~r/Listing videos/
  assert String.contains?(conn.resp_body, user_video.title)
  refute String.contains?(conn.resp_body, other_video.title)
end
```

In our setup block, we seed a user to the database by using our insert_user helper function. ConnCase takes care of running our tests in isolation. Any seeded fixtures in the database will be wiped between test blocks.

However, our new setup block causes the previous tests to break, because they expect a connection without a user logged in. To solve our test failures, let's learn a technique called *tagging* to specify which tests need logged-in users and which ones don't.

Controlling Duplication with Tagging

Some of our tests require logging in and some don't. When setup requirements are different from test to test, ExUnit *tags* can help. When you specify a tag, ExUnit makes that information available within the setup block via callbacks. We're going to use tags to determine whether to log in our user.

Let's add a tag called :login_as to signify that we should insert a user and log that user into the connection. Otherwise, we'll skip the login requirement.

testing_mvc/listings/rumbl/test/controllers/video_controller_test.change2.exs

```
Line 1  setup %{conn: conn} = config do
          if username = config[:login_as] do
            user = insert_user(username: username)
            conn = assign(conn, :current_user, user)
    5       {:ok, conn: conn, user: user}
          else
            :ok
          end
        end
   10
        @tag login_as: "max"
        test "lists all user's videos on index", %{conn: conn, user: user} do
          user_video  = insert_video(user, title: "funny cats")
          other_video = insert_video(insert_user(username: "other"), title: "another video")
   15
          conn = get conn, video_path(conn, :index)
          assert html_response(conn, 200) =~ ~r/Listing videos/
          assert String.contains?(conn.resp_body, user_video.title)
          refute String.contains?(conn.resp_body, other_video.title)
   20  end
```

On line 11, we add a :login_as tag with our username. The tag module attribute accepts a keyword list or an atom. Passing an atom is a shorthand way to set flag style options. For example @tag :logged_in is equivalent to @tag logged_in: true. We rewrite our setup block to grab the config map, which holds our metadata with the conn and tags. If login_as has a value, we use it to log the user in and return the updated connection alongside the user; otherwise, we return :ok.

Our tests now pass, because they only seed the database when necessary. We can also use the tags to run tests only matching a particular tag, like this:

```
$ mix test test/controllers --only login_as
Including tags: [:login_as]
Excluding tags: [:test]
.

Finished in 0.4 seconds (0.3s on load, 0.04s on tests)
3 tests, 0 failures, 2 skipped
```

Perfect. In short, we'll use tags anywhere we want to identify a block of tests. If many tests need to share the same tag, for example the :login_as one, we could also move it to ConnCase itself.

Our tests now exercise the video listing, but we still haven't used the controller to create a video. Let's build a test to create a video, like this:

```
testing_mvc/listings/rumbl/test/controllers/video_controller_test.change3.exs
alias Rumbl.Video
@valid_attrs %{url: "http://youtu.be", title: "vid", description: "a vid"}
@invalid_attrs %{title: "invalid"}

defp video_count(query), do: Repo.one(from v in query, select: count(v.id))

@tag login_as: "max"
test "creates user video and redirects", %{conn: conn, user: user} do
  conn = post conn, video_path(conn, :create), video: @valid_attrs
  assert redirected_to(conn) == video_path(conn, :index)
  assert Repo.get_by!(Video, @valid_attrs).user_id == user.id
end

@tag login_as: "max"
test "does not create video and renders errors when invalid", %{conn: conn} do
  count_before = video_count(Video)
  conn = post conn, video_path(conn, :create), video: @invalid_attrs
  assert html_response(conn, 200) =~ "check the errors"
  assert video_count(Video) == count_before
end
```

In this example, we want to test the successful and unsuccessful paths for creating a video. To keep things clear and easy to understand, we create some module attributes for both valid and invalid changesets. This touch keeps our intentions clear. With one tweak, we can keep our tests DRY so changes in validations require only trivial changes to our controller tests. We'll have another set of tests we can use to fully handle our changesets, but for now this strategy will work fine.

Next, we create the test case for the successful case. We use the create route with our valid attributes and then assert that we're returning the right values and redirecting to the right place. Then, we confirm that our test impacts the database in the ways we expect. We don't need to test all of the attributes, but we should pay attention to the elements of this operation that are likely to break. We assert that our new record exists and has the correct owner. This test makes sure that our happy path is indeed happy.

Writing negative tests is a delicate balance. We don't want to cover all possible failure conditions. Instead, we're handling concerns we choose to expose to the user, especially those that change the flow of our code. We test the case of trying to create an invalid video, the redirect, error messages, and so on.

Our other persistence tests will follow much the same approach. You can find the full CRUD test listing in the downloadable source code for the book.[2]

---

2. http://pragprog.com/book/phoenix/source_code

As you recall, we left a hole in our code coverage when we worked around authentication. Let's shift gears and handle the authorization cases of our controller. We must test that other users cannot view, edit, update, or destroy videos of another user. Crack open our test case and key this in:

testing_mvc/listings/rumbl/test/controllers/video_controller_test.change4.exs

```
@tag login_as: "max"
test "authorizes actions against access by other users",
  %{user: owner, conn: conn} do

  video = insert_video(owner, @valid_attrs)
  non_owner = insert_user(username: "sneaky")
  conn = assign(conn, :current_user, non_owner)

  assert_error_sent :not_found, fn ->
    get(conn, video_path(conn, :show, video))
  end
  assert_error_sent :not_found, fn ->
    get(conn, video_path(conn, :edit, video))
  end
  assert_error_sent :not_found, fn ->
    put(conn, video_path(conn, :update, video, video: @valid_attrs))
  end
  assert_error_sent :not_found, fn ->
    delete(conn, video_path(conn, :delete, video))
  end
end
```

We first insert a video for our test user, max. Then, we set up our conn to log in a newly created user named sneaky, one that doesn't own our existing video. We use the same approach that we used when we tested the basic path without logging in. We call all of the actions and ensure that they raise an error, which results in a 404 or :not_found response status. In this case, the controllers are raising the Ecto.NoResultsError, which the adapter will translate to a 404 error for our production deployment.

Though our tests don't cover every controller action, these test cases provide a pretty good cross section for the overall approach. For practice, you can use these techniques to round out our integration tests.

As we work from the top down, we have one plug that we extracted into its own module, since it plays a critical role across multiple sections of our application. We'll test that plug next, in isolation. We're going to adhere to our principle for getting the right level of isolation.

Unit-Testing Plugs

If your code is worth writing, it's worth testing. Earlier, we bypassed our authentication plug, so we should test it now. The good news is that since our plug is essentially a function, it's relatively easy to build a set of tests that will confirm that it does what we need.

Create a test/controllers/auth_test.exs and key in the following contents. We're going to break the test file into parts to keep things simple.

First, test the authenticate_user function that does the lion's share of the work:

testing_mvc/listings/rumbl/test/controllers/auth_test.exs

```
defmodule Rumbl.AuthTest do
  use Rumbl.ConnCase
  alias Rumbl.Auth

  test "authenticate_user halts when no current_user exists",
    %{conn: conn} do

    conn = Auth.authenticate_user(conn, [])
    assert conn.halted
  end

  test "authenticate_user continues when the current_user exists",
    %{conn: conn} do

    conn =
      conn
      |> assign(:current_user, %Rumbl.User{})
      |> Auth.authenticate_user([])

    refute conn.halted
  end
end
```

That's as simple as it gets. If we try to authenticate without a user, we shouldn't authenticate. Otherwise, we should. Let's run that much to make sure things continue to work:

```
$ mix test test/controllers/auth_test.exs

1) test authenticate_user halts when no current_user exists
(Rumbl.AuthTest)
test/controllers/auth_test.exs:5
** (KeyError) key :current_user not found in: %{}
stacktrace:
(rumbl) web/controllers/auth.ex:53: Rumbl.Auth.authenticate_user/2
test/controllers/auth_test.exs:8

Finished in 0.3 seconds (0.3s on load, 0.01s on tests)
2 tests, 1 failure
```

That was surprising. What happened?

Since our Auth plug assumes that a :current_user assign exists in the connection, the test errors. Let's try to quickly fix this by injecting a nil :current_user in our first test case, like this:

```
conn =
  conn
  |> assign(:current_user, nil)
  |> Auth.authenticate_user([])
```

Now let's rerun the tests:

```
$ mix test test/controllers/auth_test.exs
1) test authenticate_user halts when no current_user exists
(Rumbl.AuthTest)
test/controllers/auth_test.exs:5
** (ArgumentError) flash not fetched, call fetch_flash/2
stacktrace:
(phoenix) lib/phoenix/controller.ex:997: Phoenix.Controller.get_flash/1
(phoenix) lib/phoenix/controller.ex:982: Phoenix.Controller.put_flash/3
(rumbl) web/controllers/auth.ex:57: Rumbl.Auth.authenticate_user/2
test/controllers/auth_test.exs:11

Finished in 0.4 seconds (0.4s on load, 0.01s on tests)
2 tests, 1 failure
```

Another error. It looks like our fetch_flash raised an error because the auth_test puts a message in the flash, which isn't available. Try to simply call fetch_flash, like this:

```
conn =
  conn()
  |> fetch_flash()
  |> Auth.authenticate_user([])
```

We receive a ** (ArgumentError) session not fetched, call fetch_session/2 error. And down the rabbit hole we go.

These are the kinds of issues that integration testing through the endpoint avoids. For unit tests, Phoenix includes a bypass_through test helper to prepare a connection. The bypass_through helper that ConnCase provides allows you to send a connection through the endpoint, router, and desired pipelines but bypass the route dispatch. This approach gives you a connection wired up with all the transformations your specific tests require, such as fetching the session and adding flash messages:

testing_mvc/listings/rumbl/test/controllers/auth_test.change1.exs

```
setup %{conn: conn} do
  conn =
    conn
    |> bypass_through(Rumbl.Router, :browser)
    |> get("/")

  {:ok, %{conn: conn}}
end

test "authenticate_user halts when no current_user exists", %{conn: conn} do
  conn = Auth.authenticate_user(conn, [])
  assert conn.halted
end

test "authenticate_user continues when the current_user exists", %{conn: conn} do
  conn =
    conn
    |> assign(:current_user, %Rumbl.User{})
    |> Auth.authenticate_user([])

  refute conn.halted
end
```

We add a setup block, which calls bypass_through, passing our router and the
:browser pipeline to invoke. Then we perform a request with get, which accesses
the endpoint and stops at the browser pipeline, as requested. The path given
to get isn't used by the router when bypassing; it's simply stored in the connection. This gives us all the requirements for a plug with a valid session and
flash message support. Next, we pull the conn from the context passed to the
test macro and use our bypassed conn as the base for our test blocks. Now let's
rerun our tests:

```
$ mix test test/controllers/auth_test.exs
..

Finished in 0.4 seconds (0.4s on load, 0.02s on tests)
2 test, 0 failures
```

And boom. Now test the rest of our Auth plug, like the login and logout features:

testing_mvc/listings/rumbl/test/controllers/auth_test.change2.exs

```
test "login puts the user in the session", %{conn: conn} do
  login_conn =
    conn
    |> Auth.login(%Rumbl.User{id: 123})
    |> send_resp(:ok, "")

  next_conn = get(login_conn, "/")
  assert get_session(next_conn, :user_id) == 123
end
```

Here, we test our ability to log in. We create a new connection called login_conn. We take a basic conn, log the user in with Auth.login, and call send_resp, which sends the response to the client with a given status and response body. To make sure that our new user survives the next request, we make a new request with that connection and make sure the user is still in the session. That's easy enough. A test for logout is similar:

testing_mvc/listings/rumbl/test/controllers/auth_test.change2.exs

```
test "logout drops the session", %{conn: conn} do
  logout_conn =
    conn
    |> put_session(:user_id, 123)
    |> Auth.logout()
    |> send_resp(:ok, "")

  next_conn = get(logout_conn, "/")
  refute get_session(next_conn, :user_id)
end
```

We create a connection, put a user_id into our session, and then call Auth.logout. To make sure the logout will persist through a request, we then make a request with get, and finally make that no user_id is in the session.

Now, let's test the main interface for our plug—the call function, which calls the plug directly to wire up the current_user from the session:

testing_mvc/listings/rumbl/test/controllers/auth_test.change3.exs

```
Line 1 test "call places user from session into assigns", %{conn: conn} do
     -   user = insert_user()
     -   conn =
     -     conn
     5     |> put_session(:user_id, user.id)
     -     |> Auth.call(Repo)
     -
     -   assert conn.assigns.current_user.id == user.id
     - end
    10
     - test "call with no session sets current_user assign to nil", %{conn: conn} do
     -   conn = Auth.call(conn, Repo)
     -   assert conn.assigns.current_user == nil
     - end
```

The tests are simple and light. On line 2, we create a user for the test. Next, on line 5, we place that user's ID in the session. On line 6, we call Auth.call, and then assert that the current_user in conn.assigns matches our seeded user. We know that *logged-in users can get in.*

We have a workable positive test, but it's also important to test the negative condition. We want to make sure that *logged-out users stay out.* The test looks a lot like the positive test, but we never put any user in the session, and we match on nil instead.

The only feature left is to test our Auth.login_by_username_and_pass function. That's pretty easy:

testing_mvc/listings/rumbl/test/controllers/auth_test.change4.exs

```
Line 1  test "login with a valid username and pass", %{conn: conn} do
     -    user = insert_user(username: "me", password: "secret")
     -    {:ok, conn} =
     -      Auth.login_by_username_and_pass(conn, "me", "secret", repo: Repo)
     5
     -    assert conn.assigns.current_user.id == user.id
     -  end
     -
     -  test "login with a not found user", %{conn: conn} do
    10    assert {:error, :not_found, _conn} =
     -      Auth.login_by_username_and_pass(conn, "me", "secret", repo: Repo)
     -  end
     -
     -  test "login with password mismatch", %{conn: conn} do
    15    _ = insert_user(username: "me", password: "secret")
     -    assert {:error, :unauthorized, _conn} =
     -      Auth.login_by_username_and_pass(conn, "me", "wrong", repo: Repo)
     -  end
```

We have three basic tests. The test on line 1 seeds a user and then authenticates it. So far so good. Our positive case passes. Once again, our negative tests will closely resemble the positive ones.

We have two negative cases to cover. On line 9 we test the case where no user exists, and on line 14 we test an incorrect password.

Now let's run our tests:

```
$ mix test
....................

Finished in 4.8 seconds (0.6s on load, 4.1s on tests)
22 tests, 0 failures
```

All pass, but if you look closely, we have a problem. We're waiting five seconds for twenty-two small tests. The test time is growing quickly. You've probably been noticing how the test times have crept up as we've seeded more and more users. If your tests are slow, you won't run them as much. We have to fix it.

The reason our tests are slow is that we seed users with our registration changeset, which hashes passwords. Hashing passwords is intentionally expensive. Doing this extra bit of work makes our passwords harder to crack, but we don't need all of that security in the test environment. Let's ease up the number of hashing rounds to speed up our test suite by adding these configuration lines to config/test.exs:

```
testing_mvc/listings/rumbl/config/test.change1.exs
config :comeonin, :bcrypt_log_rounds, 4
config :comeonin, :pbkdf2_rounds, 1
```

Now let's rerun our tests:

```
$ mix test
....................

Finished in 0.6 seconds (0.5s on load, 0.2s on tests)
22 tests, 0 failures
```

Less than a second! Time to shift into views.

Testing Views and Templates

As we've said, any code worth writing is code worth testing, and your views are no exception. As you saw in Chapter 3, *Controllers, Views, and Templates*, on page 37, Phoenix templates are simply functions in a parent's view module. You can test these functions like any other. In this section, you'll see how to test views and templates in isolation.

Create a test/views/video_view_test.exs and key this in:

```
testing_mvc/listings/rumbl/test/views/video_view_test.exs
Line 1   defmodule Rumbl.VideoViewTest do
  -        use Rumbl.ConnCase, async: true
  -        import Phoenix.View
  -
  5        test "renders index.html", %{conn: conn} do
  -          videos = [%Rumbl.Video{id: "1", title: "dogs"},
  -                    %Rumbl.Video{id: "2", title: "cats"}]
  -          content = render_to_string(Rumbl.VideoView, "index.html",
  -                                     conn: conn, videos: videos)
  10
  -          assert String.contains?(content, "Listing videos")
  -          for video <- videos do
  -            assert String.contains?(content, video.title)
  -          end
  15       end
  -
  -
```

```
     test "renders new.html", %{conn: conn} do
       changeset = Rumbl.Video.changeset(%Rumbl.Video{})
20     categories = [{"cats", 123}]
       content = render_to_string(Rumbl.VideoView, "new.html",
         conn: conn, changeset: changeset, categories: categories)

       assert String.contains?(content, "New video")
25   end
   end
```

Our test needs some videos, so on line 5, we set up our required @videos assigns. With all of the prerequisites in place, we call Phoenix.View.render_to_string to render our HTML template as a simple string. Then, we make sure that all of the video titles are present on the page.

On line 18, we again set up our necessary @changeset and @categories assigns before rendering our template as a string and asserting that our render contents place us on the new video page.

Sometimes, views are simple enough that your integration tests will be enough. Many other times, you won't test the templates directly, but the functions that you create to help move the logic away from the templates and into code. Our goal with this section is to once again highlight the fact that because a template is just a function in the view, templates are easy to test because they aren't coupled with the controller layer. And this will apply to any function you create in your view, because all arguments are received explicitly. With Phoenix, you'll have all of the tools you need to do so easily. Let's move on to models.

Splitting Side Effects in Model Tests

It's time to test the M of the MVC: the model. We'll split model tests by their reliance on side effects. Phoenix, like Rumbl.ConnCase, generates a module in test/support/model_case.ex to serve as a foundation for your model tests. Crack it open so you can import our TestHelpers, like this:

testing_mvc/listings/rumbl/test/support/model_case.change1.ex

```
Line 1  defmodule Rumbl.ModelCase do
          use ExUnit.CaseTemplate

          using do
5           quote do
              alias Rumbl.Repo

              import Ecto
              import Ecto.Changeset
10            import Ecto.Query, only: [from: 1, from: 2]
```

```
        import Rumbl.TestHelpers
        import Rumbl.ModelCase
      end
    end

    setup tags do
      unless tags[:async] do
        Ecto.Adapters.SQL.restart_test_transaction(Rumbl.Repo, [])
      end

      :ok
    end

    def errors_on(model, data) do
      model.__struct__.changeset(model, data).errors
    end
  end
```

The using block serves as a place for common imports and aliases, and we again see a setup block for handling transactional tests. Recall that transactional tests run a test and roll back any changes made during the test. This allows tests to reset the database to a known state quickly between tests.

Phoenix also generates an errors_on function for quickly accessing a list of error messages for attributes on a given model. You'll see that function come into play when we write tests for our changesets.

Testing Side Effect–Free Model Code

If you're new to functional programming, recall that code with side effects changes the outside world. Some examples include writing to the database, removing a file from the filesystem, or changing some global state. Code that just transforms data, like our functions that build changesets and transform queries, is free of side effects. We start by creating a test/models/user_test.exs for holding unit tests that don't have side effects or touch the database. Open it and key this in:

testing_mvc/listings/rumbl/test/models/user_test.exs

```
defmodule Rumbl.UserTest do
  use Rumbl.ModelCase, async: true
  alias Rumbl.User

  @valid_attrs %{name: "A User", username: "eva", password: "secret"}
  @invalid_attrs %{}

  test "changeset with valid attributes" do
    changeset = User.changeset(%User{}, @valid_attrs)
    assert changeset.valid?
  end
```

```
     test "changeset with invalid attributes" do
       changeset = User.changeset(%User{}, @invalid_attrs)
15     refute changeset.valid?
     end

     test "changeset does not accept long usernames" do
       attrs = Map.put(@valid_attrs, :username, String.duplicate("a", 30))
20     assert {:username, {"should be at most %{count} character(s)", [count: 20]}} in
               errors_on(%User{}, attrs)
     end
   end
```

On line 2, we use Rumbl.ModelCase to set up our model tests. We also make sure to set our test as async: true, because one of our primary motivations for isolating side effects is that we can execute tests concurrently. Since we have side effect–free tests, we can run these in parallel for faster execution times because we can be certain they won't conflict with other tests for database or some other shared state.

As we did in previous tests, we set up a few module attributes for valid and invalid fields to keep our tests DRY and maintainable as our requirements change. Then, on lines 8 and 13, we build valid and invalid changesets and assert the expected results of changeset.valid?. You can see one of the benefits of separating change management from persistence. These tests don't require accessing the database. In this case, it's perfectly reasonable to test this code in isolation.

In the third test, on line 18, our error checking is a bit more intentional. We set a username that's too long and assert that we got a specific error back. For this test, we use the errors_on function defined on Rumbl.ModelCase. errors_on is convenient for quickly retrieving errors from the changeset function, or you can improvise something by hand if you need to test custom behavior, such as our code in the registration_changeset.

Our Rumbl.User module is small, but our password policies are important to us. We want to explicitly cover those requirements in specific test cases, like this:

testing_mvc/listings/rumbl/test/models/user_test.change1.exs

```
Line 1 test "registration_changeset password must be at least 6 chars long" do
       attrs = Map.put(@valid_attrs, :password, "12345")
       changeset = User.registration_changeset(%User{}, attrs)
       assert {:password, {"should be at least %{count} character(s)", count: 6}}
5             in changeset.errors
     end
```

```
     test "registration_changeset with valid attributes hashes password" do
       attrs = Map.put(@valid_attrs, :password, "123456")
10     changeset = User.registration_changeset(%User{}, attrs)
       %{password: pass, password_hash: pass_hash} = changeset.changes

       assert changeset.valid?
       assert pass_hash
15     assert Comeonin.Bcrypt.checkpw(pass, pass_hash)
     end
```

We first test the registration_changeset with an invalid password length. We assert that changeset.errors includes our expected error.

Next, we encode a specific security requirement. *We don't want passwords to be stored in the clear.* On line 8, we use valid user registration data, and we explicitly test that password_hash is properly hashed from the plain-text password.

Now let's run our tests:

```
$ mix test test/models/user_test.exs
.....

Finished in 0.3 seconds (0.2s on load, 0.02s on tests)
5 tests, 0 failures
```

They pass!

In the future, as we continue to build features, we'll try to make as much of our application side effect free as possible, as we do throughout Phoenix. All of these tests will go into user_test. Those tests will be easier to understand and will run faster.

Testing Code with Side Effects

Now let's handle the cases where we have side effects. We'll call these *repository tests* because the side effects manifest themselves in the repository.

In truth, most repository-related functionality will be tested with our integration tests as they insert and update records, but we want to be sure we catch some error conditions *as close to the breaking point as possible.* One such example is a uniqueness constraint checks in our changeset. It has side effects because we're going to need to explicitly create an existing record and then test against it.

Create a test/models/user_repo_test.exs file and key this in:

testing_mvc/listings/rumbl/test/models/user_repo_test.exs

```
Line 1  defmodule Rumbl.UserRepoTest do
   -      use Rumbl.ModelCase
   -      alias Rumbl.User

   5      @valid_attrs %{name: "A User", username: "eva"}

   -      test "converts unique_constraint on username to error" do
   -        insert_user(username: "eric")
   -        attrs = Map.put(@valid_attrs, :username, "eric")
   10       changeset = User.changeset(%User{}, attrs)

   -        assert {:error, changeset} = Repo.insert(changeset)
   -        assert {:username, "has already been taken"} in changeset.errors
   -      end
   15   end
```

Once again, we start by using ModelCase, but this time we go with the default async: false option because side effects prevent us from running these tests in isolation. At the top of our test, we insert a user named eric. On line 12, we attempt to add another user with the same name. Then, we assert that it was properly converted to a changeset error.

Now, let's run our test:

```
$ mix test test/models/user_repo_test.exs
.

Finished in 0.3 seconds (0.2s on load, 0.05s on tests)
1 test, 0 failures
```

And it passes! We have one more model test against our Repo. Our Category module contains an alphabetical function that composes an Ecto query. Let's test this function against Repo by creating a test/models/category_repo_test.exs:

testing_mvc/listings/rumbl/test/models/category_repo_test.exs

```
defmodule Rumbl.CategoryRepoTest do
  use Rumbl.ModelCase
  alias Rumbl.Category

  test "alphabetical/1 orders by name" do
    Repo.insert!(%Category{name: "c"})
    Repo.insert!(%Category{name: "a"})
    Repo.insert!(%Category{name: "b"})

    query = Category |> Category.alphabetical()
    query = from c in query, select: c.name
    assert Repo.all(query) == ~w(a b c)
  end
end
```

We add a single test case that inserts a few categories, then queries against the Repo to check that they're returned alphabetically as requested. We also test that our alphabetical function can compose with an existing queryable argument. Now let's run our tests:

```
$ mix test test/models/category_repo_test.exs
 .

Finished in 0.2 seconds (0.2s on load, 0.02s on tests)
1 test, 0 failures
```

Clean and green!

Though such queries' functions are just transforming data, you'll often test them with side effects because you want to verify *what the queries do*, not *how they're composed*. You can see that the code organization of models in Ecto provides an excellent separation for breaking your tests along the side-effect boundary.

Wrapping Up

With these final tests, we're finally done. We've accomplished a lot:

- We examined how tests work in Phoenix.

- We set up some basic testing functions to insert users and videos, and shared those across all of our potential test cases.

- We wrote some basic integration tests, bypassing only our authentication plug.

- We used Phoenix test helpers to make multiple assertions in a compact way.

- We tested our authentication plug in isolation.

- We tested our views.

- We tested models with and without side effects.

Raise a cheer, because we're through Part I! You should now be able to use Plug, Ecto, and Phoenix to build traditional request/response features for your application and test each of those concepts. Part II will be even more exciting, focusing on the features that prompted the creation of Phoenix. You'll see channels, OTP, and more. Get ready. We're going to push Phoenix harder.

Part II

Writing Interactive and Maintainable Applications

In Part II, we'll explore the features that will help you build a new generation of web applications. You'll learn to use channels to build highly concurrent interactive applications using a new set of abstractions. Then, you'll learn to build service layers with the OTP API, the famous Erlang library for building supervised, fault-tolerant services. You'll manage all of this with Mix, Elixir's build tool, allowing us to break a single monolithic application into smaller ones, separately maintainable but conveniently integrated. Finally, you'll learn to test channels and OTP features. You'll learn to build interactive applications that scale well and are easy to understand.

## CHAPTER 9

Watching Videos

We've accomplished quite a bit. We've built some basic web application features in a short time. We used Plug to build pipelines of functions that let us build organized, DRY code. We used Ecto to deal with our relational database in a functional way, favoring explicitness by separating the model from the repository. Phoenix wired it all together into a streamlined workflow, with live reloading, HTML support, and more.

Everything we've done so far highlights how well Phoenix encourages beautiful and maintainable applications. Those improvements bring a slightly different look to how people have done web development for the last ten years, but nothing you've seen up to now is drastically different from what you already knew.

Now you're ready to see what makes Phoenix shine. This chapter starts with preparing some common ground by adding a page to watch videos. Then you'll look into Ecto custom types, which allow you to integrate your own requirements into queries, changesets, and structs. At the close of this chapter you'll learn about the extensible power behind Elixir's protocols.

Tighten your seat belts. This ride will be unforgettable.

Watching Videos

Our rumbl application will allow us to add messages to videos in real time. We'll do some groundwork to make this process more convenient when the time comes. We'll tweak our views to make it easy to watch videos. Then, we'll create a new controller explicitly for watching a video, along with its view and template. Next, we'll tweak the router to pick up our new routes. Finally, we'll add some JavaScript to plug in to YouTube's API. You'll work through these features quickly, because they don't involve much new ground.

Let's let the user watch a video. First let's enhance our layout header with a link to My Videos for the current user in web/templates/layout/app.html.eex:

watching_videos/listings/rumbl/web/templates/layout/app.change1.html.eex

```
<div class="header">
  <ol class="breadcrumb text-right">
    <%= if @current_user do %>
      <li><%= @current_user.username %></li>
      <li><%= link "My Videos", to: video_path(@conn, :index) %></li>
      <li>
        <%= link "Log out", to: session_path(@conn, :delete, @current_user),
                         method: "delete" %>
      </li>
    <% else %>
      <li><%= link "Register", to: user_path(@conn, :new) %></li>
      <li><%= link "Log in", to: session_path(@conn, :new) %></li>
    <% end %>
  </ol>
  <span class="logo"></span>
</div>
```

Clicking My Videos routes a logged-in user directly to VideoController.index action.

This action is restricted to the current user, thanks to our scoping rules in the controller. In fact, there's no public URL we can share with our friends when it comes to watching videos. Let's address this by creating a WatchController for watching user videos, available to any user. Create a new web/controllers/watch_controller.ex file and key this in:

watching_videos/listings/rumbl/web/controllers/watch_controller.ex

```
defmodule Rumbl.WatchController do
  use Rumbl.Web, :controller
  alias Rumbl.Video

  def show(conn, %{"id" => id}) do
    video = Repo.get!(Video, id)
    render conn, "show.html", video: video
  end
end
```

Now, let's create a new template directory for the controller in web/templates/watch and add a new show.html.eex template file with these contents:

watching_videos/listings/rumbl/web/templates/watch/show.html.eex

```
<h2><%= @video.title %></h2>
<div class="row">
  <div class="col-sm-7">
    <%= content_tag :div, id: "video",
          data: [id: @video.id, player_id: player_id(@video)] do %>
```

```
      <% end %>
    </div>
    <div class="col-sm-5">
      <div class="panel panel-default">
        <div class="panel-heading">
          <h3 class="panel-title">Annotations</h3>
        </div>
        <div id="msg-container" class="panel-body annotations">

        </div>
        <div class="panel-footer">
          <textarea id="msg-input"
                    rows="3"
                    class="form-control"
                    placeholder="Comment..."></textarea>
        <button id="msg-submit" class="btn btn-primary form-control"
type="submit">
          Post
        </button>
      </div>
    </div>
  </div>
</div>
```

The template is mostly markup, with the exception of the title and the video
div, which includes the id, data-id, and data-player-id attributes. We extract the
player ID from the video url field by a function aptly named player_id. Since
templates are just functions in the view module, the view is the perfect place
to define such a function.

Create a new web/views/watch_view.ex and make it look like this:

watching_videos/listings/rumbl/web/views/watch_view.ex

```
defmodule Rumbl.WatchView do
  use Rumbl.Web, :view

  def player_id(video) do
    ~r{^.*(?:youtu\.be/|\w+/|v=)(?<id>[^#&?]*)}
    |> Regex.named_captures(video.url)
    |> get_in(["id"])
  end
end
```

Unfortunately, YouTube URLs come in a variety of formats. We need a regular
expression to extract the video ID from the URL. Regular expressions are
beyond the scope of this book, but here are the basics. A regular expression[1]
uses patterns to match specific patterns within strings. We're naming a pattern

---

1. http://www.regular-expressions.info/

called id and then piping our expression into a function called named_captures, which extracts the id field given our URL name. Then, we build a map that returns the id key with its value.

Finally, let's add an entry to our router's :browser pipeline to the new WatchController:

watching_videos/listings/rumbl/web/router.change1.ex

```
scope "/", Rumbl do
  pipe_through :browser # Use the default browser stack

  get "/", PageController, :index
  resources "/users", UserController, only: [:index, :show, :new, :create]
  resources "/sessions", SessionController, only: [:new, :create, :delete]
  get "/watch/:id", WatchController, :show
end
```

Now let's change the link for each entry in the My Videos page to point to watch instead of show. Open up web/templates/video/index.html.eex and replace show with this:

watching_videos/listings/rumbl/web/templates/video/index.change1.html.eex

```
<td class="text-right">
  <%= link "Watch", to: watch_path(@conn, :show, video),
                class: "btn btn-default btn-xs" %>

  <%= link "Edit", to: video_path(@conn, :edit, video),
                class: "btn btn-default btn-xs" %>

  <%= link "Delete", to: video_path(@conn, :delete, video),
                  method: :delete,
                  data: [confirm: "Are you sure?"],
                  class: "btn btn-danger btn-xs" %>
</td>
```

Notice the link. We use our new watch_path helper, generated by the new route.

Not much that's exciting is happening here, but this preparation will lead to a great fireworks show later. Now, things will start to get a little more interesting. Let's add the JavaScript required to let us watch videos.

Adding JavaScript

Brunch[2] is a build tool written in Node.js. We'll use Brunch to build, transform, and minify JavaScript code. Processing assets in this way makes your page load much more efficiently. Brunch not only takes care of JavaScript but also CSS and all of our application assets, such as images.

---

2. http://brunch.io

The Brunch structure is laid out in the web/static directory:

```
...
├── assets
├── css
├── js
├── vendor
...
```

We put everything in assets that doesn't need to be transformed by Brunch. The build tool will simply copy those assets just as they are to priv/static, where they'll be served by Phoenix.Static in our endpoint.

We keep CSS and JavaScript files in their respective directories. The vendor directory is used to keep any third-party tools you need, such as jQuery. This structure helps us organize code, but we're also being practical. Let's see why.

Open up web/static/js/app.js and take a look as its contents:

```
// Import dependencies
// ...
import "phoenix_html"

// Import local files
// ...
// import socket from "./socket"
```

Phoenix configures Brunch to use ECMAScript 6 (ES6)—the upcoming Java-Script version we'll use in this book—to provide the necessary import statements. Phoenix wraps the contents for each JavaScript file you add to web/static/js in a function and collects them into priv/static/js/app.js. That's the file loaded by browsers at the end of web/templates/layout.html.eex when we call static_path(@conn, "/js/app.js").

Since each file is wrapped in a function, it won't be automatically executed by browsers unless you explicitly import it in your app.js file. In this way, the app.js file is like a manifest. It's where you import and wire up your JavaScript dependencies.

The vendor directory is the exception to this rule. If you add an external Java-Script file to web/static/vendor, it'll be automatically executed at the bottom of our layout. That way, external dependencies are never imported.

You can configure the Brunch tool in the brunch-config.js file. Take a look at it on your own time. The file is heavily commented, so you can easily tell what's happening.

Brunch ships with a command-line tool, and using it is straightforward. You need to know only three commands:

```
$ brunch build
$ brunch build --production
$ brunch watch
```

The first command builds all of your static files, compiling and copying the results to priv/static. The second one builds and minifies them, doing everything you'd expect for deploying JavaScript and style sheets to production. The third command is used during development, so Brunch automatically recompiles the files as they change.

In all likelihood, you'll never type the last command directly, because Phoenix does it for you. If you open up your config/dev.exs, you see the following line:

```
watchers: [node: ["node_modules/brunch/bin/brunch", "watch", "--stdin"]]
```

That code will automatically run brunch watch --stdin when your Phoenix app starts in development. The --stdin option makes the brunch program abort when Phoenix shuts down.

With the Brunch introduction out of the way, it's time to write some Java-Script. First, we'll create a Player object to receive the data-player-id and embed the YouTube video. Later, we'll use the Player object to send and receive information about the video so we'll know exactly when an annotation is added.

Create a new file called web/static/js/player.js with these contents:

watching_videos/listings/rumbl/web/static/js/player.js

```javascript
let Player = {
  player: null,

  init(domId, playerId, onReady){
    window.onYouTubeIframeAPIReady = () => {
      this.onIframeReady(domId, playerId, onReady)
    }
    let youtubeScriptTag = document.createElement("script")
    youtubeScriptTag.src = "//www.youtube.com/iframe_api"
    document.head.appendChild(youtubeScriptTag)
  },

  onIframeReady(domId, playerId, onReady){
    this.player = new YT.Player(domId, {
      height: "360",
      width: "420",
      videoId: playerId,
      events: {
        "onReady":  (event => onReady(event) ),
        "onStateChange": (event => this.onPlayerStateChange(event) )
      }
    })
  },
```

```
  onPlayerStateChange(event){ },
  getCurrentTime(){ return Math.floor(this.player.getCurrentTime() * 1000) },
  seekTo(millsec){ return this.player.seekTo(millsec / 1000) }
}
export default Player
```

That's a fairly long example, so we should break it down piece by piece.

First, we create a Player object that wires up YouTube's special window.onY-ouTubeIframeAPIReady callback. We inject a YouTube iframe tag, which will trigger our event when the player is ready.

Next, we implement a onIframeReady function to create the player with the YouTube iframe API. We finish by adding convenience functions like getCurrent-Time and seekTo, since we want to bind messages to a point in time for the video playback.

This abstraction is more than a convenient wrapper. It builds an API for video players with the most important features for our application. Our Player API will insulate us from changes in YouTube and also let us add other video players over time. Our onYouTubeReady function needs the HTML container ID to hold the iframe. We'll pass this in from higher up in our JavaScript stack in a moment.

Chris says:
Why Brunch?

Instead of building yet another asset-build tool, the Phoenix team decided to leverage one of the many tools available in the Node.js ecosystem. We spent several weeks evaluating, using, and deploying many of the options available. Brunch was our first choice because it's simple to use, configurable, and fast.

We know this choice might not resonate with all developers, so Phoenix allows you to use the build tool of your choice. Not a single line of code in Phoenix knows about Brunch. All the configuration is in your application. You can even skip Brunch alto-gether when creating a new app by using the --no-brunch option. If you can tell your build tool to compile your static files to priv/static, you're good to go. You can even change your config/dev.exs file so Phoenix sets up a watcher for your favorite tool.

Our YouTube player is all set, but YouTube's JavaScript API expects a specific video ID, and all we have is the URL.

Remember, our player.js file won't be executed unless we import it. Let's do this in web/static/js/app.js by importing the Player and starting it with the video and player ID if one exists:

watching_videos/listings/rumbl/web/static/js/app.change1.js

```
import Player from "./player"
let video = document.getElementById("video")

if(video) {
  Player.init(video.id, video.getAttribute("data-player-id"), () => {
    console.log("player ready!")
  })
}
```

Next, let's tidy up our annotations box with a sprinkle of CSS. Create a web/static/css/video.css file and key this in:

watching_videos/listings/rumbl/web/static/css/video.css

```
#msg-container {
  min-height: 190px;
}
```

Create a new video with a YouTube URL, and you're now ready to watch it:

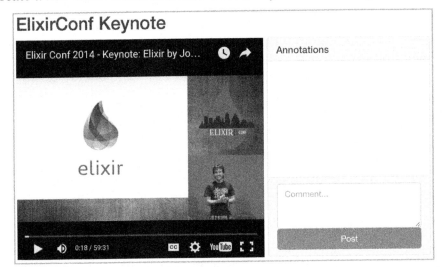

You can even start sharing the video URL with your friends with a URL that looks like /watch/13—but that's ugly. URLs for videos should use words, not numbers. Let's fix that.

Creating Slugs

We want our videos to have a unique URL-friendly identifier, called a *slug*. This approach lets us have a unique identifier that will build URLs that are friendlier to people and search engines. We need to create the slug from the title so we can represent a video titled Programming Elixir as a URL-friendly slug, such as 1-programming-elixir, where 1 is the video ID.

The first step is to add a slug column to the database:

```
$ mix ecto.gen.migration add_slug_to_video
```

We generate a new migration. Remember, your name will differ based on the timestamp attached to the front of the file, but you can find the new file in the priv/repo/migrations directory. Let's fill it in like this:

watching_videos/listings/rumbl/priv/repo/migrations/20150919152919_add_slug_to_video.exs

```elixir
def change do
  alter table(:videos) do
    add :slug, :string
  end
end
```

Our new migration uses the alter macro, which changes the schema for both up and down migrations. With the migration in place, let's apply it to the database:

```
$ mix ecto.migrate
10:28:04.589 [info]  == Running
Rumbl.Repo.Migrations.AddSlugToVideo.change/0 forward

10:28:04.590 [info]  alter table videos

10:28:04.591 [info]  == Migrated in 0.0s
```

Next, we need to add the new field to the video schema in web/models/video.ex, beneath the other fields:

```elixir
field :slug, :string
```

The whole premise of a slug is that you can automatically generate a permanent field from other fields, some of which may be updatable. Let's do this by changing the Video.changeset in web/models/video.ex, like this:

watching_videos/listings/rumbl/web/models/video.change1.ex

```elixir
def changeset(model, params \\ :empty) do
  model
  |> cast(params, @required_fields, @optional_fields)
  |> slugify_title()
  |> assoc_constraint(:category)
end

defp slugify_title(changeset) do
  if title = get_change(changeset, :title) do
    put_change(changeset, :slug, slugify(title))
  else
    changeset
  end
end
```

```
defp slugify(str) do
  str
  |> String.downcase()
  |> String.replace(~r/[^\w-]+/u, "-")
end
```

We modify the generated changeset, just as we did the changeset for the password. We build the slug field within our changeset. The code couldn't be simpler. The pipe operator makes it easy for us to tell a story with code.

If a change is made to the title, we build a slug based on the new title with the slugify function. Otherwise, we simply return the changeset. slugify downcases the string and replaces nonword characters with a - character. cast, assoc_constraint, get_change and put_change are all functions defined in Ecto.Changeset, imported by default in your model in web/web.ex.

Don't miss the importance of what we've done here. We're once again able to change how data gets into the system, without touching the controller and without using callbacks or any other indirection. All of the changes to be performed by the database are clearly outlined in the changeset. At this point, you've learned all the concepts behind changesets, and the benefits are becoming clearer:

- Because Ecto separates changesets from the definition of a given record, we can have a separate change policy for each type of change. We could easily add a JSON API that creates videos, including the slug field, for example.

- Changesets filter and cast the incoming data, making sure sensitive fields like a user role cannot be set externally, while conveniently casting them to the type defined in the schema.

- Changesets can validate data—for example, the length or the format of a field—on the fly, but validations that depend on data integrity are left to the database in the shape of constraints.

- Changesets make our code easy to understand and implement because they can compose easily, allowing us to specify each part of a change with a function.

In short, Ecto cleanly encapsulates the concepts of change, and we benefit tremendously as users. Now that we can generate slugs for the videos, let's make sure we use them in our links.

Extending Phoenix with Protocols

To use slugs when linking to the video page, let's open up the web/templates/video/index.html.eex template and see how links are generated:

```
<%= link "Watch", to: watch_path(@conn, :show, video),
                class: "btn btn-default btn-xs" %>
```

watch_path is a helper generated by the Rumbl.Router and imported into controllers and views in web/web.ex. When we pass a struct like video to watch_path, Phoenix automatically extracts its ID to use in the returned URL. To use slugs, we could simply change the helper call to the following:

```
watch_path(@conn, :show, "#{video.id}-#{video.slug}")
```

This approach may seem simple, but it has one big flaw. It's brittle because it's not DRY. Each place we build a link, we need to build the URL with the id and slug fields. If we forget to use the same structure in any of the future watch_path calls, we'll end up linking to the wrong URL. There's a better way.

We can customize how Phoenix generates URLs for the videos. Phoenix and Elixir have the perfect solution for this. Phoenix knows to use the id field in a Video struct because Phoenix defines a protocol, called Phoenix.Param. By default, this protocol extracts the id of the struct, if one exists.

However, since Phoenix.Param is an Elixir protocol, we can customize it for any data type in the language, including the ones we define ourselves. Let's do so for the Video struct. Add the following snippet to the bottom of your web/models/video.ex file:

watching_videos/listings/rumbl/web/models/video.change2.ex
```
defimpl Phoenix.Param, for: Rumbl.Video do
  def to_param(%{slug: slug, id: id}) do
    "#{id}-#{slug}"
  end
end
```

We're implementing the Phoenix.Param protocol for the Rumbl.Video struct. The protocol requires us to implement the to_param function, which receives the video struct itself. We pattern-match on the video slug and ID and use it to build a string as our slug.

The beauty behind Elixir protocols is that we can implement them for any data structure, anywhere, any time. Though we place our implementation in the same file as the video definition, it could as easily exist elsewhere. We get clean polymorphism because we can extend Phoenix parameters without changing Phoenix or the Video module itself.

Let's give this a try in IEx:

```
iex> video = %Rumbl.Video{id: 1, slug: "hello"}
%Rumbl.Video{id: 1, slug: "hello", ...}
iex> Rumbl.Router.Helpers.watch_path(%URI{}, :show, video)
"/watch/1-hello"
```

We build a video and then call watch_path, passing our video as an argument.
The new path uses both the id and slug fields. Note that we give the URI struct
to watch_path instead of the usual connection. The URI struct is part of Elixir's
standard library, and all helpers accept it as their first argument. This convenience is particularly useful when needed to build URLs outside of your web
request. Think emails, messages, and so on. Let's play a bit with this idea:

```
iex> url = URI.parse("http://example.com/prefix")
%URI{...}
iex> Rumbl.Router.Helpers.watch_path(url, :show, video)
"/prefix/watch/1-hello"
iex> Rumbl.Router.Helpers.watch_url(url, :show, video)
"http://example.com/prefix/watch/1-hello"
```

You can also ask your endpoint to return the struct_url, based on the values
you've defined in your configuration files:

```
iex> url = Rumbl.Endpoint.struct_url
%URI{...}
iex> Rumbl.Router.Helpers.watch_url(url, :show, video)
"http://localhost:4000/watch/1-hello"
```

With Phoenix.Param properly implemented for our videos, it's time to give it a
try. Access My Videos and click the Watch link for an existing video.

You see a page with an error that looks something like this:

```
value `"13-hello-world"` in `where` cannot be cast to type :id in query:

from v in Rumbl.Video,
  where: v.id == ^"13-hello-world"

Error when casting value to `Rumbl.Video.id`
```

Primary keys in Ecto have a default type of :id. For now, we can consider :id
to be an :integer. When a new request goes to /watch/13-hello-world, the router
matches 13-hello-world as the id parameter and sends it to the controller. In the
controller, we try to make a query by using the id, and it complains. Let's look
at the source of the problem:

```
def show(conn, %{"id" => id}) do
  video = Repo.get!(Video, id)
  render conn, "show.html", video: video
end
```

That's the problem. We're doing a get by using the id field. Let's fix that now.

Before doing a database query comparing against the id column, we need to cast 13-hello-world to an integer—for this particular slug, the number 13.

Extending Schemas with Ecto Types

Sometimes, the basic type information in our schemas isn't enough. In those cases, we'd like to improve our schemas with types that have a knowledge of Ecto. For example, we might want to associate some behavior to our id fields. A *custom type* allows us to do that. Let's implement one and place it in lib/rumbl/permalink.ex. Remember, there's no difference between lib and web except for code reloading. We're placing this code in lib only because it's supporting code, tied closely to Ecto. Our new *behavior*, meaning an implementation of our interface, looks like this:

```
watching_videos/listings/rumbl/lib/rumbl/permalink.ex
defmodule Rumbl.Permalink do
  @behaviour Ecto.Type

  def type, do: :id

  def cast(binary) when is_binary(binary) do
    case Integer.parse(binary) do
      {int, _} when int > 0 -> {:ok, int}
      _ -> :error
    end
  end

  def cast(integer) when is_integer(integer) do
    {:ok, integer}
  end

  def cast(_) do
    :error
  end

  def dump(integer) when is_integer(integer) do
    {:ok, integer}
  end

  def load(integer) when is_integer(integer) do
    {:ok, integer}
  end
end
```

Rumbl.Permalink is a custom type defined according to the Ecto.Type behavior. It expects us to define four functions:

type   Returns the underlying Ecto type. In this case, we're building on top of :id.

cast   Called when external data is passed into Ecto. It's invoked when values in queries are interpolated or also by the cast function in changesets.

dump   Invoked when data is sent to the database.

load   Invoked when data is loaded from the database.

By design, the cast function often processes end-user input. We should be both lenient and careful when we parse it. For our slug—that means for binaries—we call Integer.parse to extract only the leading integer. On the other hand, dump and load handle the struct-to-database conversion. We can expect to work only with integers at this point because cast does the dirty work of sanitizing our input. Successful casts return integers. dump and load return :ok tuples with integers or :error.

Let's give our custom type a try with iex -S mix. Since we changed code in lib, you need to restart any running session.

```
iex> alias Rumbl.Permalink, as: P
iex> P.cast "1"
{:ok, 1}
iex> P.cast 1
{:ok, 1}
```

Integers and strings work as usual. That's great. Let's try something more complex:

```
iex> P.cast "13-hello-world"
{:ok, 13}
iex> P.cast "hello-world-13"
:error
```

As long as the string starts with a positive integer, we're good to go.

The last step is to tell Ecto to use our custom type for the id field. This definition must go after use Rumbl.Web and before the schema call in web/models/video.ex:

watching_videos/listings/rumbl/web/models/video.change3.ex

```
@primary_key {:id, Rumbl.Permalink, autogenerate: true}
schema "videos" do
```

Because Ecto automatically defines the id field for us, customizing the primary key is done with the @primary_key module attribute. We give it a tuple, with the primary key name (:id), our new type, and the autogenerate: true option because id values are generated by the database.

And that's that. Access the page once again, and it should load successfully. By implementing a protocol and defining a custom type, we made Phoenix work exactly how we wanted without tightly coupling it to our implementation. Ecto types go way beyond simple casting, though. We've already seen the community handle field encryption, data uploading, and more, all neatly wrapped and contained inside an Ecto type.

Wrapping Up

In this chapter, we accomplished a lot. We built a controller for watching videos and laid some foundation so we can play our videos in YouTube. We also created friendly URLs. Along the way:

- You learned to use Brunch to support development-time reloading and minimization for production code.

- We used generators to create an Ecto migration.

- We used changesets to create slugs.

- We used protocols to seamlessly build URLs from those new slugs.

In the next chapter, you're going to reach the long-awaited channels topic. You'll learn to use Phoenix to build fully interactive features that show off Elixir's concurrency and consistency. Turn the page, because the energy only goes up from here!

## CHAPTER 10

Using Channels

If you dabbled in Phoenix before buying this book, at this point you're probably wondering why we've come so far and barely mentioned channels. The truth is that for the interactive applications we care about the most, channels are simpler to build so there's less to talk about.

Think about everything you've learned so far. Up until now, a browser made an isolated request and Phoenix delivered an isolated response. We had to spend plenty of time on pipelines and code organizational tools that let you do everything necessary to tie an individual user to each request and remember the exact state of the conversation. You know it well. A browser makes a request and the web server returns a response:

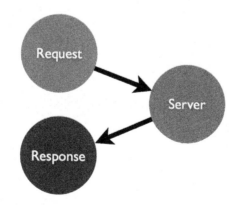

We build applications that way for a good reason. Each request is stateless, so it's easy to scale. When the programming language simply can't keep many connections around, it makes sense to do a little extra work so the web server can treat every request as a new one.

Sometimes, though, that programming model has too much overhead for the types of applications we want to build. Programs must be longer, programmers must work harder to reason about them, and the server has to work harder to process them.

This chapter will focus on the highly interactive problems that Phoenix solves so well. These problems don't lend themselves to a request/response flow. Think live chats, Google Maps, kayak.com, and foursquare.com. In that world, a single client on a page connects directly with a process on the server called a channel, like this:

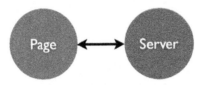

It *looks* simpler because for the programmer it *is* simpler. Since Elixir can scale to millions of simultaneous processes that manage millions of concurrent connections, you don't have to resort to request/response to make things easy to scale or even manage. A client connects to a channel and then sends and receives messages. That's it.

It's now cool again to have applications where the clients and servers just, you know, talk directly to each other. That's why this chapter is shorter than the entire request/response section of the book, and it's also why Phoenix is such a big deal.

The Channel

A Phoenix channel is a conversation. The channel sends messages, receives messages, and keeps state. We call the messages *events*, and we put the state in a struct called socket.

A Phoenix conversation is about a *topic*, and it maps onto application concepts like a chat room, a local map, a game, or in our case, the annotations on a video. More than one user might be interested in the same topic at the same time. Channels give you tools to organize your code and the communication among users. The concept that makes channels so powerful in Elixir is that *each user's conversation on a topic has its own isolated, dedicated process.*

Here's the kicker. Whereas request/response interactions are *stateless*, conversations in a long-running process can be *stateful*. This means that for more-sophisticated user interactions like interactive pages or multiplayer games, you don't have to work so hard to keep track of the conversation by using cookies, databases, or the like. Each call to a channel simply picks up where the last one left off.

This approach only works if your foundation guarantees true isolation and concurrency. True isolation means that one crashing process won't impact other subscribed users. True concurrency means lightweight abstractions that won't bleed into one another. Your channels will *scale* in the dimensions that are most important to you, including code complexity, performance, and manageability.

You may be thinking that channels can't be this simple, but they are. Your channels application will have to worry about three things, each on both the client and the server:

- Making and breaking connections
- Sending messages
- Receiving messages

In this chapter, you'll learn each of those basic building blocks in greater detail. We're primarily going to be building the interactive portion of our application. We'll allow users to build annotations in real time, and rumbl will play back all video annotations for a user. We'll do this in two parts. First, on the client side, we need to build some client code to make a connection, send messages, and receive messages. We'll write our code in ES6, the next generation of JavaScript. Then, on the server side, we'll do the same. We'll establish a connection and then write channels code to process each request in the conversation.

Let's get started.

Phoenix Clients with ES6

We're going to start on the client, using the latest ECMAScript 6[1] JavaScript features. We'll build a bare-bones client to simply establish a connection. Over time, we'll build up our client to add annotations and play them back.

Remember, each Phoenix conversation is on a topic, so we'll need to be able to identify a topic. In our case, our topics will be videos. We'll create a Video object. That client-side construct will connect to Phoenix directly.

---

1. https://babeljs.io/docs/learn-es2015/

> **Chris says:**
> # Why ES6/ES2015 JavaScript?
>
> Language features you've wished for years to land in JavaScript—string interpolation, a module system, destructuring assignment, and more—are now within reach. When you *transpile* a language, you're translating it to a more common form. Since it's possible to transpile ES6 to the widely available ES5 JavaScript, you can use ES6 today while supporting all mainstream browsers. This leaves you no reason to not go all-in on ES6. Plus, planned browser enhancements mean you have the bonus of waiting a couple years, and suddenly your ES6 code will be supported natively throughout the web.

Let's create a separate file for our Video object in web/static/js/video.js. It's a long file, but it's not too complicated, especially when broken into parts:

channels/listings/rumbl/web/static/js/video.js

```
import Player from "./player"

let Video = {

  init(socket, element){ if(!element){ return }
    let playerId = element.getAttribute("data-player-id")
    let videoId  = element.getAttribute("data-id")
    socket.connect()
    Player.init(element.id, playerId, () => {
      this.onReady(videoId, socket)
    })
  },

  onReady(videoId, socket){
    let msgContainer = document.getElementById("msg-container")
    let msgInput     = document.getElementById("msg-input")
    let postButton   = document.getElementById("msg-submit")
    let vidChannel   = socket.channel("videos:" + videoId)
    // TODO join the vidChannel
  }
}
export default Video
```

We first import our Player, the abstraction that lets us play videos and extract the exact time for any given frame so we can correctly place our annotations. Next, we define an init function to set up the player and pluck our video ID from the element attributes. We then start the socket connection with socket.connect() and initialize our player while running a this.onReady() callback when the player has loaded. Within onReady, we define a handful of DOM variables for our Video player. We have the container for annotations, the input control, and the button for creating a new annotation. Pay special attention to vidChannel, which we'll use to connect our ES6 client to our Phoenix VideoChannel. For now we just instantiate it, but we'll join the conversation with the server in a moment.

Our topics need an identifier. By convention, ours takes the form "videos:" + videoId. In our application, this topic will let us easily send events to others interested in the same topic.

Let's tweak our video player to use this new Video object.

We were previously initializing and importing our video player in web/static/js/app.js, like this:

```
import Player from "./player"
let video = document.getElementById("video")

if(video) {
  Player.init(video.id, video.getAttribute("data-player-id"))
}
```

It would be better to tweak that code to compensate for the initialization we're doing in video.js. Let's tweak it to start only the Video object, like this:

channels/listings/rumbl/web/static/js/app.change1.js

```
import socket from "./socket"
import Video from "./video"

Video.init(socket, document.getElementById("video"))
```

We import the Video object that we just created from its local module path. Next, we initialize the video with our connection called socket (more on this later) and the DOM element whose ID is video. Now load up your last video, and you should see it loaded into a YouTube player as before—but if you view your browser's JavaScript console, you see that the channel join is failing:

```
Unable to join > {reason: "unmatched topic"}
```

With our video up and running and vidChannel initialized, our client is trying to join a video channel that we haven't implemented yet. Let's flip back to the server side for a bit and fix this. It's time to create a channel and establish the conversation with our client.

Preparing Our Server for the Channel

In the request/response world, each request established a connection, which we represented in Plug.Conn. We then used ordinary functions to transform that connection until it had the response we wanted to send back to the client.

Each plug didn't use the same conn per se, but each transformation was conceptually on the same request. Each time you had a new request, you'd start from scratch with a new conn struct. Said another way, for each request, a new conn would flow through all of the pipelines and then die.

In channels, the flow is different. A client establishes a new connection with a socket. After the connection is made, that socket will be transformed through the life of the connection.

At the high level, your socket is the ongoing conversation between client and server. It has all of the information necessary to do its job. When you make a connection, you're creating your initial socket, and that same socket will be transformed with each new received event, through the whole life of the whole conversation.

You need to do a couple of things to make a connection. First, you decide whether to allow the connection. Next, you create the initial socket, including any custom application setup your application might need.

Let's hack up a quick connection to see how things work. In our ES6 example, Phoenix created a web/static/js/socket.js with an example socket connection and channel code. Replace the file contents with this minimal socket connection:

channels/listings/rumbl/web/static/js/socket.change1.js
```
import {Socket} from "phoenix"

let socket = new Socket("/socket", {
  params: {token: window.userToken},
  logger: (kind, msg, data) => { console.log(`${kind}: ${msg}`, data) }
})

export default socket
```

That simple connection is as basic as it gets. Phoenix isn't doing anything fancy for us here. You can see that the ES6 client imports the Socket object. Then let socket = new Socket("/socket", ...) causes Phoenix to instantiate a new socket at our endpoint. We pass an optional logger callback, which includes helpful debugging logging in the JavaScript console. If you peek in lib/rumbl/endpoint.ex, you can see where the "/socket" is declared. This definition is the *socket mount point*:

```
socket "/socket", Rumbl.UserSocket
```

Notice UserSocket. That module serves as the starting point for all socket connections. As you'll see later in this chapter, it's responsible for authenticating. But it's also responsible for wiring up default socket information for all channels. Peek inside the web/channels/user_socket.ex to see it in action:

```elixir
defmodule Rumbl.UserSocket do
  use Phoenix.Socket

  ## Transports
  transport :websocket, Phoenix.Transports.WebSocket
  # transport :longpoll, Phoenix.Transports.LongPoll

  def connect(_params, socket) do
    {:ok, socket}
  end

  def id(_socket), do: nil
end
```

UserSocket uses a single connection to the server to handle all your channel processes. The socket also defines the transport layers that will handle the connection between your client and the server. You see the two default transport protocols that Phoenix supports. You can build your own for more exotic use cases.

Regardless of the transport, the end result is the same. You operate on a shared socket abstraction, and Phoenix takes care of the rest. The beauty of this is that you no longer have to worry how the user is connected. Whether on older browsers over long-polling, native iOS WebSockets, or a custom transport like CoAP[2] for embedded devices, your backend channel code remains precisely the same. This is the new web. You'll be able to quickly adapt your applications as new transport protocols become important to you.

In our UserSocket, we have two simple functions: connect and id. The id function lets us identify the socket based on some state stored in the socket itself, like the user ID. The connect function decides whether to make a connection. In our case, id returns nil, and connect simply lets everyone in. We're effectively allowing all connections as anonymous users by default.

We'll be adding socket authentication with our Rumbl.Auth system in a moment, but for now, let's leave these defaults. We added socket.connect() after we initialized our Player in video.js to establish the connection to the server. If we open up the JavaScript console in our browser and refresh one of our video pages, we see the following logger output:

```
transport: connected to
ws://localhost:4000/socket/websocket?token=undefined&vsn=1.0.0
```

We have a working connection! Let's create the channel on the Phoenix side.

---

2. http://coap.technology/

Creating the Channel

It's time to write some code to process connections. To review what you know so far, a channel is a conversation on a topic. Our topic has an identifier of videos:video_id, where video_id is a dynamic ID matching a record in the database. In our application, we want a user to get all events for a topic, which to us means a user will get all annotations for a given video, regardless of who created them.

More generally, at their most basic level, topics are strings that serve as identifiers. They take the form of topic:subtopic, where topic is often a resource name and subtopic is often an ID.

Since topics are organizing concepts, we'll include topics where you'd expect: as parameters to functions and in our URLs to identify conversations. Just as the client passes a URL with an :id parameter to represent a resource for a controller, we'll provide a topic ID to scope our channel connections.

Joining a Channel

Now that we've established a socket connection, our users can join a channel. In general, when clients join a channel, they must provide a topic. They'll be able to join any number of channels and any number of topics on a channel.

We need a VideoChannel for our application, so let's start by including a channel definition in our UserSocket:

```
channels/listings/rumbl/web/channels/user_socket.change1.ex
defmodule Rumbl.UserSocket do
  use Phoenix.Socket

  ## Channels
  channel "videos:*", Rumbl.VideoChannel
```

Transports route events into your UserSocket, where they're dispatched into your channels based on topic patterns that you declare with the channel macro. Our videos:* convention categorizes topics with a resource name, followed by a resource ID.

Let's move on to the code that will process each incoming event.

Building the Channel Module

Now, it's time to create the module that will handle our specific Video channel. It'll allow connections through join and also let users disconnect and send events. For consistency with OTP naming conventions, this book sometimes refers to these features as *callbacks*. Let's start with join. Create a file called web/channels/video_channel.ex, like this:

channels/listings/rumbl/web/channels/video_channel.ex

```elixir
defmodule Rumbl.VideoChannel do
  use Rumbl.Web, :channel

  def join("videos:" <> video_id, _params, socket) do
    {:ok, assign(socket, :video_id, String.to_integer(video_id))}
  end
end
```

Here we see the first of our channel callbacks: join. Clients can join topics on a channel. We return {:ok, socket} to authorize a join attempt or {:error, socket} to deny one.

For now, we let all clients join any video topic, and we add the video ID from our topic to socket.assigns. Remember, sockets will hold all of the state for a given conversation. Each socket can hold its own state in the socket.assigns field, which typically holds a map.

For channels, *the socket is transformed in a loop rather than a single pipeline.* In fact, the socket state will remain for the duration of a connection. That means the socket state we add in join will be accessible later as events come into and out of the channel. This small distinction leads to an enormous difference in efficiency between the channels API and the controllers API.

With our channel in place, let's join it from the client. Open up web/static/js/video.js and update your listing:

channels/listings/rumbl/web/static/js/video.change1.js

```javascript
onReady(videoId, socket){
  let msgContainer = document.getElementById("msg-container")
  let msgInput     = document.getElementById("msg-input")
  let postButton   = document.getElementById("msg-submit")
  let vidChannel   = socket.channel("videos:" + videoId)

  vidChannel.join()
    .receive("ok", resp => console.log("joined the video channel", resp) )
    .receive("error", reason => console.log("join failed", reason) )
}
```

On lines 5 through 9, we create a new channel object, vidChannel, from our socket and give it our topic. We build the topic by joining the "videos:" string with our video ID, which we plucked from the div element in our WatchView's show.html.eex template.

We see our joined message in the JavaScript web console output:

```
push: videos:2 phx_join (1)
transport: connected to ws://localhost:4000/socket/websocket...
receive: ok videos:2 phx_reply (1)
joined the video channel
```

Likewise, our server output confirms that we've established our conversation:

```
[info] JOIN videos:2 to Rumbl.VideoChannel
  Transport:  Phoenix.Transports.WebSocket
  Parameters: %{}
[info] Replied videos:2 :ok
```

And we're joined!

Sending and Receiving Events

Everything we've done so far is setting us up to do one thing: process events. Just as controllers receive requests, channels receive events. With channels, we receive a message containing an event name, such as new_message, and a payload of arbitrary data.

Each channel module has three ways to receive events. You'll learn more about these callback functions in detail soon. For now, know that handle_in receives direct channel events, handle_out intercepts broadcast events, and handle_info receives OTP messages.

Taking Our Channels for a Trial Run

To test-drive everything we've put together so far, let's make our join function send our channel a :ping message every five seconds, like this:

channels/listings/rumbl/web/channels/video_channel.change1.ex

```
def join("videos:" <> video_id, _params, socket) do
  :timer.send_interval(5_000, :ping)
  {:ok, socket}
end

def handle_info(:ping, socket) do
  count = socket.assigns[:count] || 1
  push socket, "ping", %{count: count}

  {:noreply, assign(socket, :count, count + 1)}
end
```

The handle_info callback is invoked whenever an Elixir message reaches the channel. In this case, we match on the periodic :ping message and increase a counter every time it arrives.

Our new handle_info takes our socket, takes the existing count (or a default of 1), and increases that count by one. We then return a tagged tuple. :noreply means we're not sending a reply, and the assign function transforms our socket by adding the new count. Conceptually, we're taking a socket and returning a transformed socket. This implementation bumps the count in :assigns by one, each time it's called.

We've got the server-side implementation. We just need to call it now. Add the following line to video.js, immediately below your vidChannel declaration:

```
vidChannel.on("ping", ({count}) => console.log("PING", count) )
```

Now check out your web console, and you see a ping event being pushed from the server every five seconds, with an accumulated counter:

```
receive:  videos:2 ping
PING 1

receive:  videos:2 ping
PING 2

receive:  videos:2 ping
PING 3
```

Our channel process is alive and well!

handle_info is basically a loop. Each time, it returns the socket as the last tuple element for all callbacks. This way, we can maintain a state. We simply push the ping event, and the client picks up these events with the channel.on(event, callback) API. These events can arrive on the client at any time, but later you'll see how channels support synchronous messaging for handle_in responses.

This is the primary difference between channels and controllers. Controllers process a *request*. Channels hold a *conversation*.

Annotating Videos

Our channels are functioning but not doing any real work yet. Let's use them to build our real-time annotations. We'll need an Annotation model to persist our user annotations, but let's start simple and build out the channel messaging first. Later, we can circle back and persist the annotation when we're happy with our client-server channel communication.

Our WatchView's show.html.eex template is already mocked up with an annotations container and post button that we've plucked from the page to establish our msgContainer and postButton variables. Let's use these two elements to begin our real-time annotations support. Open up your video.js and update the listing below your vidChannel declaration with the following code:

channels/listings/rumbl/web/static/js/video.change3.js

```
Line 1    let vidChannel    = socket.channel("videos:" + videoId)

          postButton.addEventListener("click", e => {
            let payload = {body: msgInput.value, at: Player.getCurrentTime()}
5           vidChannel.push("new_annotation", payload)
                      .receive("error", e => console.log(e) )
            msgInput.value = ""
          })

10        vidChannel.on("new_annotation", (resp) => {
            this.renderAnnotation(msgContainer, resp)
          })

          vidChannel.join()
15          .receive("ok", resp => console.log("joined the video channel", resp) )
            .receive("error", reason => console.log("join failed", reason) )
        },

        renderAnnotation(msgContainer, {user, body, at}){
20          // TODO append annotation to msgContainer
        }
```

Let's break it down. First, we handle the click event on the post button. The push function on our vidChannel takes the contents of our message input and sends it to the server, then clears the input control.

On lines 5 and 6, you can see the channel's synchronous messaging in action. When we push an event to the server, we can opt to receive a response. It's not a true synchronous operation, but it's a big win for code readability. It lets us compose client-side messaging in line with our Elixir process handling. It also provides request/response–style messaging over a socket connection.

Now, we have to handle new events sent by the server. When users post new annotations, the server will broadcast those new events to the client, triggering a new_annotation event. On line 10, we receive those new_annotation events, calling a stubbed renderAnnotation function. Let's implement renderAnnotation to display our annotations on the page. Update your listing with the following code:

channels/listings/rumbl/web/static/js/video.change4.js

```
Line 1  esc(str){
          let div = document.createElement("div")
          div.appendChild(document.createTextNode(str))
          return div.innerHTML
5       },

        renderAnnotation(msgContainer, {user, body, at}){
          let template = document.createElement("div")
```

```
10    template.innerHTML = `
      <a href="#" data-seek="${this.esc(at)}">
        <b>${this.esc(user.username)}</b>: ${this.esc(body)}
      </a>
      `
15    msgContainer.appendChild(template)
      msgContainer.scrollTop = msgContainer.scrollHeight
    }
```

We implement the renderAnnotation function to append an annotation to our message container. First, we define an esc function on line 1 to safely escape user input before injecting values into the page. This strategy protects our users from XSS attacks. Next, on line 7, we use our esc function to safely build a DOM node with the user's name and annotation body and append it to the msgContainer list. We finish by scrolling the container to the right point.

Adding Annotations on the Server

With our client-side event handling in place, let's wire up the server side of the conversation. Replace your VideoChannel with this:

channels/listings/rumbl/web/channels/video_channel.change2.ex

```elixir
defmodule Rumbl.VideoChannel do
  use Rumbl.Web, :channel

  def join("videos:" <> video_id, _params, socket) do
    {:ok, socket}
  end

  def handle_in("new_annotation", params, socket) do
    broadcast! socket, "new_annotation", %{
      user: %{username: "anon"},
      body: params["body"],
      at: params["at"]
    }

    {:reply, :ok, socket}
  end
end
```

We ditch our ping messaging and add the second major kind of callback, handle_in. This function will handle all incoming messages to a channel, pushed directly from the remote client.

Look at the function head. This particular callback handles the new_annotation events pushed from the client. Since we aren't persisting to the database yet, we simply broadcast new_annotation events to all the clients on this topic with broadcast!

The broadcast! function sends an event to all users on the current topic. It takes three arguments: the socket, the name of the event, and a payload, which is an arbitrary map. Within the body of our callback, we can send as many messages as we'd like.

When we're done with the function, we send back a reply with a status and the socket. The status is the customary Elixir :ok or :error. We could also have used :noreply with the socket if we didn't want to reply to the client.

Let's try it out in the browser. This time, open up multiple browser windows side by side to see how broadcast! is relaying messages to all users who've joined our video topic:

It works! We now have a conversation going between client and server, and you can get a glimpse into how our real-time annotations will be orchestrated.

This Is a Bad Idea

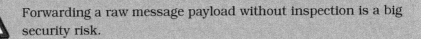

Forwarding a raw message payload without inspection is a big security risk.

Note that we didn't forward along the raw payload, such as:

```
broadcast! socket, "new_annotation", Map.put(params, "user", %{
  username: "anon"
})
```

This would have worked, but it would have been extremely dangerous. Broadcasting events delivers the payload to *all* clients on this topic. If we don't properly structure the payload from the remote client before forwarding the message along as a broadcast, we're effectively allowing a client to broadcast arbitrary payloads across our channel. If you want your application to be secure, you want to control the payload as closely as you can.

We've delivered our annotations to the client, but we've yet to persist them. Before we can do that, we need to have the current user in the socket in our channels. We've put it off as long as we can. It's time to tackle authentication.

Socket Authentication

For request/response–type applications, session-based authentication makes sense. For channels, *token authentication* works better because the connection is a long-duration connection. With token authentication, we assign a unique token to each user. Tokens allow for a secure authentication mechanism that doesn't rely on any specific transport.

Programmers often ask why they can't access their session cookies in a channel. The answer is that this would be insecure over WebSockets because of cross-domain attacks. Also, cookies would couple channel code to the WebSocket transport, eliminating future transport layers. Fortunately, Phoenix has a better way: the Phoenix.Token.

Our current_user is already authenticated in the application by our Rumbl.Auth plug. All we need to do is generate a token for our authenticated user and pass that to our socket on the front end. The first step is to expose the token to the client side in our web/templates/layout/app.html.eex layout, like this:

channels/listings/rumbl/web/templates/layout/app.change1.html.eex

```
</div> <!-- /container -->
<script>window.userToken = "<%= assigns[:user_token] %>"</script>
<script src="<%= static_path(@conn, "/js/app.js") %>"></script>
```

Just before our app.js script, we render a script tag that attaches a userToken variable to the window from our layout assigns.

Next, we need to add the :user_token to conn.assigns whenever we have a current user. We already have code to assign the current user in Rumbl.Auth, so let's handle this there:

channels/listings/rumbl/web/controllers/auth.change1.ex

```
Line 1  def call(conn, repo) do
          user_id = get_session(conn, :user_id)

          cond do
    5       user = conn.assigns[:current_user] ->
              put_current_user(conn, user)
            user = user_id && repo.get(Rumbl.User, user_id) ->
              put_current_user(conn, user)
            true ->
   10         assign(conn, :current_user, nil)
          end
        end

        def login(conn, user) do
   15     conn
```

```
     |> put_current_user(user)
     |> put_session(:user_id, user.id)
     |> configure_session(renew: true)
 end

 defp put_current_user(conn, user) do
   token = Phoenix.Token.sign(conn, "user socket", user.id)

   conn
   |> assign(:current_user, user)
   |> assign(:user_token, token)
 end
```

We add a private put_current_user function to place a freshly generated user token and the current_user into conn.assigns, which we call on lines 6 and 16. Now, any time a user session exists, both :current_user and :user_token will be set, and the :user_token will hold the signed-in user ID.

The last step is to pass the user token to the socket.connect and verify it in our UserSocket.connect callback. If you open up your web/static/js/socket.js file, you can see that we prepared for this by passing up the window.userToken value as a token parameter, like this:

channels/listings/rumbl/web/static/js/socket.change1.js

```javascript
let socket = new Socket("/socket", {
  params: {token: window.userToken},
  logger: (kind, msg, data) => { console.log(`${kind}: ${msg}`, data) }
})
```

Any :params we pass to the socket constructor will be available as the first argument in UserSocket.connect. Let's verify the params on connect and store our current_user. Update your UserSocket with the following code:

channels/listings/rumbl/web/channels/user_socket.change2.ex

```elixir
@max_age 2 * 7 * 24 * 60 * 60

def connect(%{"token" => token}, socket) do
  case Phoenix.Token.verify(socket, "user socket", token, max_age: @max_age) do
    {:ok, user_id} ->
      {:ok, assign(socket, :user_id, user_id)}
    {:error, _reason} ->
      :error
  end
end
def connect(_params, _socket), do: :error

def id(socket), do: "users_socket:#{socket.assigns.user_id}"
```

We use Phoenix.Token.verify to verify the user token provided by the client. If we want to, we can pass a max_age, ensuring that tokens are only valid for a certain period of time; in this case, we set the value to about two weeks. If the token is valid, we receive the user_id and store it in our socket.assigns while returning {:ok, socket} to establish the connection. If the token is invalid, we return :error, denying the connection attempt by the client.

Remember, the socket keeps its state for the whole duration of the connection, not just for a single response. Any socket.assigns you place in the socket during connect will be available in your channel's socket.assigns map.

Now, refresh your page. The application should work as before, but now with user authentication. We have a logged-in user. so we can move on to persist our annotations.

Persisting Annotations

Now that we have in-memory annotations going across all connected clients through an authenticated user, let's create an Annotation model. You've seen how we manage models and relationships with Ecto. In this case, we're creating annotations on videos. Each new annotation will belong to both a user and a video.

You can use the phoenix.gen.model generator, like this:

```
$ mix phoenix.gen.model Annotation annotations body:text at:integer \
user_id:references:users video_id:references:videos

* creating priv/repo/migrations/20150921162814_create_annotation.exs
* creating web/models/annotation.ex
* creating test/models/annotation_test.exs

$
```

And now you can migrate our database:

```
$ mix ecto.migrate

[info]    == Running Rumbl.Repo.Migrations.CreateAnnotation.change/0 forward
[info]    create table annotations
[info]    create index annotations_user_id_index
[info]    create index annotations_video_id_index
[info]    == Migrated in 0.9s

$
```

Our migrations are in, with our new table and two new indexes.

Next, we need to wire up our new relationships to our User and Video schemas. Both users and videos will have annotations, so add the has_many relationship to both your User and Video schema blocks in web/models/user.ex and web/models/video.ex, like this:

```
has_many :annotations, Rumbl.Annotation
```

Now, it's time to head back to our VideoChannel and persist the annotations:

```
Line 1  def join("videos:" <> video_id, _params, socket) do
          {:ok, assign(socket, :video_id, String.to_integer(video_id))}
        end

     5  def handle_in(event, params, socket) do
          user = Repo.get(Rumbl.User, socket.assigns.user_id)
          handle_in(event, params, user, socket)
        end

    10  def handle_in("new_annotation", params, user, socket) do
          changeset =
            user
            |> build_assoc(:annotations, video_id: socket.assigns.video_id)
            |> Rumbl.Annotation.changeset(params)
    15
          case Repo.insert(changeset) do
            {:ok, annotation} ->
              broadcast! socket, "new_annotation", %{
                id: annotation.id,
    20          user: Rumbl.UserView.render("user.json", %{user: user}),
                body: annotation.body,
                at: annotation.at
              }
              {:reply, :ok, socket}
    25
            {:error, changeset} ->
              {:reply, {:error, %{errors: changeset}}, socket}
          end
        end
    30 end
```

First, we ensure that all incoming events have the current user by defining a new handle_in/3 function on line 5. It catches all incoming events, looks up the user from the socket assigns, and then calls a handle_in/4 clause with the socket user as a third argument. Next, we extend our new_annotation message handling to build an annotation changeset for our user and persist it with our repo. If the insert is successful, we broadcast to all subscribers as before; otherwise, we return a response with the changeset errors. After we broadcast, we acknowledge the success with a {:reply, :ok, socket} return.

We could have decided not to send a reply with {:noreply, socket}, but it's common practice to acknowledge the result of the pushed message from the client. This approach allows the client to easily implement UI features such as loading statuses and error notifications, even if we're only replying with an :ok or :error status and no other information.

Since we also want to notify subscribers about the user who posted the annotation, we render a user.json template from our UserView on line 20. Let's implement that now:

channels/listings/rumbl/web/views/user_view.change1.ex

```
defmodule Rumbl.UserView do
  use Rumbl.Web, :view
  alias Rumbl.User

  def first_name(%User{name: name}) do
    name
    |> String.split(" ")
    |> Enum.at(0)
  end

  def render("user.json", %{user: user}) do
    %{id: user.id, username: user.username}
  end
end
```

Now let's head back to the app and post a few annotations. Watch your server logs as the posts are submitted, and you can see your insert logs:

```
[debug] INSERT INTO "annotations" ("at", "body", "inserted_at",
"updated_at", "user_id", "video_id") VALUES ($1, $2, $3, $4, $5, $6)
RETURNING "id" [0, "testing 123", {{2015, 9, 22}, {1, 20, 32, 0}},
{{2015, 9, 22}, {1, 20, 32, 0}}, 1, nil] OK query=1.6ms
[debug] COMMIT [] OK query=0.8ms
```

And we have persisted data!

We have a problem, though. Refresh your page, and the messages disappear from the UI. They're still in the database, but we need to pass the messages to the client when a user joins the channel. We could do this by pushing an event to the client after each user joins, but Phoenix provides a 3-tuple join signature to both join the channel and send a join response at the same time. Let's update our VideoChannel's join callback to pass down a list of annotations:

channels/listings/rumbl/web/channels/video_channel.change4.ex

```
alias Rumbl.AnnotationView

def join("videos:" <> video_id, _params, socket) do
  video_id = String.to_integer(video_id)
  video = Repo.get!(Rumbl.Video, video_id)

  annotations = Repo.all(
    from a in assoc(video, :annotations),
      order_by: [asc: a.at, asc: a.id],
```

```
      limit: 200,
      preload: [:user]
  )

  resp = %{annotations: Phoenix.View.render_many(annotations, AnnotationView,
                                                 "annotation.json")}
  {:ok, resp, assign(socket, :video_id, video_id)}
end
```

Here, we rewrite join to fetch the video from our repo. Then, we fetch the video's annotations. Remember, if you want to use data in an association, you need to fetch it explicitly, so we preload the :user association. We'll need to expose this information to the client. You've seen queries like this before in Chapter 6, *Generators and Relationships*, on page 91.

Then we do something new. We compose a response by rendering an annotation.json view for every annotation in our list. Instead of building the list by hand, we use Phoenix.View.render_many. The render_many function collects the render results for all elements in the enumerable passed to it. We use the view to present our data, so we offload this work to the view layer so the channel layer can focus on messaging.

Create an AnnotationView in web/views/annotation_view.ex to serve as each individual annotation, like this:

channels/listings/rumbl/web/views/annotation_view.ex

```
defmodule Rumbl.AnnotationView do
  use Rumbl.Web, :view

  def render("annotation.json", %{annotation: ann}) do
    %{
      id: ann.id,
      body: ann.body,
      at: ann.at,
      user: render_one(ann.user, Rumbl.UserView, "user.json")
    }
  end
end
```

Notice the render_one call for the annotation's user. Phoenix's view layer neatly embraces functional composition. The render_one function provides conveniences such as handling possible nil results.

Lastly, we return a 3-tuple from join of the form {:ok, response, socket} to pass the response down to the join event. Let's pick up this response on the client to build the list of messages.

Update your vidChannel.join() callbacks to render a list of annotations received on join:

channels/listings/rumbl/web/static/js/video.change5.js

```
vidChannel.join()
  .receive("ok", ({annotations}) => {
    annotations.forEach( ann => this.renderAnnotation(msgContainer, ann) )
  })
  .receive("error", reason => console.log("join failed", reason) )
```

Refresh your browser and see your history of messages appear immediately!

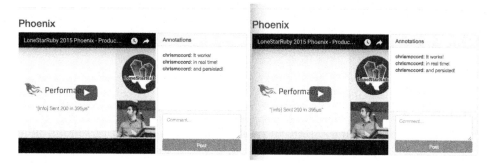

Now that we have our message history on join, we need to schedule the annotations to appear synced up with the video playback. Update video.js, like this:

channels/listings/rumbl/web/static/js/video.change6.js

```
  vidChannel.join()
    .receive("ok", resp => {
      this.scheduleMessages(msgContainer, resp.annotations)
    })
    .receive("error", reason => console.log("join failed", reason) )
},

renderAnnotation(msgContainer, {user, body, at}){
  let template = document.createElement("div")
  template.innerHTML = `
  <a href="#" data-seek="${this.esc(at)}">
    [${this.formatTime(at)}]
    <b>${this.esc(user.username)}</b>: ${this.esc(body)}
  </a>
  `

  msgContainer.appendChild(template)
  msgContainer.scrollTop = msgContainer.scrollHeight
},

scheduleMessages(msgContainer, annotations){
  setTimeout(() => {
    let ctime = Player.getCurrentTime()
```

```
    let remaining = this.renderAtTime(annotations, ctime, msgContainer)
    this.scheduleMessages(msgContainer, remaining)
  }, 1000)
},

renderAtTime(annotations, seconds, msgContainer){
  return annotations.filter( ann => {
    if(ann.at > seconds){
      return true
    } else {
      this.renderAnnotation(msgContainer, ann)
      return false
    }
  })
},

formatTime(at){
  let date = new Date(null)
  date.setSeconds(at / 1000)
  return date.toISOString().substr(14, 5)
},
```

There's a lot of code here, but it's relatively simple. Instead of rendering all annotations immediately on join, we schedule them to render based on the current player time. The scheduleMessages function starts an interval timer that fires every second. Now, each time our timer ticks, we call renderAtTime to find all annotations occurring at or before the current player time.

In renderAtTime, we filter all the messages by time while rendering those that should appear in the timeline. For those yet to appear, we return true to keep a tab on the remaining annotations to filter on the next call. Otherwise, we render the annotation and return false to exclude it from the remaining set.

You can see the end result. We have a second-by-second annotation feed based on the current video playback. Refresh your browser and let's give it a shot. Try posting a few new annotations at different points, and then refresh. Start playing the video, and then watch your annotations appear synced up with the playback time, as you can see in the screenshot on page 195.

We wired up a data-seek attribute on our renderAnnotation template, but we haven't done anything with it yet. Let's support having the annotations clickable so we can jump to the exact time the annotation was made by clicking it. Add this click handler above your vidChannel.join():

channels/listings/rumbl/web/static/js/video.change6.js

```
msgContainer.addEventListener("click", e => {
  e.preventDefault()
  let seconds = e.target.getAttribute("data-seek") ||
                e.target.parentNode.getAttribute("data-seek")
```

```
  if(!seconds){ return }
  Player.seekTo(seconds)
})
```

Now, clicking an annotation will move the player to the time the annotation was made. Cool!

Before we get too excited, we have one more problem to solve. We need to address a critical issue when dealing with disconnects between the client and server.

Handling Disconnects

Any stateful conversation between a client and server must handle data that gets out of sync. This problem can happen with unexpected disconnects, or a broadcast that isn't received while a client is away. We need to handle both cases. Let's find out how.

Our JavaScript client can disconnect and reconnect for a number of different reasons. Our server might be restarted, a rumbler might drive under a bridge, or our Internet connection may just be poor. We simply can't assume network reliability when designing our real-time systems. Fire up your server and visit one of your videos. Post a few annotations and then kill the server in your terminal. The client immediately begins trying to reestablish a connection using exponential back-off. Wait a few seconds. Then, you can restart the server with mix phoenix.server. Within a few seconds, you'll see something like this by your video:

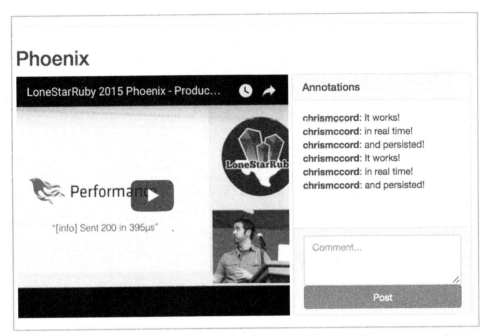

That's not good. When the client reconnected, our client rejoined our VideoChannel and the server returned all the annotations for this video, causing our client to append duplicate annotations to the ones it already had. You might be tempted to have the client detect duplicate annotations and ignore them, but we want to fetch as little data as required from the server, so there's a better way.

We can track a last_seen_id on the client and bump this value every time we see a new annotation. Then whenever we rejoin following a crash or disconnect, we can send our last_seen_id to the server. That way, we send only the data we missed. This technique keeps us from worrying about buffering messages on the server for clients that might never reconnect. We get back only the data that we need. Let's make it happen.

Open up your web/static/js/video.js and make the following changes:

channels/listings/rumbl/web/static/js/video.change7.js

```
Line 1  vidChannel.on("new_annotation", (resp) => {
   -      vidChannel.params.last_seen_id = resp.id
   -      this.renderAnnotation(msgContainer, resp)
   -    })
   5
   -    vidChannel.join()
   -      .receive("ok", resp => {
   -        let ids = resp.annotations.map(ann => ann.id)
   -        if(ids.length > 0){ vidChannel.params.last_seen_id = Math.max(...ids) }
```

```
10      this.scheduleMessages(msgContainer, resp.annotations)
      })
      .receive("error", reason => console.log("join failed", reason) )
```

On line 2, we use *channel params* for the first time. A channel on the client holds a params object and sends it to the server every time we call channel.join(). We can modify this object to store a last_seen_id whenever we receive a new_annotation event from the server.

Next, we use a similar approach on line 8 within our ok callback on join. We receive the list of annotations in the response as before, but this time we grab the max annotation ID from the list and store it in the channel params as our last_seen_id. Now, whenever we call vidChannel.join()—such as after reconnects—we provide the last_seen_id. Let's handle this new parameter on the server side within our VideoChannel. Open up your web/channels/video_channel.ex file and update the join function:

channels/listings/rumbl/web/channels/video_channel.change5.ex

```
Line 1  def join("videos:" <> video_id, params, socket) do
   -      last_seen_id = params["last_seen_id"] || 0
   -      video_id = String.to_integer(video_id)
   -      video = Repo.get!(Rumbl.Video, video_id)
   5
   -      annotations = Repo.all(
   -            from a in assoc(video, :annotations),
   -          where: a.id > ^last_seen_id,
   -        order_by: [asc: a.at, asc: a.id],
  10          limit: 200,
   -        preload: [:user]
   -      )
   -
   -      resp = %{annotations: Phoenix.View.render_many(annotations, AnnotationView,
  15                                                "annotation.json")}
   -      {:ok, resp, assign(socket, :video_id, video_id)}
   -  end
```

On line 2, we use the params as the second argument to join/3. We check for an existing last_seen_id value. To cover a fresh connection, we provide a default value of 0 since the user has yet to see an annotation.

Next, we modify our annotations query by adding a where clause on line 8 to only grab IDs greater than the last_seen_id.

That's it! If we try to re-create our duplicate entries, we'll see the client and server remain properly in sync across disconnects and reconnects using the last_seen_id approach in the channel params. Our approach is simple and direct.

We've done a lot of work in this chapter. It's time to review.

Wrapping Up

In this chapter, you learned to build simple client/server APIs with Phoenix channels. Though the problem had many layers, it was easy to understand the flow because clients connected to servers, and both sides maintained the connection until the conversation was over. Along the way:

- You learned to connect to a server-side channel through an ES6 client.

- We built a server-side channel with both long-polling and WebSocket support.

- We built a simple API to let users join a channel.

- We processed inbound messages from OTP with handle_info and channels with handle_in.

- We sent broadcast messages with broadcast!.

- We authenticated users with Phoenix.Token.

- We persisted annotations with Ecto.

Though channels are by far the most exciting feature of Phoenix, it was far easier to build this code than it was to build the request/response counter-parts for our users. We're not done yet, though! In the next chapter, you'll learn to implement reliable services with OTP. You'll also learn to better organize your applications by using umbrellas. Stay tuned!

## CHAPTER 11

OTP

You've now had your first taste of Phoenix channels and should be developing a good intuition for the strength of Phoenix for highly interactive applications. You have everything you need to create beautiful code and then run it reliably at breakneck speeds.

Phoenix isn't just about user interfaces, though. You also have the experience and elegance of Erlang's OTP framework. In general, OTP is a way to think about concurrency and distribution. It uses a few patterns that allow you to use concurrency to build state without language features that rely on mutability. OTP also has rich abstractions for supervision and monitoring. In this chapter, we'll use OTP to build an information system.

Rather than read a wave of dry prose that tells you what OTP does, you'll start with the basics by building a simple service. We'll build a counter that runs in a separate process. Then, we'll supervise it, restarting on failure. You'll see how you can hold state in an immutable world.

On its own, that knowledge will help you understand Phoenix, which is itself an OTP application. We'll use these principles to build an information service. When we're done, we'll be ready to move that service under an umbrella application in the next chapter. This neat bit of organization will let you break existing code into bite-sized pieces that are easier to manage, understand, and test.

Managing State with Processes

Functional programs are stateless, but we still need to be able to manage state. In Elixir, we use concurrent processes and recursion to handle this task. That may sound counterintuitive, but let's take a look at how it works with a simple program.

Let's create a Counter server that counts up or down. Create a lib/rumbl/counter.ex file and key this in:

otp/listings/rumbl/lib/rumbl/counter.ex

```elixir
defmodule Rumbl.Counter do

  def inc(pid), do: send(pid, :inc)

  def dec(pid), do: send(pid, :dec)

  def val(pid, timeout \\ 5000) do
    ref = make_ref()
    send(pid, {:val, self(), ref})
    receive do
      {^ref, val} -> val
      after timeout -> exit(:timeout)
    end
  end

  def start_link(initial_val) do
    {:ok, spawn_link(fn -> listen(initial_val) end)}
  end

  defp listen(val) do
    receive do
      :inc -> listen(val + 1)
      :dec -> listen(val - 1)
      {:val, sender, ref} ->
        send sender, {ref, val}
        listen(val)
    end
  end
end
```

Our module implements a Counter server as well as functions for interacting with it as a client. The *client* serves as the API and exists only to send messages to the process that does the work. It's the *interface* for our counter. The *server* is a process that recursively loops, processing a message and sending updated state to itself. Our server is the *implementation*.

Building the Counter API

Our API sends messages to increment (:inc) and decrement (:dec) the counter, and another message called :val to get the counter's value. Let's look at each one of these in turn.

:inc and :dec take only the process ID for the server process—called pid for process ID—and a single atom command. These skinny functions exist only to send :inc and :dec messages to our server process. These are asynchronous. We just send a message and don't bother to await any reply.

The val function on line 7 is a little different. It must send a request for the value of the counter and await the response. Since we need to associate a response with this particular request, we create a unique reference with make_ref(). This unique reference is just a value that's guaranteed to be globally unique. Then, we send a message to our counter with the send function. Our message payload is a 3-tuple with an atom designating the command we want to do, :val, followed by our pid and the globally unique reference.

Then, we await a response, matching on the reference. The ^ operator means that rather than reassigning the value of ref, we match only tuples that have that exact ref. That way, we can make sure to match only responses related to our explicit request. If there's no match in a given period, we exit the current process with the :timeout reason code.

We start by defining the client API to interact with our counter. First, we create inc and dec functions to increment and decrement our counter. These functions fire off an async message to the counter process without waiting for a response. Our val function sends message to the counter but then blocks the caller process while waiting for a response.

Let's take a look at our server.

As you'll see later on, OTP requires a start_link function. Ours, on line 16, accepts the initial state of our counter. Its only job is to spawn a process and return {:ok, pid}, where pid identifies the spawned process. The spawned process calls the private function named listen, which listens for messages and processes them.

Let's look at that listen function on line 20, the engine for our counter. You don't see any global variables that hold state, but our listener has a trick up its sleeve. We can exploit recursion to manage state. For each call to listen, the tiny function blocks to wait for a message. Then, we process the trivial :inc, :dec, and :val messages. The last thing any receive clause does is call listen again with the updated state.

Said another way: the state of the server is wrapped up in the execution of the recursive function. We can use Elixir's message passing to listen in on the process to find the value of the state at any time. When the last thing you do in a function is to call the function itself, the function is *tail recursive*, meaning it optimizes to a loop instead of a function call. That means this loop can run indefinitely! In many languages, burning a thread for such a trivial task can be expensive, but in Elixir processes are incredibly cheap, so this strategy is a great way to manage state.

Taking Our Counter for a Spin

This code is pretty simple, so you already know what'll happen. Still, let's try it out in IEx:

```
iex> alias Rumbl.Counter
nil
iex> {:ok, counter} = Counter.start_link(0)
{:ok, #PID<0.253.0>}
iex> Counter.inc(counter)
:inc
iex> Counter.inc(counter)
:inc
iex> Counter.val(counter)
2
iex> Counter.dec(counter)
:dec
iex> Counter.val(counter)
1
```

It works perfectly, just as you expected. Think about the techniques used:

- We used concurrency and recursion to maintain state.

- We separated the interface from the implementation.

- We used different abstractions for asynchronous and synchronous communication with our server.

As you might imagine, this approach is common and important enough for us to package it for reuse. In fact, this approach has been around a while in the form of the Erlang OTP library. Let's take a look.

Building GenServers for OTP

Though our counter is an oversimplification, the basic approach has been used for over thirty years to manage both concurrent state and behavior for most important Erlang applications. The library encapsulating that approach is called OTP, and the abstraction is called a *generic server*, or GenServer. Let's modify our counter to use OTP to create our counter, instead.

We don't need to change too much. Instead of creating specific functions to handle inc, dec, and val, we use specific OTP abstractions instead. Update your counter.ex file with these contents:

otp/listings/rumbl/lib/rumbl/counter.change1.ex

```elixir
defmodule Rumbl.Counter do
  use GenServer

  def inc(pid), do: GenServer.cast(pid, :inc)

  def dec(pid), do: GenServer.cast(pid, :dec)

  def val(pid) do
    GenServer.call(pid, :val)
  end

  def start_link(initial_val) do
    GenServer.start_link(__MODULE__, initial_val)
  end

  def init(initial_val) do
    {:ok, initial_val}
  end

  def handle_cast(:inc, val) do
    {:noreply, val + 1}
  end

  def handle_cast(:dec, val) do
    {:noreply, val - 1}
  end

  def handle_call(:val, _from, val) do
    {:reply, val, val}
  end
end
```

We've changed the terminology some, but not the implementation. When we want to send asynchronous messages such as our inc and dec messages, we use GenServer.cast, as you can see on line 4. Notice that these functions don't send a return reply. When we want to send synchronous messages that return the state of the server, we use GenServer.call as we do on line 8. Notice the _from in the function head. You can use an argument leading with an underscore, just as you'd use a _ as wildcard match. With this feature, we can explicitly describe the argument while ignoring the contents.

On the server side, the implementation is much the same: we use a handle_cast line for :inc and one for :dec, each returning a noreply alongside the new state, and we also use handle_call to handle :val, and specify the return value. We explicitly tell OTP when to send a reply and when not to send one. We also have to tweak the start_link to start a GenServer, giving it the current module name and the counter. This function spawns a new process and invokes the

Rumbl.Counter.init function inside this new process to set up its initial state. Let's take that much for a spin:

```
iex> alias Rumbl.Counter
nil
iex> {:ok, counter} = Counter.start_link(10)
{:ok, #PID<0.96.0>}
iex> Counter.dec(counter)
:ok
iex> Counter.dec(counter)
:ok
iex> Counter.val(counter)
8
```

Our first counter was split into client and server code. This segregation remains when we write our GenServer. init, handle_call, and handle_cast run in the server. All other functions are part of the client.

Our OTP counter server works exactly as before, but we've gained much by moving it to a GenServer. On the surface, we no longer need to worry about setting up references for synchronous messages. Those are taken care of for us by GenServer.call. Second, the GenServer module is now in control of the receive loop, allowing it to provide great features like code upgrading and handling of system messages, which will be useful when we introspect our system with Observer later on. A GenServer is one of many OTP behaviors. We'll continue exploring them as we build our information system.

Adding Failover

The benefits of OTP go beyond simply managing concurrent state and behavior. It also handles the linking and supervision of processes. Now let's explore how process supervision works. We'll supervise our new counter.

Though our counter is a trivial service, we'll play with supervision strategies. Our supervisor needs to be able to restart each service the right way, according to the policies that are best for the application. For example, if a database dies, you might want to automatically kill and restart the associated connection pool. *This policy decision should not impact code that uses the database.* If we replace a simple supervisor process with a supervisor tree, we can build much more robust fault-tolerance and recovery software.

In Phoenix, you didn't see too much code attempting to deal with the fallout for every possible exception. Instead, we trust the error reporting to log the errors so that we can fix what's broken, and in the meantime, we can automatically restart services in the last good state. The beauty of OTP is that it captures these clean abstractions in a coherent library, allowing us to declare the supervision properties that most interest us without bogging down the meaning of each individual application. With a supervision tree having a configurable policy, you can build *robust self-healing software* without building *complex self-healing software.*

Let's add our Counter server to our application's supervision tree by including it as a worker in our supervisor's child spec. In lib/rumbl.ex, add your new server as a worker, like this:

otp/listings/rumbl/lib/rumbl.change1.ex

```
children = [
  supervisor(Rumbl.Endpoint, []),
  supervisor(Rumbl.Repo, []),
  worker(Rumbl.Counter, [5]), # new counter worker
]

opts = [strategy: :one_for_one, name: Rumbl.Supervisor]
Supervisor.start_link(children, opts)
```

A *child spec* defines the children that an Elixir application will start. In this case, we add our new counter to our existing list of children. With the worker, we pass the arguments for the worker's start_link. In our case, we pass the initial state, or 5.

In opts, you can see the policy that our application will use if something goes wrong. OTP calls this policy the *supervision strategy.* In this case, we're using the :one_for_one strategy. This strategy means that if the child dies, only that child will be restarted. If all resources depended on some common service, we could have specified :one_for_all to kill and restart all child process if any child dies. We'll explore those strategies later on.

Now if we fire up our application with iex -S mix, we don't see anything particular, since our counter is running but we aren't interacting with it. Let's add a periodic tick to our counter to see it work in action in our supervision tree.

Modify your Counter's init function and add a new handle_info callback, like this:

otp/listings/rumbl/lib/rumbl/counter.change2.ex

```
def init(initial_val) do
  Process.send_after(self, :tick, 1000)
  {:ok, initial_val}
end

def handle_info(:tick, val) do
  IO.puts "tick #{val}"
  Process.send_after(self, :tick, 1000)
  {:noreply, val - 1}
end
```

We tweak init in the counter process to send itself a :tick message every 1,000 milliseconds, and then we add a function to process those ticks, simulating a countdown. As with channels, out-of-band messages are handled inside the handle_info callback, which sets up a new tick and decrements the state.

Now you can fire our application back up with iex -S mix and see our counter worker in action:

```
iex> tick 5
tick 4
tick 3
tick 2
tick 1
^C
```

This isn't terribly exciting, but it gets interesting when we deal with our workers crashing. Let's crash our counter if it ticks below a certain value:

otp/listings/rumbl/lib/rumbl/counter.change3.ex
```
def handle_info(:tick, val) when val <= 0, do: raise "boom!"
def handle_info(:tick, val) do
  IO.puts "tick #{val}"
  Process.send_after(self, :tick, 1000)
  {:noreply, val - 1}
end
```

We add a :tick clause for cases when the value is less than zero, and we raise an error that crashes our process. Let's fire up iex -S mix again and see what happens:

```
iex> tick 5
tick 4
tick 3
tick 2
tick 1
[error] GenServer #PID<0.327.0> terminating
** (RuntimeError) boom!
    (rumbl) lib/rumbl/counter.ex:21: Rumbl.Counter.handle_info/2
    (stdlib) gen_server.erl:615: :gen_server.try_dispatch/4
    (stdlib) gen_server.erl:681: :gen_server.handle_msg/5
    (stdlib) proc_lib.erl:239: :proc_lib.init_p_do_apply/3
Last message: :tick
State: 0
tick 5
tick 4
tick 3
tick 2
tick 1
^C
```

As expected, our server crashed—but then it restarted! That's the magic of supervision. When our counter crashed, it was restarted with its initial state of [5]. In short, our program crashed, the supervisor identified the crash, and then it restarted the process in a known good state. We don't have to add any extra code to fully supervise every process. We need only configure a policy to tell OTP how to handle each crash.

The basic building blocks of isolated application processes and a supervision structure to manage them have been the cornerstone of Erlang reliability—whether you're running a trivial counter, a server with a million processes, or a worldwide distributed application with tens of millions of processes. The principles are the same, and they've been proven to work.

To apply these principles, you need to know how to tell Elixir what supervision behavior you expect. Here are the basics.

Restart Strategies

The first decision you need to make is to tell OTP what should happen if your process crashes. By default, child processes have a restart strategy of :permanent. A supervisor will always restart a :permanent GenServer, whether the process crashed or terminated gracefully. If we wanted to explicitly specify a :permanent restart strategy, we could have done so like this:

```
worker(Rumbl.Counter, [5], restart: :permanent),
```

:permanent is the default restart strategy, and the trailing options are fully optional, so we could have written the command as worker(Rumbl.Counter, [5]). Child specifications support the following restart values:

:permanent
> The child is always restarted (default).

:temporary
> The child is never restarted.

:transient
> The child is restarted only if it terminates abnormally, with an exit reason other than :normal, :shutdown, or {:shutdown, term}.

Let's say we have a situation in which *mostly dead* isn't good enough. When a counter dies, we want it to really *die*. Perhaps restarting the application would cause harm. Let's try changing our restart strategy to :temporary and observe the crash:

```
worker(Rumbl.Counter, [5], restart: :temporary),
```

Now let's fire our project back up with iex -S mix:

```
iex(1)> tick 5
tick 4
tick 3
tick 2
tick 1
[error] GenServer #PID<0.393.0> terminating
** (RuntimeError) boom!
    (rumbl) lib/rumbl/counter.ex:21: Rumbl.Counter.handle_info/2
    (stdlib) gen_server.erl:615: :gen_server.try_dispatch/4
    (stdlib) gen_server.erl:681: :gen_server.handle_msg/5
    (stdlib) proc_lib.erl:239: :proc_lib.init_p_do_apply/3
Last message: :tick
State: 0
```

As you'd expect, when our counter dies it stays dead. The :temporary strategy is useful when a restart is unlikely to resolve the problem, or when restarting doesn't make sense based on the flow of the application.

Sometimes, you may want OTP to retry an operation a few times before failing. You can do exactly that with a pair of options called max_restarts and max_seconds. OTP will only restart an application max_restarts times in max_seconds before failing and reporting the error up the supervision tree. By default, Elixir will allow 3 restarts in 5 seconds, but you can configure these values to whatever you want. In general, you'll use the restart strategies your specific application requires.

Supervision Strategies

Just as child workers have different restart strategies, supervisors have configurable supervision strategies. The most basic and the default for new Phoenix applications is :one_for_one. When a :one_for_one supervisor detects a crash, it restarts a worker of the same type without any other consideration. Sometimes, processes depend on one another. When that happens, sometimes when a process dies, more than one must restart. In all, you have four major strategies:

:one_for_one

If a child terminates, a supervisor restarts only that process.

:one_for_all

If a child terminates, a supervisor terminates all children and then restarts all children.

:rest_for_one

> If a child terminates, a supervisor terminates all child processes defined after the one that dies. Then the supervisor restarts all terminated processes.

:simple_one_for_one

> Similar to :one_for_one but used when a supervisor needs to dynamically supervise processes. For example, a web server would use it to supervise web requests, which may be 10, 1,000, or 100,000 concurrently running processes.

These strategies are all relatively straightforward. To get a taste of them, let's change our counter-restart strategy back to the default :permanent and temporarily change our application supervisor's strategy to :one_for_all, like this:

`otp/listings/rumbl/lib/rumbl.change2.ex`
```
children = [
  supervisor(Rumbl.Endpoint, []),
  supervisor(Rumbl.Repo, []),
  worker(Rumbl.Counter, [5]),
]

opts = [strategy: :one_for_all, name: Rumbl.Supervisor]
Supervisor.start_link(children, opts)
```

Now if you start up the application with our endpoint's web server running via $ iex -S mix phoenix.server, you can see how the change in strategy cascades to all children:

```
[info] Running Rumbl.Endpoint with Cowboy on http://localhost:4000
03 Nov 20:16:51 - info: compiled 8 files into 2 files, copied 3 in 1951ms
iex> tick 5
tick 4
tick 3
tick 2
tick 1
[info] Running Rumbl.Endpoint with Cowboy on http://localhost:4000
03 Nov 20:16:57 - info: compiled 8 files into 2 files, copied 3 in 1892ms
[error] GenServer #PID<0.322.0> terminating
** (RuntimeError) boom!
...
tick 5
tick 4
^C
```

Here, you can see the :one_for_all strategy in action. Notice the Rumbl.Endpoint restart after our counter crashes. In general, the top-level strategy for our application makes sense as :one_for_one—because it houses all main services of the application with their own supervision trees and more-specific strategies—but this gives you a taste of how different strategies compose together to form resilient applications.

Now that our counter experiments are over, let's change our lib/rumbl.ex back to the original supervision tree and restart strategy:

```
otp/rumbl/lib/rumbl.ex
children = [
  supervisor(Rumbl.Endpoint, []),
  supervisor(Rumbl.Repo, []),
]

opts = [strategy: :one_for_one, name: Rumbl.Supervisor]
Supervisor.start_link(children, opts)
```

The GenServer is the foundation of many different abstractions throughout Elixir and Phoenix. Knowing these small details will make you a much better programmer. Let's see a couple more examples.

Using Agents

It turns out that a still simpler abstraction has many of the benefits of a GenServer. It's called an *agent*. With an agent, you have only five main functions: start_link initializes the agent, stop stops the agent, update changes the state of the agent, get retrieves the agent's current value, and get_and_update performs the last two operations simultaneously. Here's what our counter would look like with an agent:

```
iex> import Agent
nil
iex> {:ok, agent} = start_link fn -> 5 end
{:ok, #PID<0.57.0>}
iex> update agent, &(&1 + 1)
:ok
iex> get agent, &(&1)
6
iex> stop agent
:ok
```

To initialize an agent, you pass a function returning the state you want. To update the agent, you pass a function taking the current state and returning the new state. That's all there is to it. Behind the scenes, this agent is an OTP GenServer, and plenty of options are available to customize it as needed. One such option is called :name.

Registering Processes

With OTP, we can register a process by name. Our named process can be either local, meaning visible to a single node, or global, meaning visible to all connected nodes. OTP automatically provides this feature with the :name option in start_link. After we register a process by name, we can send messages to it using the registered name instead of the pid. Let's rewrite the previous example using a named agent:

```
iex> import Agent
nil
iex> {:ok, agent} = start_link fn -> 5 end, name: MyAgent
{:ok, #PID<0.57.0>}
iex> update MyAgent, &(&1 + 1)
:ok
iex> get MyAgent, &(&1)
6
iex> stop MyAgent
:ok
```

If a process already exists with the registered name, we can't start the agent:

```
iex> import Agent
nil
iex> {:ok, agent} = start_link fn -> 5 end, name: MyAgent
{:ok, #PID<0.57.0>}
iex> {:ok, agent} = start_link fn -> 5 end, name: MyAgent
** (MatchError) no match of right hand side value:
  {:error, {:already_started, #PID<0.57.0>}}
```

Agents are one of the many constructs built on top of OTP. You've already seen another, the Phoenix.Channel. Let's take a look.

OTP and Channels

If we were building a supervisor for a couple of application components, the simple default :one_for_one strategy might be all we'd need. Our goal is bigger, though. We don't reach occasionally for supervisors as tiny isolated services. We intentionally build all of our infrastructure with a tree of supervisors, where each node of the tree knows how to restart any major service if it fails.

When you coded your channels in the last chapter, you might not have known it, but you were building an OTP application. Each new channel was a process built to serve a single user in the context of a single conversation on a topic. Though Phoenix is new, we're standing on the shoulders of giants. Erlang's OTP has been around as long as Erlang has been popular—we know that it works. Much of the world's text-messaging traffic runs on OTP infrastructure.

That's way more than Twitter has ever experienced. You can count on this infrastructure always being up and available because it's built on a reliable foundation.

Designing an Information System with OTP

With these high-level basics demystified, let's use another OTP abstraction to enhance our application. Let's take our video annotations to another level with some OTP-backed information services. We're going to use some common web APIs to enhance our application.

For any request, we're going to ask our information system for highly relevant facts that we can inject. We'll be providing enhanced question/answer–style annotations as the video is playing. This'll give our live viewers and replayed visits alike an enhanced experience about the video that's showing.

The goal for our application is to have multiple information systems. We might pull from an API like WolframAlpha while at the same time referencing a local database. WolframAlpha is a service that allows users to ask natural-language questions and get rich responses. We'd like our design to start multiple information system queries in parallel and accumulate the results. Then, we can take the best matching responses.

Choosing a Supervision Strategy

Think about our information system requirements. We want to fetch the most relevant information for a user in real time, across different backends. Since we're fetching results in parallel, a failure likely means that the network or one of our third-party services failed. That's out of our control. It doesn't make sense for us to retry the computation. because this operation is time sensitive—a video is playing. Instead, we want to spawn processes in parallel and let them do their work, and we'll take as many results as we can get. If one of ten of our information systems crashes, it's not a problem. We'll use the results from the other nine, so we'll use the :temporary restart strategy.

Armed with our restart strategy, let's make our supervisor in lib/rumbl/info_sys/supervisor.ex, like this:

otp/listings/rumbl/lib/rumbl/info_sys/supervisor.ex

```
defmodule Rumbl.InfoSys.Supervisor do
  use Supervisor

  def start_link() do
    Supervisor.start_link(__MODULE__, [], name: __MODULE__)
  end
```

```
  def init(_opts) do
    children = [
      worker(Rumbl.InfoSys, [], restart: :temporary)
    ]

    supervise children, strategy: :simple_one_for_one
  end
end
```

Let's break it down. We use Supervisor to prepare our code to use the Supervisor API. We're actually implementing a behavior, which is an API contract. The start_link function starts the supervisor, and init is the function, required by the contract, that initializes our workers.

Similarly to GenServer.start_link, the Supervisor.start_link function requires the name of the module implementing the supervisor behavior and the initial value that we provide in init. We use the _MODULE_ compiler directive to pick up this current module's name. We also pass the initial state of an empty list, which we don't intend to use. Finally, we pass our own module name as the :name option, which is a convenient way to allow us to reach the supervisor from anywhere with the given module's name instead of using its pid.

The next function that we implement is init. In that function, we call a function supervise to begin to supervise all of our workers. We start with our child spec. The only child is a GenServer worker defined in Rumbl.InfoSys, which we'll define in a moment. It has an initial state of [] and a restart strategy of :temporary.

After we have our children identified, we can start our supervisor with supervise, passing the supervision strategy of :simple_one_for_one. That strategy doesn't start any children. Instead, it waits for us to explicitly ask it to start a child process, handling any crashes just as a :one_for_one supervisor would.

Now you're ready to add the new supervisor into our application's supervision tree in lib/rumbl.ex, like this:

otp/listings/rumbl/lib/rumbl.change3.ex

```
children = [
  supervisor(Rumbl.Endpoint, []),
  supervisor(Rumbl.InfoSys.Supervisor, []), # new supervisor
  supervisor(Rumbl.Repo, []),
]
```

With that accomplished, we're ready to code our service. Since you're new to Elixir, you don't need to hide your glee. You've just done a bunch of things that are traditionally tremendously difficult. You've ensured that a single crash in an isolated information system won't impact the rest of your application. You've also configured a supervisor that will in turn be supervised by the application. The result goes beyond simple monitoring. You've made some policy decisions to customize our transient information systems into the overall application.

Keep in mind that we're protected in both directions. Applications that crash will need to be restarted at appropriate times. Also, if the Phoenix server crashes, we'll bring down all existing information systems and all other related services so we won't have to worry about leaking resources.

Enough gloating. We still need to build the information system. You'll find that with the error behaviors out of the way, we're free to focus on the main task of the information system, and we can let the error cases crash. The real work is simpler than you think.

Building a start_link Proxy

We've chosen a supervision strategy, one that allows us to start children dynamically. Before we create our worker process, we should take a little time to decide how our supervisor works, and how we'll use it to start our service. We'd like to be able to choose from several different backends—say. one for Google, one for WolframAlpha, and so on—like this:

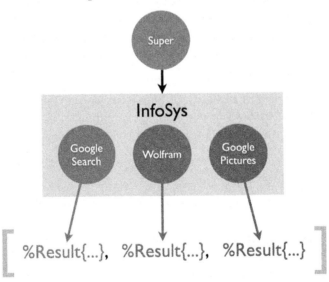

That seems right. When a user makes a query, our supervisor will start up as many different queries as we have backends. Then, we'll collect the results from each and choose the best one to send to the user. We have an open question, though. We have several different kinds of backends and only one supervisor. How can we create a single worker that knows how to start a variety of backends?

The answer is surprisingly simple. Let's use a technique called *proxying*. A proxy function is a lightweight function that stands between the original caller and the original implementation to do some simple task. Our generic start_link will proxy individual start_link functions for each of our backends. More specifically, we'll build a generic information system interface that knows about available backends and spawns a process to query each available backend service, fetches the result, and picks the best result from all possible candidates.

Create our proxy in lib/rumbl/info_sys.ex, like this:

otp/listings/rumbl/lib/rumbl/info_sys.ex

```elixir
defmodule Rumbl.InfoSys do
  @backends [Rumbl.InfoSys.Wolfram]

  defmodule Result do
    defstruct score: 0, text: nil, url: nil, backend: nil
  end

  def start_link(backend, query, query_ref, owner, limit) do
    backend.start_link(query, query_ref, owner, limit)
  end

  def compute(query, opts \\ []) do
    limit = opts[:limit] || 10
    backends = opts[:backends] || @backends

    backends
    |> Enum.map(&spawn_query(&1, query, limit))
  end

  defp spawn_query(backend, query, limit) do
    query_ref = make_ref()
    opts = [backend, query, query_ref, self(), limit]
    {:ok, pid} = Supervisor.start_child(Rumbl.InfoSys.Supervisor, opts)
    {pid, query_ref}
  end
end
```

Of the three hypothetical backends, we're going to focus on WolframAlpha. Let's break that down.

Notice that our InfoSys is a little different from typical GenServer modules. There's a good reason for that. We've built a generic module to spawn computations for queries. These backends are their own processes, but InfoSys isn't. We put all of the results into a single list, wait for each response from each spawned child, and finally pick the best one to return to the user.

At the top of our module, we use a module attribute to build a list of all the backends we support, which is initially only Rumbl.InfoSys.Wolfram. We leave this API open so we can add other backends over time.

Next, we define a Result struct to hold each search result. We have a score for storing relevance, text to describe the result, the URL it came from, and the backend to use for the computation.

On line 8, you can see our start_link function. If you're not paying attention, you can miss what's really going on here. That start_link is our proxy. It calls the start_link to the one defined in our specific backend. Our InfoSys is a :simple_one_for_one worker. Whenever our supervisor calls Supervisor.start_child for InfoSys, it invokes InfoSys.start_link. That function then starts the backend to compute its own results.

On line 12, we define compute. That function maps over all backends, calling a spawn_query function for each one. spawn_query starts a child, giving it some options including a unique reference named ref that in our case represents a single response. The function returns the child pid and the unique reference, which we'll await later on. When you consider how much this code is doing, it's a remarkably compact listing.

Let's move on to our backend.

Building the Wolfram Info System

Now that we have our generic InfoSys module in place, we can work on specific backends. We'll start with only one, our Wolfram backend. This module will call WolframAlpha to retrieve relevant information about our users' annotations.

We need an XML parser to handle WolframAlpha's XML responses. Let's add :sweet_xml to our deps list in mix.exs to take care of this:

otp/listings/rumbl/mix.change1.exs

```
{:sweet_xml, "~> 0.5.0"},
```

Next, run $ mix deps.get to grab the dependency from Hex. With our XML library in place, we're ready to sign up as a WolframAlpha API developer and retrieve our application ID. Visit the WolframAlpha developer portal,[1] sign up for a new account, and follow the instructions to get your AppID.

---

1. https://developer.wolframalpha.com/portal/signup.html

Now that we have a developer API key, we could place it directly in config/dev.exs, but there's a better way. We shouldn't check in private credentials under version control. In fact, Phoenix points us in the right direction with the generated config/prod.secret.exs file. This file is ignored from version control so we can include sensitive credentials properly. Let's use this same technique for development. Create a config/dev.secret.exs file and include your WolframAlpha key under Mix.Config, like this:

```elixir
use Mix.Config
config :rumbl, :wolfram, app_id: "12345-923429EAE6"
```

Next, add config/dev.secret.exs to the bottom of your .gitignore file so we don't check in our private development credentials:

```
/config/prod.secret.exs
/config/dev.secret.exs
```

Finally, we need to call import_config at the bottom of config/dev.exs to import our development secrets:

```elixir
import_config "dev.secret.exs"
```

With setup out of the way, now you can implement our Wolfram backend in lib/rumbl/info_sys/wolfram.ex, like this:

otp/listings/rumbl/lib/rumbl/info_sys/wolfram.ex

```elixir
Line 1  defmodule Rumbl.InfoSys.Wolfram do
          import SweetXml
          alias Rumbl.InfoSys.Result

     5    def start_link(query, query_ref, owner, limit) do
            Task.start_link(__MODULE__, :fetch, [query, query_ref, owner, limit])
          end

          def fetch(query_str, query_ref, owner, _limit) do
    10      query_str
            |> fetch_xml()
            |> xpath(~x"/queryresult/pod[contains(@title, 'Result') or
                                         contains(@title, 'Definitions')]
                              /subpod/plaintext/text()")
    15      |> send_results(query_ref, owner)
          end

          defp send_results(nil, query_ref, owner) do
            send(owner, {:results, query_ref, []})
    20    end
          defp send_results(answer, query_ref, owner) do
            results = [%Result{backend: "wolfram", score: 95, text: to_string(answer)}]
            send(owner, {:results, query_ref, results})
          end
```

```
25    defp fetch_xml(query_str) do
        {:ok, {_, _, body}} = :httpc.request(
          String.to_char_list("http://api.wolframalpha.com/v2/query" <>
            "?appid=#{app_id()}" <>
30          "&input=#{URI.encode(query_str)}&format=plaintext"))
        body
      end

      defp app_id, do: Application.get_env(:rumbl, :wolfram)[:app_id]
35   end
```

You might have spotted the start_link, but still, our module doesn't have all of the ceremony that you might have expected out of a GenServer. That's because this process is a *task*. Because GenServer's are meant to be generic servers, they hold both computation and state. However, in many cases, we want a process only to store state or only to execute a particular function. We've seen how an *agent* is a simple GenServer that manages state. A task is a simple process that executes the given function.

To start our module, we import the functions we'll need and set up a single alias. SweetXml will help us parse the XML we receive, and Result has the struct for the results we'll use.

Within our start_link on line 5, we call Task.start_link, specifying the module and function name to be invoked, as well as the arguments to be given to the function, specifying the work we want our task to do. In our case, the fetch function defines that work.

In fetch on line 9, we build a pipe to take our query, fetch the XML we'll need, extract the results using the xpath function from SweetXml, and then send the results. Next, we'll look at the functions that do each one of these tasks.

In fetch_xml on line 26, we contact WolframAlpha with the query string that interests us. We use :httpc, which ships within Erlang's standard library, to do the straight HTTP request, matching against :ok and the body that we return to the calling client. We use a private function to extract our API key from our application configuration.

In send_results on line 18, we want to send our results back to the requester. Remember that the client is waiting on our results, and we have the pid for that caller in owner.

We have two different forms of send_results, depending on whether we get results back or not. We match on the first argument in our function head. On nil, we need only send the owner an empty list. Otherwise, we build a result struct with our expected results and score. Then, we build a tuple with our results and send it back to owner.

Let's try it out with iex -S mix. First, start a query. We've designed our backend to report results to the calling process so we can issue compute requests directly. Remember, each backend will return a pid and a reference, like this:

```
iex> Rumbl.InfoSys.compute("what is elixir?")
[{#PID<0.1703.0>, #Reference<0.0.3.8938>}]
```

That query fires off a single Wolfram backend query and then presumably sends results to the calling process. That result should be waiting for us in our current process. Let's use the flush helper from IEx to see any messages we've received:

```
iex> Rumbl.InfoSys.compute("what is elixir?")
iex> flush()
[{:results, #Reference<0.0.1.9227>,
  [%Rumbl.InfoSys.Result{backend: "wolfram", score: 95,
  text: "1 | noun | a sweet flavored liquid (usually containing ...",
  url: nil}]}]
```

Brilliant. Our Wolfram service is working exactly as we expect. We get back our :results tuple with a reference and a list of results. For every result you see in the list, which may not be the same as what you see here, you get our hard-coded score of 95 percent. Remember, flush() can just return :ok if the message isn't yet in your inbox. If it happens to you, wait a few seconds and try again.

To make these services usable for our clients, we need to make a few enhancements.

First, let's detect when a backend crashes so we don't wait for results that might never arrive.

Next, we need to order the results we get from all the backends by our relevance score. Then it'll be easier to pick the best one.

Finally, we need a timeout. If the information systems take longer than we want to wait, we need to kill the processes we started and move on.

Let's make those changes now.

Monitoring Processes

We can use Process.monitor to detect backend crashes while we're waiting on results. Once a monitor is set, we'll get a message when the monitored process dies. For example, you can see this concept at work in IEx:

```
iex> pid = spawn(fn -> :ok end)
iex> Process.monitor(pid)
#Reference<0.0.2.2850>
```

We spawn a pid with a trivial function. We set up a monitor with Process.monitor. We get a reference back to identify this monitor. Meanwhile, the pid process dies immediately because it has no work to do. Let's use flush to check out our IEx mailbox, like this:

```
iex> flush()
{:DOWN, #Reference<0.0.2.2850>, :process, #PID<0.405.0>, :normal}
:ok
```

Nice! We receive a regular Elixir message as a {:DOWN, ...} tuple, informing us that our process died. We can easily apply this concept to our InfoSys client by automatically collecting results and ignoring the ones from crashed backends, making our services more predictable and safe. Extend your lib/rumbl/info_sys.ex, like this:

otp/listings/rumbl/lib/rumbl/info_sys.change1.ex

```elixir
Line 1  defmodule Rumbl.InfoSys do
          @backends [Rumbl.InfoSys.Wolfram]

          defmodule Result do
     5      defstruct score: 0, text: nil, url: nil, backend: nil
          end

          def start_link(backend, query, query_ref, owner, limit) do
            backend.start_link(query, query_ref, owner, limit)
    10    end

          def compute(query, opts \\ []) do
            limit = opts[:limit] || 10
            backends = opts[:backends] || @backends
    15
            backends
            |> Enum.map(&spawn_query(&1, query, limit))
            |> await_results(opts)
            |> Enum.sort(&(&1.score >= &2.score))
    20      |> Enum.take(limit)
          end

          defp spawn_query(backend, query, limit) do
            query_ref = make_ref()
    25      opts = [backend, query, query_ref, self(), limit]
            {:ok, pid} = Supervisor.start_child(Rumbl.InfoSys.Supervisor, opts)
            monitor_ref = Process.monitor(pid)
            {pid, monitor_ref, query_ref}
          end
    30
```

```
     defp await_results(children, _opts) do
       await_result(children, [], :infinity)
     end

35   defp await_result([head|tail], acc, timeout) do
       {pid, monitor_ref, query_ref} = head

       receive do
         {:results, ^query_ref, results} ->
40           Process.demonitor(monitor_ref, [:flush])
           await_result(tail, results ++ acc, timeout)
         {:DOWN, ^monitor_ref, :process, ^pid, _reason} ->
           await_result(tail, acc, timeout)
       end
45   end

     defp await_result([], acc, _) do
       acc
     end
50 end
```

This listing shows our revised info_sys.ex, with some changes for reliability. The compute function now automatically waits for results. When the results are retrieved, we sort them by score and report the top ones. Let's study this flow in detail.

As before, we call spawn_query for each backend. spawn_query is mostly the same, except it now monitors the child process on line 27 and returns a tuple with the child pid, the monitor reference, and the query reference.

After we spawn all children, we call await_results. This function uses a common recursive technique called *accumulation*. await_result does the bulk of the work. The first two arguments are the ones to watch. The first is a list of results to process. These are spawned backends. As we recurse, we reduce the children, one by one. Each time, we add an entry to the second argument, our accumulator. With each call to await_result, if all goes well, we add a result to the list. By the time we're done, the first list will be empty and the accumulator will have the completed result set. We pass a timeout of :infinity as the third argument, which we'll use later.

await_results recurses over all of the spawned backends. Initially, the first argument has all of the children and the accumulator is empty. We process each result, adding each to the accumulator. For each one, we receive a message.

On line 39, we first want to try to receive the next valid result. We know that valid results match {:results, ^query_ref, result}, so we receive the result and then process it. We drop our monitor. The [:flush] option guarantees that the :DOWN message is removed from our inbox in case it's delivered before we drop the monitor. Next, we recurse, using the remaining children and adding one more result to our accumulator.

On line 42, we're receiving a :DOWN message from our monitor. Notice that we're matching on the monitor's ref instead of the one for the query. That makes sense, because :DOWN messages come from the monitor, not our GenServer. We recurse with the remaining children without adding any results to our accumulator.

The second await_result clause on line 47 serves only to break our recursion after the list of children is completely consumed. That one returns the accumulated results.

Now that our code has working monitors, we're left with only results that complete successfully, ensuring that we won't wait forever for a message from a process that's already crashed. That's the beauty of monitors. They allow us a tidy way to handle resources that could otherwise leak. Let's give it a try:

```
iex> Rumbl.InfoSys.compute("what is the meaning of life?")
[%Rumbl.InfoSys.Result{backend: %Rumbl.User{...}, score: 95,
text: "42\n(according to the book The Hitchhiker", url: nil}]
```

Although monitors allow us to handle failures, a service can still take arbitrarily long. For example, we don't want to wait one minute for WolframAlpha in case its system is slow. To fix this, let's add timeouts to our information system. That way, we can terminate a backend if it takes too long.

Timing Out

Every time we attempt to receive messages, we can use the after clause to specify a time in milliseconds. That time represents the maximum amount of time we're willing to wait in a receive clause. Let's try it out:

```
iex> receive do
...>    :this_will_never_arrive -> :ok
...> after
...>    1_000 -> :timedout
...> end
:timedout
```

We could use this mechanism in our information system, specifying a timeout for every message we expect from each information system, but there's a hidden problem. This approach is cumulative. Imagine that we changed receive in await_result to use a timeout of 5_000 milliseconds. If we have three information systems and all of them time out, we'll wait five seconds *for every backend*, halting altogether for a total of fifteen seconds.

We need to use a slightly different approach. Instead of using the after clause, we'll use Process.send_after to send ourselves a :timedout message. At first, we'll collect messages from the backends as usual, using the timeout of :infinity until we receive the :timedout message. When we reach the timeout, we'll flip the timeout from :infinity to 0, indicating that we're no longer willing to wait for the backend response. In other words, we'll use the :timedout message to indicate if we should wait for the reply or not. Let's check our new await_results function:

```
otp/listings/rumbl/lib/rumbl/info_sys.change2.ex
```

```elixir
defp await_results(children, opts) do
  timeout = opts[:timeout] || 5000
  timer = Process.send_after(self(), :timedout, timeout)
  results = await_result(children, [], :infinity)
  cleanup(timer)
  results
end

defp await_result([head|tail], acc, timeout) do
  {pid, monitor_ref, query_ref} = head

  receive do
    {:results, ^query_ref, results} ->
      Process.demonitor(monitor_ref, [:flush])
      await_result(tail, results ++ acc, timeout)
    {:DOWN, ^monitor_ref, :process, ^pid, _reason} ->
      await_result(tail, acc, timeout)
    :timedout ->
      kill(pid, monitor_ref)
      await_result(tail, acc, 0)
  after
    timeout ->
      kill(pid, monitor_ref)
      await_result(tail, acc, 0)
  end
end

defp await_result([], acc, _) do
  acc
end

defp kill(pid, ref) do
  Process.demonitor(ref, [:flush])
  Process.exit(pid, :kill)
end
```

```
    defp cleanup(timer) do
      :erlang.cancel_timer(timer)
      receive do
40      :timedout -> :ok
      after
        0 -> :ok
      end
    end
```

The new await_results retrieves the timeout option and uses Process.send_after to send itself a message after the given timeout value, on line 3. We handle this new message in our receive call in the await_result function on line 18. Every time a timeout occurs, we kill the backend we are currently waiting on and move on to await the next one. When we receive the :timedout message, we change the call to await_result to use a timeout of 0. That timeout triggers the after branch of the receive call for subsequent backends unless a reply is already in the process inbox.

In both the :timedout and after clauses, we use the kill function defined on line 32 to shut down the backend. The function simply removes the monitor and sends a :kill exit signal to the backend process.

Finally, after we collect all results, we call the cleanup function with the timer returned by Process.send_after. The cleanup function, on line 37, uses :erlang.cancel_timer to cancel the timer, in case it wasn't yet triggered, and flush the :timedout message from our inbox if it was already sent.

Our information system now handles timeouts exactly as we desire. We were able to add complexity such as monitoring and timeouts to the information system altogether without changing the backends themselves. Because each backend is a new process, we could leverage everything in OTP to make our system resilient without changing the business code.

Integrating OTP Services with Channels

Now that we have a complete information system, let's integrate it with our VideoChannel.

Make the following changes to your web/channels/video_channel.ex. Our goal is to call into our information system any time a user posts an annotation, to see if we have relevant results to add to that user's conversation. Since the compute function is a blocking call, we want to make it asynchronous in our channel so our user gets the annotation broadcast right away. Let's first use a task to spawn a function call for our InfoSys computation:

> **José says:**
> # What About Task.async/await?
>
> If you're familiar with Elixir, you may be wondering why we haven't used Task.async and Task.await to write our information system. One of the criteria for our information system is that, if one of the backends crashes, we don't want it to affect the caller. If we used async/await, that's exactly what would happen, because async/await automatically links the spawned task to the caller.
>
> In Elixir v1.2, the standard library ships with a Task.Supervisor.async_nolink function that will start a task as a child process of a supervisor without links, much like our information system. However, we don't plan to update this section to use such features, because the goal of this chapter is to explore OTP foundations and patterns.

otp/listings/rumbl/web/channels/video_channel.change1.ex

```elixir
Line 1   def handle_in("new_annotation", params, user, socket) do
           changeset =
             user
             |> build_assoc(:annotations, video_id: socket.assigns.video_id)
      5      |> Rumbl.Annotation.changeset(params)

           case Repo.insert(changeset) do
             {:ok, ann} ->
               broadcast_annotation(socket, ann)
     10        Task.start_link(fn -> compute_additional_info(ann, socket) end)
               {:reply, :ok, socket}

             {:error, changeset} ->
               {:reply, {:error, %{errors: changeset}}, socket}
     15    end
         end

         defp broadcast_annotation(socket, annotation) do
           annotation = Repo.preload(annotation, :user)
     20    rendered_ann = Phoenix.View.render(AnnotationView, "annotation.json", %{
             annotation: annotation
           })
           broadcast! socket, "new_annotation", rendered_ann
         end
```

On line 9, we extract our broadcast to a shared broadcast_annotation function so our information system can make use of it when it has relevant results to share. Next, we spawn a task on line 10 to asynchronously call a new compute_additional_info function, which we'll write in a moment. We use Task.start_link because we don't care about the task result. It's important that we use a task here so we don't block on any particular messages arriving to the channel.

Now, let's write compute_additional_info to ask our InfoSys for relevant results:

otp/listings/rumbl/web/channels/video_channel.change1.ex

```
defp compute_additional_info(ann, socket) do
  for result <- Rumbl.InfoSys.compute(ann.body, limit: 1, timeout: 10_000) do
    attrs = %{url: result.url, body: result.text, at: ann.at}
    info_changeset =
      Repo.get_by!(Rumbl.User, username: result.backend)
      |> build_assoc(:annotations, video_id: ann.video_id)
      |> Rumbl.Annotation.changeset(attrs)

    case Repo.insert(info_changeset) do
      {:ok, info_ann} -> broadcast_annotation(socket, info_ann)
      {:error, _changeset} -> :ignore
    end
  end
end
```

First, we call into our information system, asking it for only one result, and telling it we are willing to wait ten seconds for an answer. Next, we comprehend over the results and query the database for a user representing each search result backend. Then we insert a new changeset and use our shared broadcast_annotation function on line 18 to report the new annotation to all subscribers on this topic. The integration is tight and smooth, and it's done.

We need to seed our database with a wolfram user to post annotations along with our real user conversations. Create a priv/repo/backend_seeds.exs, like this:

otp/listings/rumbl/priv/repo/backend_seeds.exs

```
alias Rumbl.Repo
alias Rumbl.User

Repo.insert!(%User{name: "Wolfram", username: "wolfram"})
```

Now, you can run these seeds with mix run, like this:

```
$ mix run priv/repo/backend_seeds.exs
[debug] BEGIN [] OK query=143.4ms queue=4.1ms
[debug] INSERT INTO "users" ("inserted_at", "name", ...
[debug] COMMIT [] OK query=2.3ms
```

Given that the preceding text made such a big deal about changesets, you may have had to choke down a gasp, or at least a snicker. In this case, we're controlling our user input directly. Since we're not dealing directly with user input, this script is no more or less safe than any other code in our codebase.

Let's try it out on the front end:

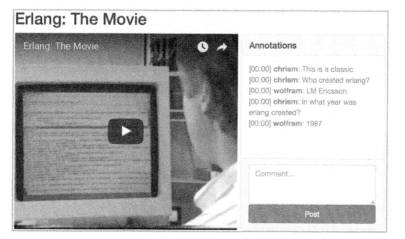

It works!

At this point, you can use this template to add services to our information system. Bing has an API that you might use to retrieve search results for linking. You could also build your own service. The important thing is that you have a framework to add services to.

We're at a convenient breaking point. It's time to wrap up.

Wrapping Up

In this chapter dedicated to OTP services, we first took our time so you could build a solid understanding of how OTP uses concurrency and message passing to safely encapsulate state without implicit state, or instance or global variables. Then, we built an information system for our annotations. Along the way:

- We built a counter that demonstrates how some OTP behaviors work.

- You looked at several OTP supervision and restart strategies.

- You saw examples of a full OTP service as GenServer.

- You learned how tasks wrap behavior and agents encapsulate state.

- We implemented an information system abstract front end with concrete backends.

- You learned to fetch WolframAlpha results from an HTTP service and share them with our channels.

Next, we'll see how to break our application into manageable pieces. When we're done, you'll be able to develop and test the pieces in isolation.

## CHAPTER 12

Observer and Umbrellas

As we add sophistication to our rumbl application, you should begin to notice that the information system isn't like some of the other parts of the application. For the first time, we have a feature that's reasonably complete on its own—one that's both robust and complex. It would be nice to separate this feature out as a project that can live side by side with the rest of our project but can be developed and tested independently.

If we were working with code, we'd refactor it. In this chapter, you'll see how to refactor your whole application. Umbrella projects allow you to develop and test multiple child applications in isolation side by side while providing conveniences for configuring and building them only once. The combination of Mix and OTP make this abstraction a good one for separating core concerns and dealing with complexity.

Introspecting with Observer

We're considering using an umbrella because our rumbl application is growing wider in terms of responsibilities and becoming more complex. We not only serve web requests, but we also now provide a complete information system that might provide dozens of backends in the future. As this grows, it would be great to be able to build and test this project in isolation.

Right now, we only have a gut feeling. Let's try to visualize this growing concern in a more concrete way. Once we can see it, we can act on it with much more confidence. Luckily, Erlang ships with a fantastic tool called Observer. To take it for spin, start a new iex -S mix session and run this command:

```
iex> :observer.start
nil
```

That command opens up an application that looks like this:

Observer is a great tool for understanding all running processes for your application. When you open it up, the initial tab gives you general information about Erlang and also statistics about your system and your application. The tabs let you access charts to visualize different aspects of your system, check out memory allocation, look at running processes, and the like.

You Might Not Have Observer Installed

Some package managers like to break the Erlang standard library into multiple packages. If :observer.start doesn't work, you might be missing the erlang-observer (or similar) package.

Consider the Processes tab. You can see a list of all running processes in your system, providing a tremendous amount of visibility into the system. Remember that in Elixir, all state exists in your processes. With Observer, we can see the state of our entire system and who's responsible for each piece.

There's more. Since communication happens with message passing, you can easily identify bottlenecks by finding the processes with the largest message queues. From there, you can double-click any process row to get more information about it.

You won't explore all tabs now, but let's look at one more in particular: Applications. There, you can see the applications that run on your system as well as each application's supervision tree. Click the Applications tab and then the Rumbl link on the left-side panel. You can see something like this:

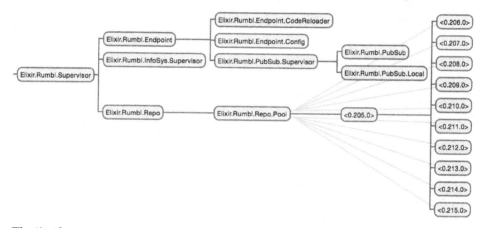

That's the rumbl supervision tree, more or less. Because we started iex -S mix and not iex -S mix phoenix.server, the server is missing from the tree. Inspecting our supervision trees is a great way to analyze how complex our systems are. If a supervision tree is growing too big or too wide, it's a great opportunity to act on it.

Furthermore, the supervision tree tells us exactly how to break a big system apart. We can find a robust branch from a supervision tree. When we find a convenient logical separation point, we can break it out into another application. All of the initial state and initialization is inside the supervision tree, so that subtree is easy to extract because we know where all of the complex parts of the system reside.

Let's do that now. We're going to extract the newly built information system from our rumbl application. When we're done, we'll effectively have two applications: :rumbl and :info_sys. However, instead of breaking them into multiple applications in distinct source-code repositories, which would add too much overhead to our development workflow, we are going to rely on Elixir umbrella projects.

Using Umbrellas

Now that we've confirmed our intuition by using Observer, we can get down to the work of splitting these applications. Each umbrella project has a parent directory that defines:

- The shared configuration of the project
- The dependencies for that project
- The apps directory with child applications

To get started, let's create an umbrella project called rumbrella. Instead of using mix phoenix.new to build a Phoenix application, we'll use mix new, which ships with Elixir, and pass it the --umbrella flag. Let's run the command outside of the rumbl application, like this:

```
$ mix new rumbrella --umbrella

* creating .gitignore
* creating README.md
* creating mix.exs
* creating apps
* creating config
* creating config/config.exs

Your umbrella project was created successfully.
```

You can see that the structure is much simpler than a full Phoenix project. You get a mix.exs file, a config directory with config.exs, and the apps directory. That's it.

Moving InfoSys Under rumbrella

Now that we've created our umbrella, we can work on the umbrella projects. rumbrella is our umbrella. The projects underneath it will be InfoSys, our information system, and rumbl, the rest of our application.

Let's create a regular Elixir application inside the apps directory that will host the information system. Since this application has a supervision tree, let's pass the --sup flag to mix new, like this:

```
$ cd rumbrella/apps
$ mix new info_sys --sup

* creating README.md
* creating .gitignore
* creating mix.exs
* creating config
* creating config/config.exs
* creating lib
* creating lib/info_sys.ex
* creating test
* creating test/test_helper.exs
* creating test/info_sys_test.exs

    Your Mix project was created successfully.
    You can use "mix" to compile it, test it, and more:
```

```
    cd info_sys
    mix test

  Run "mix help" for more commands.
```

$ **cd info_sys**

Notice that what we're doing now has little to do with Phoenix. We're building a basic blank Elixir application with a supervisor tree. All we need to do now is extract our information system from rumbl and then add it to info_sys. Open up the info_sys/lib/info_sys.ex file:

```
defmodule InfoSys do
  use Application

  # See http://elixir-lang.org/docs/stable/elixir/Application.html
  # for more information on OTP Applications
  def start(_type, _args) do
    import Supervisor.Spec, warn: false

    children = [
      # Define workers and child supervisors to be supervised
      # worker(InfoSys.Worker, [arg1, arg2, arg3]),
    ]

    # See http://elixir-lang.org/docs/stable/elixir/Supervisor.html
    # for other strategies and supported options
    opts = [strategy: :one_for_one, name: InfoSys.Supervisor]
    Supervisor.start_link(children, opts)
  end
end
```

This file is similar to the one that Phoenix created at rumbl/lib/rumbl.ex. It's responsible for starting the InfoSys supervision tree. We already have a supervisor, so replace the one in the previous listing with the following:

```
defmodule InfoSys do
  use Application

  def start(_type, _args) do
    InfoSys.Supervisor.start_link()
  end
end
```

This module starts the application. Recall that for OTP, that means that it starts the supervision tree. You may have noticed that the InfoSys module is no longer in the same namespace as Rumbl.InfoSys. Let's remedy that now. We're going to move some things around and change the name of references to our InfoSys module. We are not strictly required to do so, but since we're breaking the applications apart, we think it's worth it.

You're Moving Code Without the Help of Corresponding Listings

If you're following along but mostly paying attention to listings, it'll be easy for you to miss these next few changes, because the listings for the code you'll be moving aren't shown. Make sure you follow the directions in the following paragraph and numbered sequence.

Let's migrate the supervisor and the rest of the information system. We're going to do two things. We'll change the names of references to our new module in our code, and we'll move all information system code to our new umbrella structure. Let's do that now:

1. Rename the Rumbl.InfoSys module at rumbl/lib/rumbl/info_sys.ex to InfoSys and move it to info_sys/lib/info_sys.ex. Remember to keep the use Application and the start function that we defined in the preceding listing.

2. Rename the Rumbl.InfoSys.Supervisor module at rumbl/lib/rumbl/info_sys/supervisor.ex to InfoSys.Supervisor and move it to info_sys/lib/info_sys/supervisor.ex.

3. Rename the Rumbl.InfoSys.Wolfram module at rumbl/lib/rumbl/info_sys/wolfram.ex to InfoSys.Wolfram and move it to info_sys/lib/info_sys/wolfram.ex.

4. Use your editor to find and replace all occurrences of Rumbl.InfoSys in your project with InfoSys.

Our information system is almost ready to go, but we need to make two final changes.

First, let's retrieve Wolfram's application ID from the :info_sys application instead of :rumbl. In the file lib/info_sys/wolfram.ex, find this line:

```
defp app_id, do: Application.get_env(:rumbl, :wolfram)[:app_id]
```

Change it to this:

```
defp app_id, do: Application.get_env(:info_sys, :wolfram)[:app_id]
```

That way, we'll fetch the :wolfram application key from the right application. We also need to make :sweet_xml a dependency of InfoSys. That's done in the mix.exs file—specifically, the one for the :info_sys application. In rumbrella/apps/info_sys/mix.exs, add :sweet_xml to deps, like this:

```
def deps do
  [{:sweet_xml, "~> 0.5.0"}]
end
```

Let's make sure that the code compiles and the system boots by fetching dependencies and running tests for info_sys, from the root of rumbrella, like this:

```
$ mix deps.get
$ mix test
==> info_sys
.

Finished in 0.06 seconds (0.06s on load, 0.00s on tests)
1 test, 0 failures
```

Excellent! We've successfully extracted our information system from rumbl. Now, we can develop and test those features in isolation. As a bonus, we can use that umbrella project in other projects as well.

Making rumbl an Umbrella Child

Now that info_sys is a child application under our rumbrella project, we can safely move rumbl to the apps directory. Before we do so, let's take a look at the project function generated inside InfoSys's mix.exs:

```elixir
def project do
  [app: :info_sys,
   version: "0.0.1",
   build_path: "../../_build",
   config_path: "../../config/config.exs",
   deps_path: "../../deps",
   lockfile: "../../mix.lock",
   elixir: "~> 1.2",
   build_embedded: Mix.env == :prod,
   start_permanent: Mix.env == :prod,
   deps: deps]
end
```

You can see the configurations for :build_path, :config_path, :deps_path, and :lockfile. That's *all* it takes to make something an umbrella child. At the end of the day, Elixir simply configures the project to use the configuration, dependencies, and build paths from the parent application.

This List Will Look Different for Earlier Versions of Elixir

If you are using Elixir v1.1 or earlier, you'll notice that the :build_path and :config_path path keys won't be generated for your mix.exs file. That's expected, because those options aren't supported on earlier versions. Therefore, don't add those options to your rumbl application. Just copy the :deps_path and :lockfile keys.

Since we don't need to change any module names this time, it'll be easy to convert this application to an umbrella child application. We're just changing a line here and there, so we'll give you only the changes:

1. Move the rumbl directory into apps. Now, you should have two projects in apps: rumbl and info_sys.

2. Change rumbl's rumbrella/apps/rumbl/mix.exs project function to include the same configurations as InfoSys, like this:

    ```
    build_path: "../.._build",
    config_path: "../../config/config.exs",
    deps_path: "../../deps",
    lockfile: "../../mix.lock",
    ```

3. Since the rumbl application depends on InfoSys, we need to *add it to our application list*. Inside the application function in mix.exs, add:

    ```
    def application do
      [mod: {Rumbl, []},
       applications: [:phoenix, :phoenix_html, :cowboy, :logger, :gettext,
                      :phoenix_ecto, :postgrex, :comeonin, :info_sys]]
    end
    ```

4. Update your dependencies. Since we no longer need :sweet_xml, *we can remove it*. And since the rumbl application depends on InfoSys, we need to *add it as a dependency*. Inside the deps function, add info_sys and remove sweet_xml, like this:

    ```
    {:info_sys, in_umbrella: true}
    ```

5. Change the rumbl/lib/rumbl.ex supervision tree to remove the Rumbl.InfoSys worker—because starting it is now the responsibility of the InfoSys application—like this:

    ```
    children = [
      supervisor(Rumbl.Endpoint, []),
      supervisor(Rumbl.Repo, []),
    ]
    ```

6. Change the compute_additional_info function in web/channels/video_channel.ex to call InfoSys instead of Rumbl.InfoSys

    ```
    for result <- InfoSys.compute(ann.body, limit: 1, timeout: 10_000) do
    ```

7. Change the config/dev.secrets.exs file from config :rumbl, :wolfram, app_id: ... to config :info_sys, :wolfram, app_id: ...

Whew. Let's review what we did. We physically moved our application to our rumbrella project, under the apps directory. We made some changes to mix.exs to tell Elixir where to find the umbrella files, which applications to start, and which dependencies to track. We then removed info_sys from our supervisor child list, because starting that project is the responsibility of the umbrella project now. We then changed Rumbl.InfoSys references to InfoSys to conform to our namespace changes. And finally, we changed our :wolfram project key to pull it from the umbrella project to remove our product key.

Now we need to tweak the paths in our front-end code. Because we moved the dependencies directory to the umbrella, we need to tell Brunch, our assets builder, to look for phoenix and phoenix_html in their new location. Open up package.json and change the phoenix and phoenix_html keys to the following:

```
"phoenix": "file:../../deps/phoenix",
"phoenix_html": "file:../../deps/phoenix_html"
```

As always, you can fetch your dependencies with mix deps.get and then run mix test to verify that our tests still pass:

```
$ cd rumbrella
$ mix deps.get
...
$ mix test
==> info_sys
.

Finished in 0.06 seconds (0.06s on load, 0.00s on tests)
1 test, 0 failures

Randomized with seed 344855
==> rumbl

....................................

Finished in 0.1 seconds
37 tests, 0 failures
```

Notice that you can run mix test from the umbrella root, testing all projects at once, or in isolation inside each application directory.

Take note of the big win here. All of our work for our clean InfoSys interface has paid off. We can treat this service as if someone else had built it. Whenever you're developing code for the project, you can focus your efforts on a single place. As your project grows—if you pay attention to clean, logical interfaces—you can continue to extract services to their own umbrella projects.

It's a good time to wrap up what we've done.

Wrapping Up

In this chapter, we took some time to break our growing project into bite-sized pieces. We used umbrellas, an Elixir construct that allows us to develop and test projects in isolation but integrate them into a whole. Along the way:

- We used Observer to view our application.

- We found a convenient place to split our application.

- We moved our information system into its own child umbrella project.

- We moved rumbl into its own child umbrella project.

- We learned to identify configuration changes, including dependencies, supervision trees, and application configuration.

In the next chapter, you'll look at how to test your applications. You'll see how to test channels and OTP, and also how our umbrella project will help us manage all of it. Don't stop now—you're almost done!

CHAPTER 13

Testing Channels and OTP

The last few chapters were packed with new features. We've spent quite a bit
of time and effort establishing new features that are interactive, compelling,
and fast. Our information system uses an external API with flexible backends.
Our channels-based API offers real-time web support for a rich user interface,
one extremely sensitive to good server performance. Our channels allow peer-
to-peer messaging. We're missing only one thing. Tests.

In this chapter, you'll see how to test OTP processes in isolation. You'll learn
to use the Phoenix helpers to simplify channels testing. Before we dive in,
let's briefly talk about what you can expect.

Recall that in Part I, the test cases for our controllers used Phoenix test helpers
in ConnCase. We tested our HTTP-backed features, the router, controller, and
views. Our integrated tests also hit the database. We used helpers such as
html_response to remove some of the boilerplate from our typical tests.

In Part II, our code stack is fundamentally different. The MVC code gave way
to channels and OTP. Still, the basic approach will be the same. We'll build
tests that hit a single channel call, one that integrates everything down to
the database.

We'll draw the line at the external requests. Since we want to run our integration tests within our sphere of control, we'll want our usual test stack to focus
on everything we've built *except our external HTTP request to WolframAlpha*.
We'll want to isolate our tests from that piece of code.

Let's start our testing process with our information system.

Testing the Information System

We'll start with perhaps our most significant testing challenge. We have quite
a bit of behavior to cover, such as timeouts and forced backend termination.

You'll be surprised at how quickly we can cover all this functionality with a few short and sweet test cases. Let's get started.

A natural first step for testing our InfoSys is to simply look for successful results. Replace your rumbrella/apps/info_sys/test/info_sys_test.exs with the following code:

testing_otp/listings/rumbrella/apps/Info_sys/test/info_sys_test.change1.exs

```
Line 1  defmodule InfoSysTest do
          use ExUnit.Case
          alias InfoSys.Result

    5     defmodule TestBackend do
            def start_link(query, ref, owner, limit) do
              Task.start_link(__MODULE__, :fetch, [query, ref, owner, limit])
            end
            def fetch("result", ref, owner, _limit) do
   10         send(owner, {:results, ref, [%Result{backend: "test", text: "result"}]})
            end
            def fetch("none", ref, owner, _limit) do
              send(owner, {:results, ref, []})
            end
   15     end

          test "compute/2 with backend results" do
            assert [%Result{backend: "test", text: "result"}] =
                   InfoSys.compute("result", backends: [TestBackend])
   20     end

          test "compute/2 with no backend results" do
            assert [] = InfoSys.compute("none", backends: [TestBackend])
          end
   25   end
```

We start off by defining a stub TestBackend module on line 5. This module will act like our Wolfram backend, returning a response in the format that we expect. Since we don't use the URL query string to do actual work, we can use this string to identify specific types of results we want our test backend to fetch.

We'll use this module to test specific behavior like returning successful results or no results based on the query it gets. With our stub in place, on line 17, we define a test case for computing successful results. We pass a query string of "result", which we handle in our TestBackend to send fake results. Finally, we assert that the result set is what we expect.

That takes care of the cases in which backends properly report results. Next, we need to cover the edge cases, like backend timeouts.

Chris says:
What's the Difference Between a Stub and a Mock?

Stubs and mocks are both testing fixtures that replace real-world implementations. A *stub* replaces real-world libraries with simpler, predictable behavior. With a stub, a programmer can bypass code that would otherwise be difficult to test. Other than that, the stub has nothing to say about whether a test passes or fails. For example, a http_send stub might always return a fixed JSON response. In other words, a stub is a simple scaffold implementation standing in for a more complex real-world implementation.

A *mock* is similar, but it has a greater role. It replaces real-world behavior just as a stub does, but it does so by allowing a programmer to specify expectations and results, playing back those results at runtime. A mock will fail a test if the test code doesn't receive the expected function calls. For example, a programmer might create a mock for http_send that expects the test argument, returning the value :ok, followed by the test2 argument, returning :ok. If the test code doesn't call the mock first with the value test and next with the value test2, it'll fail. In other words, a mock is an implementation that records expected behavior at definition time and plays it back at runtime, enforcing those expectations.

Incorporating Timeouts in Our Tests

A backend might time out. To test timeouts, we need a way to simulate a backend taking longer than expected. We also need to be able to make sure that the information system terminates the backend in such cases, as we expect it to. We want to do all of this in a fast test.

You might be tempted at this point to write a test using refute Process.alive?(pid) to verify that the backend is down, but we would be introducing a race condition. Let's examine why. In the event of a timeout, the information system calls the Process.exit function to terminate the backend with an asynchronous exit signal. If the exit signal arrives before the refute call, your test will pass; if not, your test will fail, leading to intermittent test failures. The worst answer a computer can ever give you is *maybe*, so we should rarely use Process.alive?(pid) in our tests. Instead, call Process.monitor to deliver a DOWN message when the monitored process exits. We used the same technique to monitor backends in Chapter 11, *OTP*, on page 199.

Fortunately, our TestBackend and ExUnit testing helpers make writing this test super simple. Update your test with the following code:

testing_otp/listings/rumbrella/apps/info_sys/test/info_sys_test.change2.exs

```elixir
Line 1  defmodule TestBackend do
          def start_link(query, ref, owner, limit) do
            Task.start_link(__MODULE__, :fetch, [query, ref, owner, limit])
          end
    5     def fetch("result", ref, owner, _limit) do
            send(owner, {:results, ref, [%Result{backend: "test", text: "result"}]})
          end
          def fetch("none", ref, owner, _limit) do
            send(owner, {:results, ref, []})
   10     end
          def fetch("timeout", _ref, owner, _limit) do
            send(owner, {:backend, self()})
            :timer.sleep(:infinity)
          end
   15   end

        test "compute/2 with timeout returns no results and kills workers" do
          results = InfoSys.compute("timeout", backends: [TestBackend], timeout: 10)
          assert results == []
   20     assert_receive {:backend, backend_pid}
          ref = Process.monitor(backend_pid)
          assert_receive {:DOWN, ^ref, :process, _pid, _reason}
          refute_received {:DOWN, _, _, _, _}
          refute_received :timedout
   25   end
```

As you might expect, we solve this problem by cheating with our fetch parameter, passing a specific string that makes our stub time out. The technique works because our testing stub isn't built to deliver information based on the fetch parameter, as our information system is. Our test stub is built to simulate difficult behavior based on the fetch parameter. It may feel like cheating a little bit, but we do so with a clear conscience.

On line 11, we add a fetch clause to match on a "timeout" query string. Our test performs a :timer.sleep(:infinity) to simulate a request that takes too long. So that the client can monitor our backend process, we send our own pid before sleeping.

With a long request properly simulated, on line 17, we add a test case for timeouts and call InfoSys.compute with a short timeout of 10ms. We ensure that we get zero results back after our timeout period.

That's not enough. We need to make sure that our backend receives the data we expect. ExUnit provides the assert_receive assertion for this purpose. We also need to make sure we receive our {:backend, backend_pid} message on line 20. With that backend_pid, we monitor the backend process and verify that we receive a :DOWN message, ensuring that our code successfully killed the backend after timing out.

assert_receive keeps our tests compact, allowing us to simultaneously verify that we successfully receive a message and match the result. assert_receive by default waits for 100ms before failing the test. You can explicitly pass a timeout as an optional second argument for cases when you're willing to wait a longer period.

After the test, call refute_received to confirm that no further :DOWN or :timedout messages are in our inbox. When we wrote the compute function, we made sure that the code cleans up after itself, guaranteeing it doesn't leave messages in the process inbox. Those assertions help us validate our cleanup code.

Notice that we use refute_received instead of refute_receive. These functions are different. Use refute_receive to wait 100ms and make sure that no matching message arrives at the inbox. Because we don't expect messages to arrive in the first place, calling refute_receive multiple times can quickly become expensive, because each call waits 100ms. Since we've already made sure that the backend is down, we needn't wait, because the messages we're refuting would already be in our inbox if they leaked. We can use refute_received for this purpose. Saving a few milliseconds might not seem like much, but across hundreds of tests, they add up.

Managing Crashes

Another edge case is a crashing backend. We want to ensure that the crash is isolated from the caller and that the compute function doesn't leave extra messages in our inbox. As with our "timeout" request, let's stub a query that simulates a crash, like this:

testing_otp/listings/rumbrella/apps/info_sys/test/info_sys_test.change3.exs

```
Line 1  defmodule TestBackend do
          def start_link(query, ref, owner, limit) do
            Task.start_link(__MODULE__, :fetch, [query, ref, owner, limit])
          end
     5    def fetch("result", ref, owner, _limit) do
            send(owner, {:results, ref, [%Result{backend: "test", text: "result"}]})
          end
          def fetch("none", ref, owner, _limit) do
            send(owner, {:results, ref, []})
    10    end
          def fetch("timeout", _ref, owner, _limit) do
            send(owner, {:backend, self()})
            :timer.sleep(:infinity)
          end
```

```
15    def fetch("boom", _ref, _owner, _limit) do
        raise "boom!"
      end
    end

20  test "compute/2 discards backend errors" do
      assert InfoSys.compute("boom", backends: [TestBackend]) == []
      refute_received {:DOWN, _, _, _, _}
      refute_received :timedout
    end
```

Again, we cheat. Our fetch clause matches a specific query string, in this case, "boom". On line 15, our new clause simply raises an exception any time we send the "boom" query string to simulate a crash. Then, on line 20, we define a test that passes our "boom" query, and we assert that our code returns an empty list for our results.

Now let's run the tests:

```
$ mix test
==> info_sys
..[error] Task #PID<0.270.0> started from InfoSys.Supervisor terminating
** (RuntimeError) boom!
    test/info_sys_test.exs:21: InfoSysTest.TestBackend.fetch/4
    (elixir) lib/task/supervised.ex:89: Task.Supervised.do_apply/2
    (stdlib) proc_lib.erl:239: :proc_lib.init_p_do_apply/3
Function: &InfoSysTest.TestBackend.fetch/4
    Args: ["boom", #Reference<0.0.2.2806>, #PID<0.269.0>, 10]
....

Finished in 0.3 seconds (0.1s on load, 0.1s on tests)
4 tests, 0 failures

Randomized with seed 291545
==> rumbl
...................................

Finished in 0.3 seconds
31 tests, 0 failures
```

If you look closely, you can see that our tests pass, but we got a wicked error message. The [error] report is the logged crash of the Wolfram worker process. Cleanup on aisle 12!

Let's silence this error by adding the @tag :capture_log before our test. With this tag, we can capture all log messages, and they'll only be shown for failing tests. Now our test output is kept nice and tidy:

```
@tag :capture_log
test "compute/2 discards backend errors" do
  assert InfoSys.compute("boom", backends: [TestBackend]) == []
  refute_received {:DOWN, _, _, _, _}
  refute_received :timedout
end
```

You can find more about log capturing in the ExUnit.CaptureLog module. Besides supporting tags, it also provides a function named capture_log that returns the log entries as a string so we can match against a specific result in our tests. This module, along with its sibling ExUnit.CaptureIO, is useful for testing logs and I/O in your tests.

And now let's rerun the tests:

```
$ mix test
==> info_sys
......

Finished in 0.4 seconds (0.2s on load, 0.2s on tests)
4 tests, 0 failures

Randomized with seed 262462
==> rumbl
................................

Finished in 0.3 seconds
31 tests, 0 failures
```

Our new tests are nice and tidy, just like we want them. We've done pretty well with our generic information system, but there's still some supporting Wolfram code that we'd like to test in isolation.

Isolating Wolfram

We'd like to keep our Wolfram tests isolated, but we have a problem. Our code makes an HTTP request to the WolframAlpha API, which isn't something we want to perform within our test suite. You might be thinking, "Let's write a bunch of mocks!"

Within the Elixir community, we want to avoid mocking whenever possible. Most mocking libraries, including dynamic stubbing libraries, end up changing global behavior—for example, by replacing a function in the HTTP client library to return some particular result. *These function replacements are global,* so a change in one place would change all code running at the same time. That means *tests written in this way can no longer run concurrently.*

These kinds of strategies can snowball, requiring more and more mocking until the dependencies among components are completely hidden.

The better strategy is to identify code that's difficult to test live, and to build a configurable, replaceable testing implementation rather than a dynamic mock. We'll make our HTTP service pluggable. Our development and production code will use our simple :httpc client, and our testing code can instead use a stub that we'll call as part of our tests. Let's update our Wolfram backend to accept an HTTP client from the application configuration, or a default of :httpc. Update rumbrella/apps/info_sys/lib/info_sys/wolfram.ex with this code:

testing_otp/listings/rumbrella/apps/info_sys/lib/info_sys/wolfram.change1.ex

```
Line 1  @http Application.get_env(:info_sys, :wolfram)[:http_client] || :httpc
     2  defp fetch_xml(query_str) do
     3    {:ok, {_, _, body}} = @http.request(
     4      String.to_char_list("http://api.wolframalpha.com/v2/query" <>
     5        "?appid=#{app_id()}" <>
     6        "&input=#{URI.encode_www_form(query_str)}&format=plaintext"))
     7    body
     8  end
```

We've made only a minor change to this file. First, we look up an :http_client module from our mix configuration and default it to the :httpc module. We bake that module into an @http module attribute at compile time for speedy runtime use. Next, we replace our :httpc.request call with an @http.request invocation.

The result is simple and elegant. We simply call the function as before, using our environment's HTTP client instead of hard-coding the HTTP client. This way, our behavior remains unchanged from before, but we can now stub our HTTP client as desired.

Now let's update our test configuration to use our stubbed client. Create a new rumbrella/apps/info_sys/config/test.exs file, like this:

testing_otp/listings/rumbrella/apps/info_sys/config/test.exs

```
use Mix.Config

config :info_sys, :wolfram,
  app_id: "1234",
  http_client: InfoSys.Test.HTTPClient
```

Next, enable configuration loading in rumbrella/apps/info_sys/config/config.exs by uncommenting your last line, so Elixir will load your configuration file for the current environment:

```
import_config "#{Mix.env}.exs"
```

So we can load configuration for each environment, create bare configuration files for config/dev.exs and config/prod.exs with the following contents:

```
use Mix.Config
```

Now on to the tests. To test our stubbed WolframAlpha API results, we need an example XML payload. Wolfram conveniently includes an API explorer[1] that accepts a search query and displays the XML response. We've grabbed a result for you for a query of "1 + 1". Copy the entire XML file that follows into a new rumbrella/apps/info_sys/test/fixtures/ directory and save it as wolfram.xml:

testing_otp/listings/rumbrella/apps/info_sys/test/fixtures/wolfram.xml

```
<?xml version='1.0' encoding='UTF-8'?>
<queryresult success='true'
    error='false'
    numpods='6'
    datatypes='Math'
    timedout=''
    timedoutpods=''
    timing='0.922'
    parsetiming='0.136'
    parsetimedout='false'
    recalculate=''
    id='MSPa24041ic5a62926318g34000048gd708f8iid6h17'
    host='http://www4b.wolframalpha.com'
    server='7'
    related='http://www4b.wolframalpha.com/api/v2/relatedQueries.jsp'
    version='2.6'>
```

With our fixture in place, let's create the stubbed HTTP client that returns fake XML results using our fixture. Create a new rumbrella/apps/info_sys/test/backends/ directory and add the following module to a new rumbrella/apps/info_sys/test/backends/http_client.exs file:

testing_otp/listings/rumbrella/apps/info_sys/test/backends/http_client.exs

```
Line 1  defmodule InfoSys.Test.HTTPClient do
     2    @wolfram_xml File.read!("test/fixtures/wolfram.xml")
     3    def request(url) do
     4      url = to_string(url)
     5      cond do
     6        String.contains?(url, "1+%2B+1") -> {:ok, {[], [], @wolfram_xml}}
     7        true -> {:ok, {[], [], "<queryresult></queryresult>"}}
     8      end
     9    end
    10  end
```

---

1.   http://products.wolframalpha.com/api/explorer.html

We define an InfoSys.Test.HTTPClient module that stubs our request function and returns fake Wolfram results. We cheat as we did before. We check the fetched url for the URI-encoded "1 + 1" string. If it matches, we simply return the XML contents of our wolfram.xml fixture. For any other case, we return a fake request for empty XML results.

Our goal isn't to test the Wolfram service, but make sure we can parse the data that Wolfram provides. This code elegantly lets us write tests at any time that return a result. To confirm our HTTPClient module is loaded for both our rumbl and InfoSys applications, let's require the file in each test suite. Add the following line to the top of your rumbrella/apps/info_sys/test/test_helper.exs:

testing_otp/listings/rumbrella/apps/info_sys/test/test_helper.change1.exs

```
Code.require_file "backends/http_client.exs", __DIR__
ExUnit.start()
```

Next, do the same for your rumbrella/apps/rumbl/test/test_helper.exs file, but with the appropriate path:

testing_otp/listings/rumbrella/apps/rumbl/test/test_helper.change1.exs

```
Code.require_file "../../info_sys/test/backends/http_client.exs", __DIR__
ExUnit.start

Mix.Task.run "ecto.create", ~w(-r Rumbl.Repo --quiet)
Mix.Task.run "ecto.migrate", ~w(-r Rumbl.Repo --quiet)
Ecto.Adapters.SQL.begin_test_transaction(Rumbl.Repo)
```

With our HTTP client in place, create a new rumbrella/apps/info_sys/test/backends/wolfram_test.exs file with the following contents:

testing_otp/listings/rumbrella/apps/info_sys/test/backends/wolfram_test.exs

```
Line 1  defmodule InfoSys.Backends.WolframTest do
   -      use ExUnit.Case, async: true
   -      alias InfoSys.Wolfram
   -
   5      test "makes request, reports results, then terminates" do
   -        ref = make_ref()
   -        {:ok, _} = Wolfram.start_link("1 + 1", ref, self(), 1)
   -
   -        assert_receive {:results, ^ref, [%InfoSys.Result{text: "2"}]}
  10      end
   -    end
```

Using our stubbed HTTP client, we add our first test case on line 5. First, we spawn a Wolfram backend with start_link. Next, we use assert_receive to ensure that the backend reports the successful %InfoSys.Result{} that we asked for.

Now let's run the test:

```
$ mix test
..

Finished in 0.2 seconds (0.1s on load, 0.09s on tests)
5 tests, 0 failures
```

And they pass. Next, we'll need to make sure that our backend terminates after its work is complete. Let's use Process.monitor again to test our Wolfram termination. Update your test with the following listing:

testing_otp/listings/rumbrella/apps/info_sys/test/backends/wolfram_test.change1.exs

```elixir
test "makes request, reports results, then terminates" do
  ref = make_ref()
  {:ok, pid} = Wolfram.start_link("1 + 1", ref, self(), 1)
  Process.monitor(pid)

  assert_receive {:results, ^ref, [%InfoSys.Result{text: "2"}]}
  assert_receive {:DOWN, _ref, :process, ^pid, :normal}
end
```

We add Process.monitor(pid) to monitor our newly spawned Wolfram process. Next, we assert that the process terminates normally with assert_receive.

Let's run our tests again:

```
$ mix test
..

Finished in 0.2 seconds (0.1s on load, 0.09s on tests)
5 tests, 0 failures
```

José says:

At What Level Should We Apply Our Stubs/Mocks?

For the WolframAlpha API case, we chose to create a stub that replaces the :httpc module. However, you might not be comfortable with skipping the whole HTTP stack during the test. You'll have to decide the best place to stub the HTTP layer. No single strategy works for every case. It depends on your team's confidence and the code being tested. For example, if the communication with the endpoint requires passing headers and handling different responses, you might want to make sure that all of those parameters are sent correctly.

One possible solution is the Bypass[a] project. Bypass allows us to create a mock HTTP server that our code can access during tests without resorting to dynamic mocking techniques that introduce global changes and complicate the testing stack.

---

a.   https://github.com/PSPDFKit-labs/bypass

They're green, and they'll be consistently green because we make sure that our measurements await the completion of our tests.

We have one more edge case. A query might return zero results from the API. Let's add a new test case to complete our coverage:

testing_otp/listings/rumbrella/apps/info_sys/test/backends/wolfram_test.change2.exs

```
test "no query results reports an empty list" do
  ref = make_ref()
  {:ok, _} = Wolfram.start_link("none", ref, self(), 1)

  assert_receive {:results, ^ref, []}
end
```

As before, we start a new Wolfram process, but this time we give it a different query string, causing our HTTPClient.request function to return a fake response with zero API results. Next, we assert that the backend reported in with an empty list of results, as expected.

Let's run the tests:

```
$ mix test
..

Finished in 0.2 seconds (0.1s on load, 0.09s on tests)
6 tests, 0 failures
```

Perfect once again. You may have noticed that these tests are more involved than the typical single-process tests you might be used to. But by using the specific helpers that ExUnit provides and thinking through possible outcomes and orderings, you'll quickly get the hang of writing tests that aren't too much more difficult than synchronous ones. When you're done, you'll have one major advantage. Your tests will run concurrently, meaning they'll finish much more quickly than their synchronous counterparts.

With our Wolfram backend covered, it's time to move on to the last part of our application: the channels. You'll learn how to use the testing tools from Phoenix.ChannelTest.

Adding Tests to Channels

We started this chapter by testing our information system, including unit-testing our supporting code for the Wolfram backend. Now it's time to test our channels code. Remember that underneath, channels are also OTP servers. Phoenix includes the Phoenix.ChannelTest module, which will simplify your testing experience. With it, you can make several types of common assertions. For example, you can assert that your application pushes messages to a client, replies to a message, or sends broadcasts. Let's look at some code.

The rumbrella/apps/rumbl/test/support/channel_case.ex is a file that was generated by Mix when we generated the rumbl application. You've already seen a couple of similar test cases with model_case and conn_case in Chapter 8, *Testing MVC*, on page 129. Let's take a deeper look at how those files work. Crack it open now:

testing_otp/rumbrella/apps/rumbl/test/support/channel_case.ex

```elixir
defmodule Rumbl.ChannelCase do
  use ExUnit.CaseTemplate

  using do
    quote do
      # Import conveniences for testing with channels
      use Phoenix.ChannelTest

      alias Rumbl.Repo
      import Ecto
      import Ecto.Changeset
      import Ecto.Query, only: [from: 1, from: 2]

      # The default endpoint for testing
      @endpoint Rumbl.Endpoint
    end
  end

  setup tags do
    unless tags[:async] do
      Ecto.Adapters.SQL.restart_test_transaction(Rumbl.Repo, [])
    end

    :ok
  end
end
```

Knowing what's happening here in basic broad strokes is enough. First you see use ExUnit.CaseTemplate, which establishes this file as a test case. Next is a using block to start an inline macro, and a quote to specify the template for the code that we want to inject. The use Phoenix.ChannelTest statement establishes Phoenix.ChannelTest as the foundation for our test file. Then, we do a few imports and aliases for convenience, and so on.

The result is a file that prepares your tests for the features you're most likely to use in your channel tests. Our application has just one channel: the VideoChannel, which supports features like real-time annotations and integration with our InfoSys layer. All of our tests go through a single endpoint.

Before we test the VideoChannel, let's start where the channel process begins by testing the UserSocket behavior.

Authenticating a Test Socket

Most of our channels code relies on an authenticated user. We'll start our tests with the socket authentication. Let's do that now.

Create a rumbrella/apps/rumbl/test/channels/user_socket_test.exs file containing:

testing_otp/listings/rumbrella/apps/rumbl/test/channels/user_socket_test.exs

```
Line 1  defmodule Rumbl.Channels.UserSocketTest do
          use Rumbl.ChannelCase, async: true
          alias Rumbl.UserSocket

      5   test "socket authentication with valid token" do
            token = Phoenix.Token.sign(@endpoint, "user socket", "123")

            assert {:ok, socket} = connect(UserSocket, %{"token" => token})
            assert socket.assigns.user_id == "123"
     10   end

          test "socket authentication with invalid token" do
            assert :error = connect(UserSocket, %{"token" => "1313"})
            assert :error = connect(UserSocket, %{})
     15   end
        end
```

On line 5, we make sure that a user with a valid token can open a new socket connection. The test is pretty simple. We generate a valid token, use the connect helper to simulate a UserSocket connection, and ensure that the connection succeeds. That's not enough. We also make sure that the socket's user_id is placed into the socket. With the happy path tested, we can move on to the negative condition.

On line 12, we test the opposite case. We first try to log in with a nonexistent token. Next, we test a simple edge condition, attempting to connect with no token at all. Since these tests don't require side effects such as database calls, they can run independently and concurrently. In the use line, we set :async to true, and we can feel a little happier inside. Our tiny test saves milliseconds, but when we aggregate thousands of tests, we'll be saving full minutes or more. These tiny savings can add up to hours every day.

We can see the finish line. It's finally time to test our video channel.

Communicating with a Test Channel

Let's see how easy it is to test our VideoChannel features. Our plan is simple. We're going to set up some data to share across our tests and then sign the user in within our setup block. Then, we can write some independent tests against that live connection.

Create a new rumbrella/apps/rumbl/test/channels/video_channel_test.exs file that looks like this:

testing_otp/listings/rumbrella/apps/rumbl/test/channels/video_channel_test.exs

```
Line 1  defmodule Rumbl.Channels.VideoChannelTest do
   -      use Rumbl.ChannelCase
   -      import Rumbl.TestHelpers
   -
   5      setup do
   -        user = insert_user(name: "Rebecca")
   -        video = insert_video(user, title: "Testing")
   -        token = Phoenix.Token.sign(@endpoint, "user socket", user.id)
   -        {:ok, socket} = connect(Rumbl.UserSocket, %{"token" => token})
  10
   -        {:ok, socket: socket, user: user, video: video}
   -      end
   -
   -      test "join replies with video annotations", %{socket: socket, video: vid} do
  15        for body <- ~w(one two) do
   -          vid
   -          |> build_assoc(:annotations, %{body: body})
   -          |> Repo.insert!()
   -        end
  20        {:ok, reply, socket} = subscribe_and_join(socket, "videos:#{vid.id}", %{})
   -
   -        assert socket.assigns.video_id == vid.id
   -        assert %{annotations: [%{body: "one"}, %{body: "two"}]} = reply
   -      end
  25  end
```

On line 5, we add a setup block to prepare our tests with a user and video. Next, we use connect to start a simulated socket connection. We can use that connection for each of our tests. We put the user, the video, and the connected socket into our test context, one that we'll be able to match for individual tests.

On line 14, we write our first test. Our function head matches the connected socket and video, so our test can take advantage of the setup work we've done. We first build a couple of annotations. Then we call the subscribe_and_join test helper to attempt to join the channel responsible for the "video:#{vid.id}" topic. If the join is successful, this helper function returns {:ok, reply, socket}. An unsuccessful join fails the match and forces an error for our test.

Next, we make sure we've joined the right topic by comparing the video ID from our connected test socket with the one returned from our test helper.

Then we make sure that the right annotations are in our reply by matching them against our reply.

Let's try this much:

```
$ mix test
==> info_sys
......

Finished in 0.2 seconds (0.1s on load, 0.09s on tests)
6 tests, 0 failures

Randomized with seed 231514
==> rumbl
..................................

Finished in 0.3 seconds
35 tests, 0 failures
```

No problem! Our tests pass, and we know the following:

- Our user can successfully connect.
- Our user successfully joined a topic.
- The topic is the correct one.
- The reply has all of the annotations in the video.

That's a good start. Now that we've tested that we can join the VideoChannel, we can test a conversation with the client. Let's test the incoming new_annotation event. We want to simulate the creation of a new annotation, and we want to make sure we correctly augment the state in the socket.

Code the new test in rumbrella/apps/rumbl/test/channels/video_channel_test.exs, like this:

testing_otp/listings/rumbrella/apps/rumbl/test/channels/video_channel_test.change1.exs

```
test "inserting new annotations", %{socket: socket, video: vid} do
  {:ok, _, socket} = subscribe_and_join(socket, "videos:#{vid.id}", %{})
  ref = push socket, "new_annotation", %{body: "the body", at: 0}
  assert_reply ref, :ok, %{}
  assert_broadcast "new_annotation", %{}
end
```

As before, our function head matches the vid and socket we created in setup. Like last time, we subscribe and join with our helper. This time, we use the push helper function to push a new event to the channel. We use assert_reply to make sure we get a :ok response. We could also pass in additional key/value pairs, but we don't need to do so in this case, so we pass an empty map.

Finally, we use the assert_broadcast function to make sure that our annotation gets broadcast to any waiting subscribers. The assert_reply and assert_broadcast functions are provided by Phoenix and built on top of the assert_receive function that we used in the previous section.

Notice how our test process works as a client of the channel, because we were able to establish a test connection using subscribe_and_join. In the same way, the browser is a channel client. That's why we can assert that we've received some particular reply. The test process also subscribes to the same topic as its channel, explaining why we can assert that something was broadcast.

Let's test the integration with our information system. Crack your test open once again, and add this test to the end:

`testing_otp/listings/rumbrella/apps/rumbl/test/channels/video_channel_test.change2.exs`

```
test "new annotations triggers InfoSys", %{socket: socket, video: vid} do
  {:ok, _, socket} = subscribe_and_join(socket, "videos:#{vid.id}", %{})
  ref = push socket, "new_annotation", %{body: "1 + 1", at: 123}
  assert_reply ref, :ok, %{}
  assert_broadcast "new_annotation", %{body: "1 + 1", at: 123}
  assert_broadcast "new_annotation", %{body: "2", at: 123}
end
```

As before, our function head picks off the things our test needs. We subscribe and join, push a new annotation, and check the response. This time, use the special stubbed "1 + 1" query to return fake answers. We verify that the original response and the InfoSys annotation are both broadcast successfully.

Let's try it out:

```
$ mix test

1) test new annotations triggers information system
(Rumbl.Channels.VideoChannelTest)
test/channels/video_channel_test.exs:40
** (EXIT from #PID<0.373.0>) an exception was raised:
** (Ecto.NoResultsError)
expected at least one result but got none in query:

  from u in Rumbl.User,
    where: u.username == ^"wolfram"
```

Sad face. If you recall, our VideoChannel.compute_additional_info function fetches a user by backend name when we insert an annotation. That Wolfram user becomes a necessary part of our testing setup. Let's take a look at that function again to refresh our memory:

```
testing_otp/rumbrella/apps/rumbl/web/channels/video_channel.ex
```

```
Line 1  defp compute_additional_info(ann, socket) do
          for result <- InfoSys.compute(ann.body, limit: 1, timeout: 10_000) do
            attrs = %{url: result.url, body: result.text, at: ann.at}
            info_changeset =
     5        Repo.get_by!(Rumbl.User, username: result.backend)
              |> build_assoc(:annotations, video_id: ann.video_id)
              |> Rumbl.Annotation.changeset(attrs)

            case Repo.insert(info_changeset) do
     10       {:ok, info_ann} -> broadcast_annotation(socket, info_ann)
              {:error, _changeset} -> :ignore
            end
          end
        end
```

On line 5, we fetch a user based on the result.backend name.

That's easy enough to fix. You can just insert a new Wolfram user to satisfy our tests, like this:

```
testing_otp/listings/rumbrella/apps/rumbl/test/channels/video_channel_test.change3.exs
```

```
test "new annotations triggers InfoSys", %{socket: socket, video: vid} do
  insert_user(username: "wolfram")
  {:ok, _, socket} = subscribe_and_join(socket, "videos:#{vid.id}", %{})
  ref = push socket, "new_annotation", %{body: "1 + 1", at: 123}
  assert_reply ref, :ok, %{}
  assert_broadcast "new_annotation", %{body: "1 + 1", at: 123}
  assert_broadcast "new_annotation", %{body: "2", at: 123}
end
```

With our new Wolfram user safely in the database, let's retry our test:

```
$ mix test
==> info_sys
......

Finished in 0.2 seconds (0.1s on load, 0.09s on tests)
6 tests, 0 failures

Randomized with seed 602949
==> rumbl
................................

Finished in 0.3 seconds
36 tests, 0 failures
```

And we pass!

As you can see, Phoenix provides plenty of support for testing your channels code. These testing features are first-class features for our ecosystem. It's a good time to see how far we've come.

Wrapping Up

Amazingly, this is the last chapter wrapup in our book! In this chapter, we tested the most sophisticated features in our entire application stack. You probably noticed that the functional nature of Phoenix made testing the application much easier than you might have expected. Our tests run quickly, and they're compact, thanks to the helpers that abstract concepts like assert_reply, assert_broadcast, and assert_receive. Here's what we accomplished:

- We tested our OTP layer for our InfoSys OTP application.

- We built a specific backend rather than a dynamic stub or mock to keep our tests isolated, as our unit and integration tests should be.

- We tested our sockets authentication code.

- We used the Phoenix testing support to test our channels, just as our end users would, through our endpoints.

By no means is this testing story complete. We didn't cover user acceptance testing. Nor did we cover performance testing. We did accomplish quite a bit in a short time. These kinds of concurrent, interactive applications are notoriously difficult to test.

You're almost done! Turn the page, and we'll start wrapping up.

## CHAPTER 14

What's Next?

We hope you've enjoyed reading this book as much as we've enjoyed putting it together for you. The Phoenix story is an incredible one, and the telling is nowhere near done. If you've coded along with us, you should have a better handle on how the bits of your code fit together to form scalable, reliable applications. Let's review what we've done so far.

First, we built a toy application so you could learn where to put each piece of code. You worked with the Phoenix router table. You learned how connections flowed through plugs to controllers and views. You built a trivial controller and a simple view that rendered a template.

Next, we started working on our rumbl application, one that you used throughout the rest of the book. We created a controller, and rather than integrating a full database right away, we built a simple repository stub for our application so we could focus on the controller. We then created a couple of actions, and some views and templates to render our results.

With that out of the way, we dove into Ecto to replace our in-memory stub with a full database-backed repository. Initially, we focused on the initial model for users. We built a migration and a changeset to help us manage change. In the next few chapters, we used this model in our controller. We created a plug to help integrate authentication in our application, and then we built some more-sophisticated models with relationships. Then, we tested the work we'd done so far.

Next, we moved into Part II. We built a channel to handle the real-time features of our application. We learned that the Phoenix messaging allows us to build applications with state, but without the performance penalties you generally see with similar frameworks. We used these features to deliver real-time features, allowing users to comment on a playing video in real time. We worked on the server in Elixir and paired it with an ES6 JavaScript client. We used channels to let users post messages, and then broadcast those messages to all other interested users. Then, we extended our authentication system, adopting token-based authentication.

With the working interactive user interface built, we crafted an information system service. We used OTP—a mechanism for building state into our applications with concurrency, message passing, and recursive functions. We also learned to use supervisors to keep our system reliable and take action when things break.

We then extracted our information system into an umbrella application. Along the way, we used Observer to get a full picture of what was happening with our application in real time. The umbrella application let us isolate the development and testing of individual units. Finally, we tested our channels and OTP services.

We tried to build a broad and exciting application, but it was impossible to cover all of the useful projects happening in the language, the Phoenix project, or the community. Here are some of the things you can explore.

Other Interesting Features

In any successful development ecosystem, a tension always exists between currency and stability. We've tried to walk as closely to currency as we could without stepping over. Still, exciting things are happening, many of which weren't ready to include in this text. These are some exciting developments you may want to explore.

Supporting Internationalization with Gettext

In version v1.1, Phoenix added integration with Gettext, an internationalization (i18n) and localization (l10n) system commonly used for writing multilingual programs. Gettext can automatically extract translations from your source code, reducing the burden on the developer. Furthermore, since the Gettext standard is used by so many communities, you can take advantage of a rich set of tooling for both developers and translators.

When you ran mix phoenix.new rumbl, Phoenix generated a Rumbl.Gettext module at web/gettext.ex. You can see it in use in the web/views/error_helpers.ex file, used to translate the error messages coming from Ecto. Since programmers often organize translations into namespaces called domains, Phoenix places Ecto messages in the errors domain by default.

The translations for different languages are in the priv/gettext directory. There you'll find a default template for Ecto messages called errors.pot. A translation for each language is placed in directories such as priv/gettext/en/LC_MESSAGES.

To learn more about the integration between Phoenix and Gettext, we recommend this fantastic article by Rebecca Skinner entitled "Internationalization using Gettext in the Phoenix framework."[1] For general information, check out the Gettext documentation.[2]

Next, we'll move from internationalization to intercept and handle, a couple of functions that make it easier to manage channel messages.

Intercepting on Phoenix Channels

When you broadcast a message, Phoenix sends it to the Publish and Subscribe (PubSub) system, which then broadcasts it directly to all user sockets. We call this approach *fastlaning* because it completely bypasses the channel, allowing us to encode the message once. Phoenix channels also provide a feature called intercept, which allows channels to intercept a broadcast message before it's sent to the user.

For example, maybe we'd like to let the video's creator edit all of its annotations. For such a feature, we could append an is_editable field to the annotation map when we broadcast it so the front end can adapt accordingly. Using intercept, we could build this feature like this:

```
intercept ["new_annotation"]

# For every new_annotation broadcast,
# append an is_editable value for client metadata.
def handle_out("new_annotation", msg, socket) do
  %{video: video, user_id: user_id} = socket.assigns
  push socket, "new_annotation",
      Map.merge(msg, %{is_editable: video.user_id == user_id})
  {:noreply, socket}
end
```

For each event that we specify in intercept, we must define a handle_out clause to handle the intercepted event. You can also intercept an event and choose not to push it at all, in case you want to make sure that some clients don't receive specific events.

intercept is a nice feature, but you need to be careful. Imagine that you have 10,000 users watching a video at the same time. Instead of using intercept,

---

1. http://sevenseacat.net/2015/12/20/i18n-in-phoenix-apps.html
2. http://hexdocs.pm/gettext

you could write a few extra lines of code to include a :video_user_id field in the message, letting the client decide whether the message is editable. For that implementation, Phoenix would encode the broadcast once and send the message to all sockets.

With the intercept implementation, Phoenix would send the message to the first 10,000 channel processes, one for each client. While processing the intercept, each channel would independently modify the intercepted message and push it to the socket to be encoded and sent. The cost of intercept is 10,000 extra messages, one per channel, as well as encoding those messages 9,999 times—again. one per channel—compared to the one-time encoding of the implementation without intercept. For those reasons, we recommend using intercept with care.

On the other hand, intercept can be tremendously useful when we're evolving code. Imagine that in the future you build a new version of the annotations feature, with new front-end and backend code, including a different payload when new annotations are broadcast. However, imagine that you also have old clients that can take a while to migrate. You could use the new annotation-broadcast format throughout the new code and use intercept to retrofit the new_annotation broadcast into the old one. For these cases, intercept would be an ideal solution. You'd pay a temporary performance price to make your code easier to build and understand.

For more information on intercept and handle, check the Phoenix documentation on channels.[3] Next, we'll move on to live code reload.

Understanding Phoenix Live Reload

One of the features we used throughout the entire book was Phoenix Live Reload, which allows us to see changes propagated to the browser as soon as we save them to the filesystem. Phoenix Live Reload is composed of:

- A dependency called fs that watches the filesystem for changes

- A channel that receives events from the fs application and converts them into broadcasts

- A plug that injects the live-reload iframe on every request and serves the iframe content for web requests

There isn't much to Live Reload, and that's exactly why we recommend that you to study its source code to learn more on how simple it is to extend

---

3. http://hexdocs.pm/phoenix/Phoenix.Channel.html

Phoenix. If the feature is something you might want to customize, you might consider reading more or even following the project. You can find the source code in our Phoenix Live Reload GitHub project.[4]

While we're on the subject of customization, let's see how you might customize the Phoenix PubSub adapter.

Phoenix PubSub Adapter

By default, Phoenix PubSub uses Distributed Erlang to ensure that broadcasts work across multiple nodes. This requires all machines to be connected together according to the Erlang Distribution Protocol. Setting up Distributed Erlang is straightforward, but it might not be directly supported in some deployment platforms. For example, Heroku only recently launched a feature called Private Spaces[5] that would support such.

You needn't worry, though. Phoenix PubSub is extensible—it supports multiple adapters. One is the Redis adapter,[6] maintained by the Phoenix team, which empowers the PubSub system by using Redis as its message-distribution mechanism. You can use one of these options or even write your own.

You've seen how to customize Phoenix messaging on the server side. Some interesting things are happening on the client side too.

Phoenix Clients for Other Platforms

In our channels chapter, you saw how we customized the Phoenix transport to work with our ES6 code. Phoenix channels support the nearly ubiquitous JavaScript and also a wide range of other clients and platforms, including C#, Java, Objective-C, and Swift.[7]

All these clients use WebSockets, but don't forget that Phoenix channels are transport agnostic. If you have special requirements, as in embedded software or working on special platforms, you can always use a custom protocol to talk to Phoenix. We also expect to see some exotic front-end options, such as the Elm language, show up soon.

Let's shift gears from the web layer to the database layer. Ecto has some interesting features you can use today but that we didn't have room to cover.

---

4. http://github.com/phoenixframework/phoenix_live_reload
5. https://blog.heroku.com/archives/2015/9/10/heroku_private_spaces_private_paas_delivered_as_a_service
6. https://github.com/phoenixframework/phoenix_pubsub_redis
7. https://github.com/livehelpnow/CSharpPhoenixClient, https://github.com/eoinsha/JavaPhoenixChannels, https://github.com/livehelpnow/ObjCPhoenixClient, and https://github.com/davidstump/SwiftPhoenixClient.

Casting Ecto Associations

We've covered all the main Ecto concepts in this book, from repositories to queries and changesets. Although we also discussed associations, we haven't shown one feature: the ability to cast or change an association at the same time that we modify its parent model.

This feature neatly integrates Phoenix and Ecto, allowing developers to build different form sections for each associated record. For more information, we recommend the walk-through written by the Plataformatec team called "Working with Ecto associations and embeds."[8] That paper explores associations and Ecto's support for embeds.

We've only scratched the surface. New features from this vibrant community are emerging faster than we can write about them. Let's talk about features that are on the roadmap but weren't available at the time of this printing.

What's Coming Next

Phoenix was able to extend its reach beyond our wildest dreams in its first few years, but we're even more excited about what's coming next. We've ordered the next sections by delivery, highlighting first the changes we believe will be released sooner, but we offer no guarantees!

Ecto 2.0

The Ecto team is working on Ecto v2.0, and it brings many and great improvements to Ecto:

- Support for many_to_many associations will make it easier than ever to model relationships like *a post has many tags* and *tags have many posts*.

- Support for concurrent transactional tests will allow faster tests. When we wrote our model tests, we had to split our model tests into the ones with side effects, which relied on the database, and the ones without, which were database independent. One of the benefits of this split was that the tests without side effects could run concurrently. Ecto v2.0 will ship with an ownership-based mechanism that will allow even tests with side effects to run concurrently, speeding up not only our model tests but also any controller or integration test we write. Concurrency is important, and Ecto v2.0 will allow us to leverage it in all of our tests.

---

8. http://blog.plataformatec.com.br/2015/08/working-with-ecto-associations-and-embeds/

- Support for insert_all will allow batch inserts. Ecto repositories support update_all and delete_all to update multiple entries simultaneously but provide no mechanism for inserting many entries. Ecto v2.0 will rectify that by introducing insert_all.

Those are the major improvements. Expect many other features to be part of Ecto v2.0, making developers more productive and your web applications faster. Next, we'll talk about one of the most often requested features in Phoenix, called *presence*.

Phoenix Presence

Social interactive platforms often require some kind of answer to the question, Who is using this channel right now? The Phoenix team is working on a feature called Phoenix Presence that lets developers track which users are connected to which channel. Such a feature would allow our rumbl application to answer the question, Who is currently watching a video?

The Phoenix Presence will be built on top of the Phoenix PubSub system, allowing developers to run clusters of Phoenix applications without needing to configure extra dependencies like Redis.

Stay tuned!

Phoenix Components

One tool gathering a lot of attention on the front-end side is called GraphQL.[9] Although the Phoenix team doesn't plan to integrate GraphQL directly into Phoenix, we believe GraphQL contains great ideas that may make building real-time Phoenix applications simpler than it is today.

One such idea is GraphQL's specification of templates with the data it needs, all in the same place. If we bring similar ideas to Phoenix, developers could provide components, which combine templates with a specification for the data it requires. With components, Phoenix could automatically cache templates and provide real-time updates based on the true state of the data, allowing Phoenix to automatically push data to clients whenever a record is added, removed, or updated in your application.

This is an area we are actively researching, and we hope to have more news on the topic in upcoming conferences and blog posts.

---

9. http://graphql.org

Good Luck

That's a brief taste of what's happening in the Phoenix ecosystem right now. With the rapid growth in this space, we hope and fully expect the community to contribute ideas faster than we can write about them. We also expect that you, our readers, will use the ideas in this book to change the way the world thinks about what's possible.

Good luck.

Index

Put the "Fun" in Functional

Elixir puts the "fun" back into functional programming, on top of the robust, battle-tested, industrial-strength environment of Erlang.

Programming Elixir 1.2

You want to explore functional programming, but are put off by the academic feel (tell me about monads just one more time). You know you need concurrent applications, but also know these are almost impossible to get right. Meet Elixir, a functional, concurrent language built on the rock-solid Erlang VM. Elixir's pragmatic syntax and built-in support for metaprogramming will make you productive and keep you interested for the long haul. This book is *the* introduction to Elixir for experienced programmers.

Maybe you need something that's closer to Ruby, but with a battle-proven environment that's unrivaled for massive scalability, concurrency, distribution, and fault tolerance. Maybe the time is right for the Next Big Thing. Maybe it's *Elixir*.

This edition of the book has been updated to cover Elixir 1.2, including the new with expression, the exrm release manager, and the removal of deprecated types.

Dave Thomas
(354 pages) ISBN: 9781680501667. $38
https://pragprog.com/book/elixir12

Metaprogramming Elixir

Write code that writes code with Elixir macros. Macros make metaprogramming possible and define the language itself. In this book, you'll learn how to use macros to extend the language with fast, maintainable code and share functionality in ways you never thought possible. You'll discover how to extend Elixir with your own first-class features, optimize performance, and create domain-specific languages.

Chris McCord
(128 pages) ISBN: 9781680500417. $17
https://pragprog.com/book/cmelixir

Exercises and Teams

From exercises to make you a better programmer to techniques for creating better teams, we've got you covered.

Exercises for Programmers

When you write software, you need to be at the top of your game. Great programmers practice to keep their skills sharp. Get sharp and stay sharp with more than fifty practice exercises rooted in real-world scenarios. If you're a new programmer, these challenges will help you learn what you need to break into the field, and if you're a seasoned pro, you can use these exercises to learn that hot new language for your next gig.

Brian P. Hogan
(118 pages) ISBN: 9781680501223. $24
https://pragprog.com/book/bhwb

Creating Great Teams

People are happiest and most productive if they can choose what they work on and who they work with. Self-selecting teams give people that choice. Build well-designed and efficient teams to get the most out of your organization, with step-by-step instructions on how to set up teams quickly and efficiently. You'll create a process that works for you, whether you need to form teams from scratch, improve the design of existing teams, or are on the verge of a big team re-shuffle.

Sandy Mamoli and David Mole
(102 pages) ISBN: 9781680501285. $17
https://pragprog.com/book/mmteams

The Joy of Mazes and Math

Rediscover the joy and fascinating weirdness of mazes and pure mathematics.

Mazes for Programmers

A book on mazes? Seriously?

Yes!

Not because you spend your day creating mazes, or because you particularly like solving mazes.

But because it's fun. Remember when programming used to be fun? This book takes you back to those days when you were starting to program, and you wanted to make your code do things, draw things, and solve puzzles. It's fun because it lets you explore and grow your code, and reminds you how it feels to just think.

Sometimes it feels like you live your life in a maze of twisty little passages, all alike. Now you can code your way out.

Jamis Buck
(286 pages) ISBN: 9781680500554. $38
https://pragprog.com/book/jbmaze

Good Math

Mathematics is beautiful—and it can be fun and exciting as well as practical. *Good Math* is your guide to some of the most intriguing topics from two thousand years of mathematics: from Egyptian fractions to Turing machines; from the real meaning of numbers to proof trees, group symmetry, and mechanical computation. If you've ever wondered what lay beyond the proofs you struggled to complete in high school geometry, or what limits the capabilities of the computer on your desk, this is the book for you.

Mark C. Chu-Carroll
(282 pages) ISBN: 9781937785338. $34
https://pragprog.com/book/mcmath

Past and Present

To see where we're going, remember how we got here, and learn how to take a healthier approach to programming.

Fire in the Valley

In the 1970s, while their contemporaries were protesting the computer as a tool of dehumanization and oppression, a motley collection of college dropouts, hippies, and electronics fanatics were engaged in something much more subversive. Obsessed with the idea of getting computer power into their own hands, they launched from their garages a hobbyist movement that grew into an industry, and ultimately a social and technological revolution. What they did was invent the personal computer: not just a new device, but a watershed in the relationship between man and machine. This is their story.

Michael Swaine and Paul Freiberger
(424 pages) ISBN: 9781937785765. $34
https://pragprog.com/book/fsfire

The Healthy Programmer

To keep doing what you love, you need to maintain your own systems, not just the ones you write code for. Regular exercise and proper nutrition help you learn, remember, concentrate, and be creative—skills critical to doing your job well. Learn how to change your work habits, master exercises that make working at a computer more comfortable, and develop a plan to keep fit, healthy, and sharp for years to come.

This book is intended only as an informative guide for those wishing to know more about health issues. In no way is this book intended to replace, countermand, or conflict with the advice given to you by your own healthcare provider including Physician, Nurse Practitioner, Physician Assistant, Registered Dietician, and other licensed professionals.

Joe Kutner
(254 pages) ISBN: 9781937785314. $36
https://pragprog.com/book/jkthp

Long Live the Command Line!

Use tmux and Vim for incredible mouse-free productivity.

tmux

Your mouse is slowing you down. The time you spend context switching between your editor and your consoles eats away at your productivity. Take control of your environment with tmux, a terminal multiplexer that you can tailor to your workflow. Learn how to customize, script, and leverage tmux's unique abilities and keep your fingers on your keyboard's home row.

Brian P. Hogan
(88 pages) ISBN: 9781934356968. $16.25
https://pragprog.com/book/bhtmux

Practical Vim, Second Edition

Vim is a fast and efficient text editor that will make you a faster and more efficient developer. It

Drew Neil
(354 pages) ISBN: 9781680501278. $29
https://pragprog.com/book/dnvim2

The Pragmatic Bookshelf

The Pragmatic Bookshelf features books written by developers for developers. The titles continue the well-known Pragmatic Programmer style and continue to garner awards and rave reviews. As development gets more and more difficult, the Pragmatic Programmers will be there with more titles and products to help you stay on top of your game.

Visit Us Online

This Book's Home Page
https://pragprog.com/book/phoenix
Source code from this book, errata, and other resources. Come give us feedback, too!

Register for Updates
https://pragprog.com/updates
Be notified when updates and new books become available.

Join the Community
https://pragprog.com/community
Read our weblogs, join our online discussions, participate in our mailing list, interact with our wiki, and benefit from the experience of other Pragmatic Programmers.

New and Noteworthy
https://pragprog.com/news
Check out the latest pragmatic developments, new titles and other offerings.

Save on the eBook

Save on the eBook versions of this title. Owning the paper version of this book entitles you to purchase the electronic versions at a terrific discount.

PDFs are great for carrying around on your laptop—they are hyperlinked, have color, and are fully searchable. Most titles are also available for the iPhone and iPod touch, Amazon Kindle, and other popular e-book readers.

Buy now at *https://pragprog.com/coupon*

Contact Us

Online Orders:	*https://pragprog.com/catalog*
Customer Service:	*support@pragprog.com*
International Rights:	*translations@pragprog.com*
Academic Use:	*academic@pragprog.com*
Write for Us:	*http://write-for-us.pragprog.com*
Or Call:	+1 800-699-7764

CPSIA information can be obtained
at www.ICGtesting.com
Printed in the USA
BVOW11s1200220616
453050BV00011B/100/P